point

GODS, DEMIGODS & DEMONS AN ENCYCLOPEDIA OF GREEK MYTHOLOGY

Bernard Evslin

SCHOLASTIC INC.
New York Toronto London Auckland Sydney

ISBN 0-590-41448-8

21 20 19 18   1 2/0

Printed in the U.S.A.   01

For Tom and Bill

**whose way of listening made
wonder more wonderful**

NOTE TO THE READER

The keys to pronunciation and principal sounds are those used in Scholastic Magazines' classroom periodicals. For most readers they are easier to understand than the diacritical marks usually found in encyclopedias.

KEY TO PRONUNCIATION

The pronunciation of a word is indicated in parentheses following the word in the encyclopedia.

The system used translates each syllable into the nearest common English equivalent. (A syllable is several letters taken together so as to form one sound.)

Short, familiar words are used occasionally to make the pronunciation of a syllable easier. These words are:

dew	less
ice	sell
jay	urn
lay	us

A syllable in capital letters is the syllable that is accented.

Examples: Lucretia   loo KREE shih uh
          Leto   LEE toh
          Saturn   SAT urn

Often the unaccented syllable has the neutral sound, uh.

Examples: the a in sofa
                the e in silent
                the i in charity
                the o in connect
                the u in circus

KEY TO PRINCIPAL SOUNDS:

a	(as in add, cat)
ay	(as in hay, ale)
ah	(as in all, arm)
air	(as in hair, care, there)
aw	(as in soft)
ch	(as in chair)
ee	(as in Eve, eat, Lee)
eh	(as in end, hen, met)
g	(as in game, go, gone)
ih	(as in ill, is, into)
j	(as in jay, joke)
k	(as in ache, can, keep)
oh	(as in oh, old)
oo	(as in food, mood, rude, the owl's oo, you)
or	(as in oar, or, orb)
ow	(as in out)
s or ss	(as in miss, this, us)
t	(as in at, Thomas, tin, Tom)
th	(as in thigh, thin)
u	(as in few, cube, use)
uh	(as in charity, circus, connect, silent, sofa)
ur	(as in lure, your)
y	(as in eye, high, pie)
z	(as in is, tease)

Abas (AH buhs): An early king of Argos; great-grandfather of Perseus. He was a special favorite of Hera who blessed his shield, making it resistant to any sword-stroke. Thus favored by the goddess, Abas proved himself a fearsome warrior. His reputation persisted after his death, and the very sight of his shield, it is said, carried by one of his descendants, was enough to strike fear into the foes of Argos.

Acantha (uh KAN thuh): A nymph who disdained Apollo. Despite her refusals he kept pursuing her until she turned upon him and scratched his face. Enraged, he turned her into a thorny plant which we still know today as the "acanthus."

Achelous (uhk uh LOH uhs): A river-god; son of Oceanus and Tethys. He competed with Heracles for the favor of the beautiful Deianira. Achelous transformed himself into a river and raged over his banks, trying to drown Heracles. When that failed, he turned into a serpent, and, finally, into a bull. But Heracles withstood all these metamorphoses, and hurled Achelous, senseless, to the ground. The defeated god slunk off to his underground springs — but it is said that he still swells angrily in the springtime at the memory of his defeat, and spitefully floods the villages of the plain.

Achilles (uh KILL eez): Son of Peleus and Thetis, and the greatest of all Greek warriors. When Achilles was an infant his sea-goddess mother, wishing him to share her immortality, dipped him into the river Styx. However, in doing so, she held him by the heel, and the part of his heel covered by her thumb became his one vulnerable spot. Otherwise, his hide was stronger than any armor. He could not be wounded by any weapon wielded by man. Even without this magic hide, however, he would have been a most fearsome adversary. For no one whom he engaged in combat lived long enough to get a blow in. He was masterful with spear, sword, bow and arrow — and, even weaponless, fighting with bare hands, he could disarm any foe. He could run faster than any horse — except his own two immortal stallions. Yellow-haired, gray-eyed, thin-lipped, sleek-muscled, he was beautiful to look upon as he moved in the fatal ballet of sword-stroke and spear-thrust. His very appearance on the field struck his foes with terror. When he charged, even the bravest scattered like sheep. The gods themselves, it is said, were loath to meet him weapon in hand. Indeed, on the morning that he killed Hector, he first overcame the river-god Scamander. His feud with Agamemnon almost cost the Greeks the war. For Achilles refused to do any fighting so long as Agamemnon led the army. But Ulysses persuaded Achilles to lend his golden armor to his beloved friend, Patroclus, so that the Trojans, believing that Achilles had taken the field, would yield some of the ground they had won. Achilles agreed and Patroclus was slain by Hector, whereupon Achilles was moved to vengeance. He joined the battle, killed Hector, and turned the tide in favor of the Greeks. He did this despite the Fates' decree that he would not outlive Hector by more than three days. Three days later he was ambushed by Hector's brother Paris, who sent an arrow into the tendon above his heel, his one vulnerable spot — still called the Achilles tendon. The hero fell, but the tale of his deeds lives a stubborn life of its own, partaking of the immortality that Thetis meant to bestow upon her marvelous son.

Actaeon (uhk TEE uhn): A hunter unfortunate enough to glimpse the goddess Artemis bathing in the river. Angered at being seen in her nakedness by a mortal, the maiden goddess changed him into a stag. He was torn to pieces by his own hounds.

Adamanthea (ad uh man THEE uh): A nymph entrusted with the care of the infant Zeus. She concealed the new-born god among the olive groves which grew on the slopes of Mt. Ida so that he would be safe from his father, Cronus, who had formed the habit of devouring his children.

Admetus (ad MEE tuhs): A king of Thessaly whose herds were tended by the exiled Apollo. The king, ignorant that his new herdsman was a god, treated him, as he did all men, with great kindness. Apollo vowed that he would return the favor one day. When Admetus was called to an untimely death, Apollo intervened with the Fates, arguing his case so persuasively that the fatal crones broke their own rule. They agreed that Admetus might return to life if he could find someone to take his place among the dead. The wife of Admetus, the lovely Alcestis, eagerly volunteered. But she was rescued from death by Heracles, who also owed Admetus a favor, and who wished to measure his strength against the one opponent he had never met — death. In all mythology, these two, Admetus and Alcestis, are perhaps the archetypes of the happily married — each bringing to their union love, faithfulness, and a capacity for self-sacrifice.

Adonis (uh DAHN uhs; uh DOH nuhs): Prince of Phoenicia, a youth of surpassing beauty, fruit of the union between King Cynyaras and his daughter, Myrrh. Adonis was adopted by Aphrodite and tutored in the arts of love. But she could not woo him away from his passion for hunting dangerous beasts — which led to his death. The jealous Ares turned himself into a giant boar and gored Adonis to death. From his blood sprang the red flower anemone, which still carpets the slopes of Mt. Lebanon. And Aphrodite's voice still mourns among the trees, calling, "Adon ... Adon...."

Aegeus (EE juhs; EE jee uhs): King of Athens; father of Theseus. When Theseus went to Crete to fight the Minotaur, it was arranged that the homeward-bound ship would bear a white sail if Theseus had prevailed — but would keep its black sail if he had been killed by the monster. Theseus, young and heedless, drunk with victory, forgot to raise the white sail. His father, watching from a hilltop near Athens, saw the black sail appear on the horizon. Grief-stricken at the thought of his hero-son's death, he leaped into the sea, drowning himself, and giving that sea its name — the Aegean.

Aegis (EE jihs): The magical goat-skin which Zeus used to cover his shield. Later, he gave it to his daughter, Athena, who hung the head of Medusa (a present to her from Perseus) from it and was able to turn her enemies to stone.

Aegisthus (ee JIHS thuhs): Key figure in a classic triangle. During the ten years that Agamemnon spent leading the Greek forces against Troy, his cousin, Aegisthus, made himself at home in Mycenae, wooing Queen Clytemnestra, and usurping the king's authority. His success was complete. When Agamemnon returned from Troy, Aegisthus validated his claims by helping Clytemnestra kill her huband. Then he in turn was killed by Agamemnon's avenging children, Orestes and Electra. Clytemnestra shared his fate.

Aeneas (ee NEE uhs): A prince of Troy; son of Aphrodite and Anchises. He was one of the heroes of the Trojan forces, second in fighting ability only to the mighty Hector. He escaped death in the sack of Troy, and saved the life of his old father — carrying him on his back through the flaming city. His wanderings after the fall of Troy are the subject of Virgil's great epic, the *Aeneid*, which concludes with Aeneas landing on the shore of Italy and founding Rome.

Aeolus (EE oh luhs): King of the winds, a stormy red-faced god with disheveled white hair and beard. He dwelt on the island of Aeolia, which he surrounded with a brass wall so that no stranger could come to interfere with his duties. He kept the winds pent in a cave, and dispatched them at his will — sometimes as gentle breezes, sometimes as strong trade winds, and sometimes as gales, hurricanes, or typhoons — according to his temper. Upon certain rare occasions he sewed up the winds in leather bags and lent them to a sailor who could use them as he wished to speed his journey. But this happened only when Aeolus admired the voyager or had been offered a huge bribe. He bagged the winds for Ulysses once, but the favor miscarried, and the trip ended disastrously.

Aetna (ET nuh): A volcanic mountain in Sicily. Its smoky crater was used as a workshop by Hephaestus; the smith-god stoked its fires to temper the thunderbolts he forged for Zeus. Aetna was originally the name of a nymph who made her home on a slope of the mountain. At first, Hephaestus disliked this nymph because she had sided with his sister, Demeter, in a family quarrel. Later, his wrath was melted by her beauty. She bore him twin

5

sons, the Palici — and Hephaestus gave her name to the mountain.

Agamemnon (ag uh MEM nuhn): Son of Atreus, brother of Menelaus, and leader of the Greek expedition against Troy. This king of Mycenae was one of the dominant figures of his age, a formidable battle-chief, but his abilities were marred by his vices. He was lecherous and swinish to the last degree. His insistence on claiming for himself a Trojan girl, captured by Achilles, led to the quarrel which kept Achilles on the sidelines until the Greeks had almost lost the war. On Agamemnon's return from Troy, he was murdered by his queen, Clytemnestra, and her lover, Aegisthus.

Aglaia (uh GLAY yuh): Youngest of the Graces, this beautiful, gentle daughter of Zeus and Eurynome, according to some legends, became the second wife of Hephaestus after he had tired of Aphrodite's infidelities.

Ajax (AY jax): A prince of Salamis, who was, next to Achilles, the most powerful warrior among the Greeks. This huge, beefy, red-faced brawler used the mast of a ship as a spear and hurled enormous boulders as if they were pebbles. He fought a draw with Hector and lived through the bloodiest battles of the war only to fall by his own hand. Legend says he went mad when Odysseus cheated him out of the dead Achilles' golden armor — with the last glimmer of his reason he chose to slay himself rather than run amok and destroy his comrades.

Albion (AL bih uhn): Most honorable of Poseidon's mischievous brood. According to one legend he flew to the Western rim of the world to fetch a golden apple from Hera's tree as a present for his mother, Amphitrite. Homeward bound, he found a mist-shrouded island just east of the Hesperides. It was inhabited by blue-painted tribesmen who immediately recognized him as a god and did him much honor. He lingered on the island teaching its people the arts of boat-building and navigation. Since then, the islanders have been the ablest boatwrights and bravest sailors in the entire world. They named their island Albion in honor of the kindly sea-god; it is now called England.

Alcestis (al SES tihs): Beautiful wife of Admetus, who offered to die if her husband's life might be spared. Her offer was accepted, but Heracles wrested her from the clutches of Hades, and she was joyfully reunited with her husband, King Admetus.

Alcmene (alk MEE nee): Princess of Argos, and mother of Heracles. Loveliest woman of her time, Alcmene was known as the "Lady of the Light Footstep." It was said of her that she could run over a field of grass without bending a blade. Zeus fell in love with her but, knowing her reputation for virtue, put on the form of her husband before visiting her. Heracles was the product of this impersonation.

Alcyone (al SY oh nee): Daughter of Aeolus; princess of the winds. She married Ceyx, son of the Morning Star. They were so happy they aroused the envy of the unhappily wed Hera, who sent a storm to wreck the ship on which Ceyx was voyaging. His ghost appeared to Alcyone, and she drowned herself to keep him company. But Zeus pitied them and turned them into a pair of kingfishers. Each winter thereafter Aeolus forbade his winds to blow for a space of seven days so that his daughter, now a beautiful white kingfisher, could lay her eggs in a nest which floated on the sea. It is from this episode that we derive the word "halcyon," meaning a period of calm and golden days.

Alectryon (uh LEK trih uhn): The unlucky sentinel. He was assigned by Ares to watch for daybreak so that he might awaken the war-god who was trysting with Aphrodite and did not wish the sun to spy upon his doings. But Alectryon fell asleep — and Apollo, charioteer of the sun, observed the dalliance, and the secret was a secret no more. Enraged, Ares turned Alectryon into a rooster, who must wake himself earlier than any other creature to proclaim sunrise.

Alpheus (al FEE uhs): A river-god who fell in love with a nymph named Arethusa. He pursued her over the field and through the wood and was about to catch her when she claimed the aid of Artemis, who changed her into a stream. Whereupon Alpheus changed himself into a river and sought to mingle his waters with the stream. But Artemis dammed him up and left him in thwarted flood. It was this river, Alpheus, which Heracles later diverted from its course to flush out the Augean Stables.

Amalthea (am uhl THEE uh): A she-goat whose milk nourished the infant Zeus on the slope of Crete's Mt. Ida. Zeus was always grateful to this compassionate creature whom he viewed as his foster-mother. He honored her in three ways. After her death he used her hide to cover his shield. This was the sacred "aegis," later given to Athena. He also filled her horn with golden fruit from the Garden of the Hesperides; when the fruit was eaten, it would magically replenish itself. This was the "cornucopia." Later, he set goat and horn among the stars, where they shine as the constellation "Capricorn."

Amazons (AM uh zuhnz): A nation of warrior women, said to have originated in Scythia. They trained their bodies for warfare, did all the hunting and fighting, and used men only for breeding purposes and menial tasks. They attained matchless skill in horseback riding and

8

archery and became the most fearsome cavalry of ancient times. They enter many legends. Heracles and Theseus raided them and carried off two of their queens. A detachment of Amazons fought for Priam before the walls of Troy, and wrought much destruction among the Greeks until finally vanquished by Achilles. They invaded Lycia, and would have overrun that land had they not been defeated by Bellerephon, who rode above them on the flying horse Pegasus, and dropped huge boulders on them. On their most successful expedition they swept over the entire Peloponnese, and laid seige to Athens — which almost fell to them before they were turned back by Theseus.

Amphitrite (am fih TRY tee): Wife of Poseidon; queen of the sea. This joyous daughter of Oceanus loved to frisk among the blue waves and come out at low tide to dance on the shore. Poseidon glimpsed her dancing on Naxos and fell violently in love with her. But she feared his stormy wooing, and fled him to the depths of the sea. Whereupon he changed his tactics and tried to win her with gifts. Of coral and pearl and the bullion off sunken treasure ships, he wrought her marvelous ornaments, but she spurned them all. Finally, he created something entirely new for her — a talking dancing fish. He dubbed the creature "dolphin," and sent it to Amphitrite. The dolphin pleaded Poseidon's cause with such wit and eloquence that Amphitrite yielded. She reigned as queen of the sea for many centuries and bore Poseidon scores of children, among them Triton of the wreathed horn. The dolphin remained her favorite of all the creatures of the deep and she employed a string of them to pull her crystal chariot.

Amphitryon (am FIHT rih uhn): Husband of Alcmene; stepfather of Heracles. His courtship of Alcmene was extremely eventful. She refused to marry him unless

9

he avenged her eight brothers who had been killed by a certain Pterelaus, king of Taphos. To mount an expedition against Taphos, however, he needed the help of King Creon of Thebes. Creon refused to help him unless he first killed a giant, man-eating fox. This fox was deemed uncatchable, but Amphitryon borrowed a hound from Artemis. With this wolfish black and silver hound he was able to track the fox to its lair and there slay it. Nevertheless, his invasion against Taphos would have failed had he not won the love of Princess Comaetho — who betrayed her father to him. For her father, the king, was invincible until he should lose a single golden hair that grew among his white hairs. The princess plucked this golden hair as her father lay asleep and presented it to Amphitryon, who thereupon defeated the king's army and killed the king. However, he disappointed the princess. He left Taphos and married Alcmene, whose conditions he had now fulfilled. Their marriage was very happy. He never blamed Alcmene for bearing Zeus an illegitimate child. He treated Heracles as his own son and viewed the strategy of Zeus as a compliment to himself. For Alcmene had broken all precedent by resisting the mighty god until he deceived her by assuming the form of her husband. Amphitryon and Alcmene remained happily united after the birth of Heracles.

Anchises (an KY seez): Father of Aeneas. This handsome young prince of Troy boasted that he had enjoyed the favors of Aphrodite. Zeus heard him bragging and hurled a thunderbolt at him — laming the young man and so disfiguring him that he was ignored by Aphrodite thereafter. Nevertheless, she bore him a son, the hero Aeneas, who, after fighting very gallantly against the Greeks, saved his father from the sack of Troy by carrying him on his shoulders through the flaming city. Anchises lived long enough to accompany his marvelous son on the beginning of that voyage which was to culminate in the founding of Rome.

Andromache (an DRAHM uh kee): Hector's wife. One of the most attractive figures in mythology. All during the ordeal of the Trojan war she was constantly encouraging her husband and helping him in everything he did. After the fall of Troy she was taken into slavery by Neoptolemus, son of Achilles.

Andromeda (an DRAHM ee duh): A princess of Joppa, whose mother, Cassiopeia, boasted that she was more beautiful than those lovely ocean nymphs, called Nereids. This angered Poseidon, who was partial to Nereids, and he sent a sea-monster to ravage the coast. An oracle informed the king that the monster would not be appeased until Andromeda was sacrificed to him. Thereupon, the maiden was bound to a rock to be devoured by the monster. But Perseus happened to be passing that way with the newly killed Medusa's head in his pouch. He flashed the head at the monster turning it to stone, struck the shackles from Andromeda, and took her home to Sephiros to be his wife. After her death, Andromeda found a place in heaven among the stars and became a constellation, as did her mother, Cassiopeia, her father, Cepheus, and the sea-monster.

Antaeus (an TEE uhs): A giant who figured in one of Heracles' most famous adventures. This huge creature was a son of Mother Earth. He was tall as a tree and was reputed to be the most fearsome wrestler in the world. In addition to his titanic strength he held a magical advantage. He could not be pinned. Every time he touched earth he drew new strength from his mother and arose, more terrible than ever, to face his adversary. Heracles, during their bout, was unable to defeat him

11

until he understood that Antaeus was being refreshed by every fall. Then Heracles lifted the giant from earth and held him there, out of contact with his mother, so that he could not renew his strength. And, holding him suspended, Heracles strangled him.

Antigone (an TIHG uh nee): Daughter of Oedipus. This young girl became a model for filial piety and family loyalty. She insisted on accompanying her blind father as he wandered homeless from Thebes, and stayed with him until he died at Colonnus. Then she returned to Thebes to find that her brother, Polynices, had been killed in a combat with his brother. Creon, their uncle, had declared the young man a rebel and refused him burial. Antigone stole her brother's body and buried it with proper ceremony, knowing that she was risking her own life in doing so. Nevertheless, she took the risk and paid the price: Creon ordered her to be buried alive.

Antiope (an TEE uh pee): An Amazon princess who married Theseus. She objected strenuously when he decided to put her aside for a second wife, Phaedra. Theseus met her objections by killing her. However, her ghost was avenged. For Phaedra, young wife of Theseus, fell in love with Antiope's son, Hippolytus, who was about her own age. But Hippolytus disdained her. He was interested only in taming horses. Phaedra, in a fury, lied to Thesus, saying the boy had assaulted her. Theseus killed his son and Phaedra hanged herself.

Aphrodite (af ruh DY tee): Goddess of love. Unlike the other Olympians, she was charged with only one duty — to incite desire. She did nothing else. Love was her profession, her pleasure, her hobby. She had no parents. Aphrodite means "foam-born." In the beginning of time, Cronus killed his father, Uranus, and flung the gigantic body into the sea. The blood of the dismembered god drifted in the sun, whitening into foam. From the foam rose a tall yellow-haired maiden who came ashore at Cyprus. Where she walked, flowers bloomed and birds circled, singing. Thus, in the legend, love was born out of the primal murder, expressing the Greek belief in the final indestructibility of life. Aphrodite was courted by all the gods, but surprised everyone by marrying the ugliest of the Pantheon, Hephaestus, the little lame smith-god. As goddess of love, which is the mainspring of human activity, she enters more legends than any other god or goddess. She bore many children, who had almost as many fathers: Eros (the archer of love), son of Zeus; Phobos (Fear), and Harmonia, mother of the Amazons, both sired by Ares; the misshapen Priapus, son of Dionysus; and her encounter with Hermes produced the self-sufficient monster, Hermaphroditus. After every adventure, however, she returned to Hephaestus — who always forgave her. Apple, rose, myrtle, and the dove were sacred to her. In Roman mythology, Aphrodite was known as Venus.

Antinuous (an TIHN oh uhs): Most persistent and obnoxious of Penelope's suitors — and the first one killed by the avenging Odysseus.

Apollo (uh PAHL oh): The sun-god. Also god of medicine and music; patron of poetry, mathematics, and prophecy. This radiantly beautiful son of Zeus and Leto bears many names: Phoebus, or the Bright One; King of minstrels; Prince of oracles; Lord of the golden bow. His first act was to take up his golden bow and hunt down the Python, which, upon the orders of jealous Hera, had harried his mother from one end of the earth to the other. The giant serpent fled to its cave at Delphi. But Apollo pursued it into the depths of the cavern and there slew it with his golden arrows. He seized the cave for his own and raised a temple at Delphi, served by oracular priestesses, who were called Pythonesses. Each morning Apollo rose from his couch in his eastern palace, bridled his fiery-maned stallions, and drove the golden chariot of the sun across the blue meadows of the sky along the path marked by white-winged dawn. Then, finally, he descended among festive pennants of fire and dipped beneath the western horizon, where he stabled his horses. Of all the gods of the Pantheon, Apollo resembles most closely the Greek ideal — eternally youthful, lovely to look upon, potent in battle, warm-hearted, and cool-thinking. He was beloved of mankind and used his influence very wisely, preaching always the middle way, counseling against excess. Once, his twin sister, Artemis, who always disapproved of his paramours, accused him of hypocrisy. "You preach moderation," she cried. "But you let your own passions run away with you!" And Apollo replied: "I preach moderation in all things — including moderation." It was this sunny jesting quality, combined with serene wisdom, that endeared him to god and man. There are conflicting claims as to which of his sons Zeus loved best, but it is agreed that he entrusted Apollo with more significant powers than any other god.

Apple of Discord (AP l uhv DIHS kord): A golden apple wrought by Hephaestus that triggered the Trojan War. The war-god, Ares, had a sister named Eris who was an ugly shrew. It was her pastime to ride beside her brother in his war-chariot, screaming for blood, laughing at the spectacle of violent death. She was unpopular among the gods and was left off the invitation list for the wedding of Peleus and Thetis, the most brilliant fête ever held on Olympus. Eris vowed vengeance. She stole the golden apple from Hephaestus's workshop and engraved it with these words: "To the Fairest." Then, when the festivities were at their height, she entered unseen and rolled the apple on the banquet table. It was immediately claimed by Hera, Aphrodite, and Athena. They appealed to Zeus for judgment. But the king of the gods, knowing that his choice of one would lead to endless recrimination on the part of the others, refused to judge the matter. He passed it on to Paris, young prince of Troy, for adjudication. Each of the goddesses offered bribes. Hera offered him limitless power; Athena offered him wisdom. Aphrodite simply took his hand and whispered to him, and he promptly awarded her the apple. What she had promised him was a woman as beautiful as herself — Queen Helen of Sparta. It was the abduction of Helen by Paris that launched the Greek invasion of Troy. During that war, Hera and Athena showed marked partiality for the Greek side.

Arachne (uh RAK nee): A young girl of Lydia, who was so proud of her skill at weaving that she dared challenge Athena herself to a contest. When the contest was joined, Arachne wove marvelous tapestries depicting scandalous incidents from the lives of the gods, and all the spectators thought she must surely win though she was matched against the goddess who had invented the spindle. But then Athena stood with her giant spindle on a hilltop; she gathered the rosy fleece of the sunset and the first blue and silver strands of starlight, and wove scenes of the world's creation. She flung her starry brocades across the rafters of heaven so that the whole sky was hung with her handiwork, and the spectators fell on their knees and worshipped. In despair at her defeat Arachne killed herself. But Athena took pity and changed her into a spider — a little creature who spins the hours away but does not brag about it.

Ares (AIR eez): Son of Zeus and Hera; god of war. The Olympians were by no means peaceable, nevertheless they disliked Ares whom they regarded as a bloody-minded butcher. He killed for the pleasure of it; incited men to warfare, then gloated over the battlefield. He was accompanied by his sister, Eris, goddess of discord, and two sons — Deimos (Fear), and Phobos (Terror). Terror was also the name of one of his chariot horses; the others were Fire, Flame, and Trouble. Only three gods were friendly to Ares: Aphrodite, who was fascinated by violence and thought him handsome in a brutal kind of way; Eris, his sister, who rode beside him in his war-chariot, shrieking; and Hades, god of the dead, whose kingdom was greatly enlarged by the wars that Ares started.

Argonauts (AHR guh nawts): The crew of heroes recruited by Jason for his quest of the Golden Fleece.

Argos (AHR guhs): Master shipwright, supposed to have been the author of such nautical refinements as the leather-socketed oar-port for easier rowing, a sail that could be tilted on the mast for quartering winds, and the first rudder — a pivoted steering-board used instead of the helm oar. The ship that he built for Jason, called the *Argo*, was able to outrace and outmaneuver any other ship in the sea.

Argosy (AHR guh see): Name given to Jason's quest for the Golden Fleece. The term was later applied to Spanish treasure ships.

Argus (AHR guhs): A hundred-eyed giant employed by Hera to spy upon Zeus and observe his trysting places. He was killed by Hermes upon the instigation of Zeus when he proved over-zealous in guarding Io.

Ariadne (air ih AD nee): Eldest daughter of Minos, king of Crete. She helped Theseus find his way out of the labyrinth by unreeling a ball of magical thread. She eloped with Theseus after he slew the Minotaur, but

16

tiring of her, he abandoned her on the island of Naxos, where she was consoled by the voyaging Dionysus.

Arion (uh RY uhn): Singer and musician second only to Orpheus; inventor of the dithyramb, or poem of praise. He sang so beautifully that the fish would rise from the depths of the sea to listen to him — a phenomenon that was to save his life. When thrown overboard by pirates he was rescued by a music-loving dolphin.

Aristaeus (ahr ihs TEE uhs): Son of Apollo and Cyrene. Eurydice, wife of Orpheus, was fleeing Aristaeus when she was fatally bitten by a snake and began that journey to Hades which led to her husband's famed excursion into death.

Artemis (AHR tuh mihs): The moon-goddess. Silver belonged to Artemis as gold belonged to her brother, Apollo. She was the moon-maiden who rode the night sky in a silver chariot drawn by white stags, and bent her silver bow shooting arrows of silver light. Although Poseidon was king of the sea, this slender moon-princess owned a mystic power over his demesne; for she and she alone swung the tides on a silver leash — now hurling the waves onto the shores, now letting them subside in silvery ripples. She was the goddess of the hunt also, and ran in silver sandals down mountain slopes and through forest glades, followed by a troop of laughing dryads. She was also the Lady of Wild Things, and punished those who killed more than they could eat. She caused them to be thrown from their horses or to lose their way in the wood and be eaten by wolves. She was cold and disdainful and held herself aloof, disliking crowds and loathing cities. She admired her half-sister, Athena, and took similar vows of chastity — which she imposed upon her dryads with mixed results. She was less demanding of mortals, however, and in some legends was the patroness of young lovers — lending torches for their revels and casting shadows so they could hide. Wild animals were sacred to her, especially lion, bear, wolf, and all kinds of wild birds. In Roman mythology, Artemis was known as Diana.

Asclepius (ass KLEE pee uhs): Son of Apollo; father of medicine. Apollo held domain over medicine and passed the gift of healing to his son, Asclepius, who became such a marvelous doctor that he could bring the dead back to life. He did this so often that Hades, king of Tartarus, whose subjects are the dead, became enraged because so few were crossing over into his kingdom. Hades complained to Zeus that Asclepius was robbing him, thus attacking the dignity of all gods. Zeus nodded, took up a thunderbolt, and hurled it at Asclepius, killing him. Apollo, infuriated, stormed into the volcano and slew all the Cyclopes who labored there forging thunderbolts. Then Apollo went to Zeus and pleaded his son's case so eloquently that Zeus recalled Asclepius to life. In return, Asclepius patched up the Cyclopes, who returned to forge thunderbolts for Zeus.

Astreus (ass TREE uhs): A titan. In an early legend he trysted in a corner of the sky with Eos, goddess of the dawn, siring the four winds and a litter of stars.

Astyanax (ass TY uh nax): Infant son of Hector and Andromache. During the sack of Troy he was flung off the wall to his death. Some say Menelaus committed this crime; others accuse Neoptolemus, son of Achilles.

Atalanta (at uh LAN tuh): When Arcadians saw this long-legged maiden racing across the fields and through the trees they thought she was the goddess Artemis, descended from heaven. Indeed, anyone seeing her run down a stag in full stride or wrestle a bear would have sworn that she was more than mortal. Abandoned in infancy by her father, the king, she was adopted by a she-bear who suckled her. Bear cubs were her brothers and sisters. She played with them, wrestled with them, hunted with them, and grew up wild and solitary as a wood-nymph. She was able to outrace and outfight any man she met. When Meleager, the only lad she had ever loved, was killed because his mother disapproved of the match, Atalanta vowed never to accept any other suitor. But she was surpassingly beautiful, and suitors swarmed. She devised a method to curtail their wooing. She promised to marry the first man to beat her in a foot-race, but warned that losers must pay with their lives. One by one, her suitors raced her and lost; one by one they lost their heads. Finally, one young man, Hippomanes, had the wit to pray to Aphrodite before the race. The goddess of love gave him three golden apples which he bore to the starting post under his tunic. One by one he dropped them. Each time that Atalanta stooped to retrieve a rolling apple, he gained ground. He won the race and Atalanta became his wife. There are those who say, however, that she was fast enough to have retrieved the apples and still have beaten him, but that she was tired of living alone. According to legend, she and Meleager spent their first year together traveling with Jason on his Argosy.

Ate (ay TEE): Daughter of Zeus and Eris. In some legends she is the daughter of Discord, a self-sufficient spite, immortal sower of quarrels. In other tales, Ate is a variant name for Eris herself. Her mischief-making finally infuriated Zeus, who hurled her from Olympus. She then took up residence on earth and caused more trouble than ever, sowing suspicion among men and provoking them to feuds and bloody quarrels.

Athamas (ATH uh muhs): This king of Thebes was

unfortunate enough to be involved in a quarrel among the gods. He had married Ino, daughter of Cadmus, and sister to Semele, whom Zeus had courted, and who bore the infant god, Dionysus. After the jealous Hera had contrived Semele's death, Zeus gave the orphaned Dionysus to Ino to raise. Hera's wrath was turned upon her and upon her husband, Athamas. She drove them mad. In their madness they murdered their children.

Athena (uh THEE nuh): Daughter of Zeus and goddess of wisdom. Athena's mother was Metis, a daughter of the Titans. But it had been prophesied of Metis that if she bore a son he would kill his father. Zeus, unwilling to take any chances, swallowed Metis whole. He was immediately stricken by a headache so terrible that he began to batter his head against a rock. Hephaestus sprang to his aid, and split his father's head open with a blow of his mallet. From Zeus' skull sprang a tall gray-eyed maiden, brandishing a spear. Born in this way, Athena naturally became goddess of wisdom, patroness of intellectual activities, and protector of Athens, which was named after her and where she was particularly honored. She was called Pallas Athena, the Maiden Goddess, and remained a virgin forever. She is depicted always as wearing a helmet and breastplate, carrying lance and shield. She worked very assiduously to make men wise. She taught her favorites to invent the plough, the spinning wheel, and the sail. Scholars prayed to her for enlightenment, inventors for inspiration, judges for clarity and fair-mindedness. Captains, seeking to sharpen their tactics on the eve of battle, prayed to her also. The olive tree was sacred to her, also the owl. In Roman mythology, Athena was known as Minerva.

Atlas (AT luhs): A powerful Titan. He fought bravely in the war against Zeus, so bravely that when Cronus was defeated and the Titans exiled, Atlas was singled out for special punishment. He was condemned to station himself on the far western margin of the world and bear the rim of the sky on his shoulders. There he stood as the centuries turned, seas boiled and receded, and mountains were worn to pebbles — standing always under his burden, shoulders bowed, legs braced, enduring his punishment. In happier days he had married the Titaness Pleione, and fathered the Pleiades, the Hyades, Calypso, and the Hesperides. These last were three beautiful daughters, the apple nymphs, who accompanied their father into exile and guarded Hera's golden tree that had been planted under the shadow of Atlas. He once rid himself of his burden when Heracles came upon his eleventh labor to fetch a golden apple. Atlas persuaded Heracles to take the sky upon his shoulders, promising to take it back again after he had stretched his aching muscles. He fully intended to break his promise, but Heracles guesssed his purpose and tricked him into resuming his burden. The suffering Titan was never again able to find anyone strong enough to relieve him of his awful weight. Some say the ordeal of Atlas ended when Perseus, remembering his own visit to the Garden of the Hesperides and struck by belated pity, left the Elysian Fields, and traveled west again with his Medusa head. He showed the head to Atlas and turned him to stone. Thenceforth he was known as Mt. Atlas; he still bore the sky on his snowy shoulders, but without suffering.

Atreus (AY tree us): Son of Pelops; king of Mycenae and head of the most tragic house in Greek mythology. Atreus' wife, Aerope, fell in love with his twin brother, Thyestes, and bore him two children. Atreus took a terrible vengeance: He killed the two children, roasted them, and served them to his brother at a banquet. For this horrid crime the gods fastened a curse upon Atreus and all his descendants. His son, Menelaus, married

Helen and became the most famous cuckold in the world. His other son, Agamemnon, leader of the Greek forces against Troy, was murdered by his own wife upon his return from the wars. His grandson, Orestes, killed his mother, Clytemnestra, to avenge his father's death, and was himself torn by the Furies. The misadventures of the House of Atreus have been a treasure trove for writers for almost three thousand years. Of the thirty-three Greek dramas which have come down to us intact, eight of them are concerned with members of this accursed family. Scores of later writers, including many contemporaries, have also mined the riches of this tragic tale.

Atropos (AT roh pohss): Eldest of the Fates, and most fearsome of the three sisters. She waits with her shears to cut the thread of life after it has been spun by Clotho and measured by Lachesis.

Augean Stables (uh GEE uhn STAY b'lz): The sixth labor of Heracles was to clean these stables in one day. Now King Augeas of Elis was a man of very filthy habits. For thirty years he had kept three thousand cattle housed in a huge system of barns and byres, and never once in all those thirty years were the cattle allowed outside, nor were the stables cleaned. The result was a stinking midden that defied imagination. Heracles reversed the flow of the river Alpheus, lifting it from its bed and hurling its waters through the stables, flushing them out in a mighty torrent. He left the stables clean, but to this day the river still runs the wrong way.

Autolycus (oh TAHL uh kuhs): Son of Hermes, grandfather of Odysseus. He inherited Hermes' craftiness and talent for thievery. His cattle grazed on the lush slopes of Mt. Parnassus, but his herds had a disquieting way of expanding overnight. He would raid his neighbors' herds in the dark of night, so swiftly and so silently he was able to cut out the best beeves and drive them onto his own grazing grounds before his neighbors detected anything amiss. Not only that, but he could change the appearance of a bull or heifer so that no herdsman was able to identify his own property. He changed the color of the animals' coats, the length and shape of their horns, or dehorned them completely. His techniques were a secret, but their effectiveness was notorious. Hermes was entertained by the exploits of this crafty son, and many times intervened to save him from sudden death at the hands of his outraged neighbors.

Avernus (uh VUR nuhs): The somber lake whose underwater caves, the ancients believed, opened into Tartarus, the Land Beyond Death.

Bacchantes (buh KAHN teez): Worshippers of Dionysus (Bacchus), son of wine, and bestower of ecstasy. Ivy-crowned and joyous, these women danced in the moonlight, abandoning themselves to adoration of their radiant young lord.

Balius (BAY lih- us): One of Achilles' wonderful horses. It spoke Greek, and was in the habit of unyoking itself from the chariot to fight at its master's side. Its partner was Xanthus, an equally remarkable horse.

Baucis and Philemon (BAH sihs) (fih LEE mahn): An old couple who, despite their poverty, lavishly entertained Zeus and Hermes while they were wandering the earth in mortal guise. The gods, deeply moved by this unassuming generosity, granted the aged pair their dearest wish — that they remain united even in death. They were transformed into trees whose branches ever after intermingled.

Bellerephon (buh LAIR uh fuhn): A hero who bridled Pegasus and slew the Chimaera. Bellerephon was a young Corinthian who, unknowingly, offended the king of Lycia. The king was in the habit of killing those who displeased him, but Bellerephon was a guest, and the laws of hospitality forbade outright murder. Therefore the king sent the young man on a mission he believed would be fatal — to slay a monster that had been ravaging the countryside. Called the Chimaera, it was half ram, half dragon; it flew on leathery wings and breathed flame. The youth, who was very innocent, thought it entirely proper that he be sent upon such an errand. He prayed to Athena, queen of tactics, for such aid as she might believe him to merit. Athena, much impressed by his modesty and uprightness, appeared to him in a dream, and instructed him to capture the winged horse Pegasus, before battling the Chimaera. When Bellerephon awoke, he found a golden bridle lying on the bed and knew that the dream had been a divine visitation. Bellerephon found the marvelous horse grazing on the slope of Mt. Helicon. He was a gorgeous creature — snow-white, with coral-red nostrils, gold wings, and brass hooves, with a mane of bright gold. When the stallion saw Bellerephon, he neighed, beat his wings, and began to fly away, but Bellerephon threw Athena's bridle over his head — whereupon he descended and allowed the youth to mount. Inspired by Athena, Bellerephon had made a careful battle plan. Nothing, he knew, could withstand the flaming breath of the monster; he must find a way to turn this deadly quality to his own advantage. He affixed a lump of lead to the point of his spear, and spurred Pegasus to rise above the Chimaera. Then he made Pegasus fold his wings and side-slip, diving suddenly out of the sun and appearing beside the monster's head before it realized it was being attacked. The surprise was complete. The Chimaera opened its terrible jaws, but before it could lick Bellerephon with its tongue of flame, he thrust his spear between its jaws. The lump of lead was melted by the fiery breath, and flowed down the Chimaera's throat, scorching its liver and killing it instantly. The Chimaera folded its wings and dropped like a stone. Bellerephon coasted down to the plain where a multitude of people had assembled to watch the battle. He was hailed as their champion, and the king forgave him. He also gave him his daughter, the princess Philinoe, in marriage. Bellerephon fought many other battles, always riding Pegasus into the fray, always triumphant. But as his fame grew, his modesty shrank. He became very vain, and decided to ride Pegasus as high as Olympus, and there boast to the gods of the deeds he had done. But the gods discouraged such displays. Zeus sent a gadfly which stung Pegasus in mid-flight, causing the horse to buck suddenly, throwing his rider. Bellerephon fell as the Chimaera had fallen. He was not killed by the fall, but was terribly lamed — and had to drag out the rest of his life as a beggar. Pegasus was stabled among the horses of Zeus. But those charming daughters of Zeus, the Muses, were struck by the beauty of the steed, and coaxed him away from their father, who could refuse them nothing. The Muses kept Pegasus as their own, riding him from Olympus to Parnassus, and back again. Sometimes, it was said, they lent him to young artists in need of help. But he still sometimes bucked suddenly when he felt that his rider had grown too vain.

Biblis (BIHB luhs): The ancient Phoenician city which gave its name to books. Some say it is the oldest city in the world. Phoenicia took its name from King Phoenix (Cinyras), father and grandfather of Adonis.

Boreas (BOH reh uhs; boh REE uhs): A name for the North Wind. The Romans called it *Aquilo*, the eagle-wind. It was the most unruly denizen of Aeolus' cave. It loved storm and trouble, exulted in shipwrecks, and was more feared than any of its brothers.

Briareus (bry AHR ee uhs): A hundred-handed giant who won the eternal favor of Zeus by releasing him from captivity. The king of the gods had been surprised by a rebellious faction of Olympians led by Hera, and lay bound and helpless. But Briareus searched for his master and untied the hundred knots that bound Zeus, allowing him to escape and suppress the rebellion. Zeus trussed Hera in golden chains and hung her upside down from the rafters of heaven — and kept her hanging until she pleaded for forgiveness, vowing never to rebel agin. Thereafter, Zeus ruled unchallenged, retaining Briareus as his most trusted servant.

Briseis (bry SEE uhs): A beautiful Trojan girl captured by Achilles. When Agamemnon unfairly claimed her, Achilles quit the war. He did not return until the Greeks had suffered huge losses and Agamemnon had been humiliated.

Brize (BRY zee): A horrid little spite who served Hera. She was a gadfly, large as a sparrow — with a sting as long as a dagger. She was sent by Hera to torment the nymph Io, to whom Zeus had been attentive. Hermes killed this gadfly when he saved Io.

Brontes (BRAHN teez): A Cyclops who labored underwater making horse troughs for Poseidon. He wrought the silver new-moon bow for Artemis, even though she had rejected him as a suitor.

Butes (BU teez): One of the Argonauts. Bee-keeper extraordinary, the honey made by his swarms was sweeter than any other; he supplied it to Olympus for the gods' repast.

Cabeiri (kuh BY ry): Archaic gods whose legends were told long before the tales of the Olympians. Their attributes are lost in the mists of unrecorded time, but they are associated with the most ancient ceremonies of planting, fishing, and toolmaking. The Cabeirian Mysteries were performed in Thebes, and on the islands of Imbros, Lemnos, and Samothrace. The secrets of these rites were disclosed only to initiates, who were forbidden to speak of them upon pain of death.

Cacus (KAY kuhs): A three-headed giant; son of Hephaestus and Medusa. He was unwise enough to steal cattle from Heracles, who pursued the giant, withstood the flame that issued from each of his three mouths, and decapitated him one head at a time.

Cadmus (KAD muhs): An early hero of mythology; brother of Europa. This young prince of Phoenicia entered legend when his sister was abducted by Zeus, who had turned himself into a white bull for the occasion. Cadmus immediately set off in search of his sister, even though he had been told that the most powerful god had claimed her as his own. Cadmus searched all the lands of the known world, following the trail of Europa, whose name has been given to that Western land mass. Finally, Cadmus prayed to Athena, who answered him and said she could not help him reclaim his sister, who now belonged to Zeus. But she also told him that with her counsel he could found a great nation. She filled him with such courage that he was able to kill a dragon that attacked him when he came to Thebes. Then, still following instructions of the goddess, he sowed the dragon's teeth. A legion of iron-clad men sprang from the furrows. He hid himself and threw stones at them. They began to fight among themselves and fought until there were only a handful of survivors. Then Cadmus came out of hiding and proclaimed himself their king. With these men he founded Thebes, fought off invading chieftains, and built a prosperous and warlike nation. He became so powerful a monarch that Aphrodite gave him her daughter, Harmonia, to be his queen. Their daughters were Semele, mother of Dionysus, and the ill-fated Ino.

Caduceus (kuh DOO see uhs): The serpent-wreathed staff carried by Hermes. Since he was the messenger-god, this staff was later carried by all heralds. It is said that the original staff belonged to Apollo, who gave it to Hermes in return for the lyre Hermes had invented. Apollo was also god of medicine and so the caduceus became the insignia for the healing art, and is still used in that way.

Calais (KAL ay uhs): A son of the North Wind. With his twin brother, Zetes, he accompanied Jason on the Argosy. It was these twins who delivered Phineus from the Harpies who were tormenting him. In gratitude, the king of Trace gave them each a pair of wings. At their deaths the gods changed them into a pair of birds.

Calchas (KAL kuhs): A soothsayer whose expert prophecies guided the Greeks in their war against the Trojans. It was he who advised Agamemnon to sacrifice

29

Iphigenia in order to bring fair winds that would carry his fleet to Troy. He warned that the Greeks could not win without the presence of Achilles, and it was his timely counsel that stopped the plague Apollo had sent as punishment for Agamemnon's impiety. He also foretold that the war would last ten years. However, he was undone by his high opinion of himself. Challenged to a guessing contest by Mopsus, he failed to estimate the number of figs on a tree. When his opponent guessed correctly, Calchas strangled on his own vanity.

Calliope (kuh LIE oh pee): The Muse of epic poetry. This stalwart daughter of Zeus and Mnemosyne was the most assertive of the eight sisters. She loved to sing of heroes, wars, and glorious victories. Later, she bore a son, Orpheus, who was the sweetest singer of his age.

Callisto (kuh LISS toh): She was a princess of Arcadia and an attendant of Artemis. Now Artemis, the Maiden Goddess, imposed strict vows of chastity on her court and enforced them stringently. Zeus, however, pursued Callisto, and persuaded her to break her vows. Thereupon, Hera turned Callisto into a bear and set her in the path of Artemis when the goddess was out hunting. Artemis killed the bear, but Zeus snatched her from the dead and set her among the stars as the constellation of the Great Bear.

Callirhoe (kuh LIHR oh ee): Daughter of the river-god Achelous, and second wife of Alcmaeon, an Argive chieftain, who was assassinated by the father of his first wife. The widow Callirhoe thirsted for vengeance. She prayed to Zeus that her infant sons grow to manhood in a single day so that they might avenge their father's murder. Zeus granted her prayer, and the children, growing six feet in one day, took up arms and killed their father's murderer.

Calydonian Boar Hunt (KAL uh DOH nih uhn BOHR HUHNT): A key incident in the legend of Atalanta. The king and queen of Calydon had angered Artemis, who sent a wild boar to waste their kingdom. This beast was huge, larger than an elephant, with razor-sharp tusks and an incredibly vicious temper. It defied the efforts of anyone to trap or kill it. Prince Meleager sent messages to the best hunters in all the lands that bordered Calydon, proclaiming a gala boar hunt. The ablest hunters and warriors of the time responded, including Theseus, Castor, Polydeuces, Peleus, and many of those who later became Argonauts. Now, the fleet-footed maiden Atalanta, who had been raised by a she-bear and could hunt and fight better than most men, was Meleager's beloved. They always hunted together and at the Calydonian Boar Hunt they cornered the boar and, working in tandem, killed the beast. Meleager courteously presented her with the boar's hide. His angry uncles objected, and insulted Atalanta, whereupon Meleager slew his uncles. This led to his own death at the hands of his mother who had been driven half-mad by the prospect of her son marrying a wild girl from the hills.

Calypso (kuh LIHP soh): A daugher of Atlas. This beautiful Titaness dwelt on an island all alone, occasionally amusing herself with shipwrecked sailors whom she pulled from the sea. The most noted of these was Odysseus. She rescued him after one of his misadventures, and made life very sweet for the wanderer. After seven years, however, he grew restless and insisted on departing. She pleaded with him, offering him immortality and eternal youth, but he refused all her offers, and sailed away from her island on a raft she had sorrowfully built for him.

Carya (KAHR ih uh): A girl beloved of Dionysus. She

returned his love, and when she died the grieving god turned her into a walnut tree. Thereafter, the word "caryatid," was applied to a female statue used as a temple column — these columns were carved of walnut.

Cassandra (kuh SAN druh): Daughter of Priam and Hecuba. This beautiful, shy, yet witty princess had the misfortune to be loved by Apollo. He promised her great gifts if she would yield to him, and caressed her with sun-stroke — under the influence of which she uttered startling prophecies. But when she would still not warm to his advances he added a fatal twist to his gift: She would prophecy truly, but no one would ever believe her. And so, she read the future with total accuracy, but could not communicate her vision; her utterances were ignored. She warned that if Paris were to visit Sparta, he would bring disaster on Troy. She warned against bringing the Wooden Horse through the gates into Troy. She foretold that she would be taken into slavery. And she further warned the man who enslaved her that he would be dishonored and killed on his return from Troy. This man was Agamemnon — but he did not believe her either. Her only happy prophecy on record concerned her cousin, Aeneas; she foretold that he would surmount all perils and found a great nation.

Cassiopeia (kas ih uh PEE uh): Mother of Andromeda. She also became a constellation after her death, together with her husband, her daughter, her throne, and the sea-monster sent by Poseidon to ravage the shores of her country.

Castor and Polydeuces (KASS ter) (pawl ih DEW seez): The Spartan Twins; sons of Leda; brothers of Helen. Castor was the greatest wrestler of ancient times, and Polydeuces the greatest boxer (excepting Heracles). It is said that Polydeuces stormed into Hephaestus' workshop and forced the smith-god to cut off his hands at the wrist, and then forge him a pair of iron hands. When these iron hands were clenched into iron fists, Polydeuces alone was worth a phalanx of heavily armed warriors. The twins accompanied Jason on his Argosy and helped him win the Golden Fleece. They were admired by the gods, who valued good fighting men. When they died, Zeus placed them among the stars as the constellation Gemini, the Twins.

Cecrops (SEE krahps): An early king of Attica. Despite the fact that he was half dragon, half human, he proved to be a very pious king. It was during his reign that Athena and Poseidon contended for the overlordship of Attica. A council of gods decided in favor of Athena, and she planted an olive tree on the site of what was to become the principal city of Attica — Athens. According to legend, it was Cecrops who led the people in worship of Athena. It is said also that he substituted barley cakes for human sacrifices in the worship of Zeus. A large and handsome moth, the Cecropia, takes its name from Cecrops.

Celmus (SELL muhs): The son of very old Phrygian gods, and a playfellow of the young Zeus on the slopes of Mt. Ida. Now Celmus and his brothers were the first to smelt iron and were very proud of their skill. He challenged Zeus to a fencing match, each to use his favorite weapon — thunderbolt against iron club. But even in his youth, the dignity of Zeus was too great to brook challenge. Thunder crashed, lightning sizzled. A voltage of the divine rays passed through the iron club, up through the arm of Celmus, and through his body, so that duelist and club became one weld, an iron statue welding an iron club.

Centaurs (SEHN torz): Legendary creatures, half man

and half horse, who roamed the plains of Thessaly. In some tales they combine the best qualities of both species; occasionally, they display the worst characteristics of man and horse. Their legend is echoed by followers of Cortez, who reported that the Aztecs — who had never seen mounted men before the Spanish invasion — thought the Spaniards were divisible monsters who could separate at will into man and horse. Thus the myth of the Centaurs must have arisen when the Thessalian peasants saw their first mounted men, the nomad Dorian invaders from the north. One extremely wise Centaur, Chiron, enters the legends of Heracles, Peleus, Achilles, Jason, and Aeneas. He tutored these heroes, teaching them riding, archery, and the secrets of medicinal herbs.

Cephalus (SEHF uh luhs): A son of Hermes whose beauty troubled the dawn. Eos, the dawn-goddess, fell in love with the beautiful lad and bore him to her castle east of the sun. But he spurned the flame-haired goddess, declaring that he was affianced to Procris, daughter of the king of Athens, and intended to remain faithful. Eos protested, telling him that Procris was false-hearted and unworthy of his love. When he continued to disdain her, Eos changed his appearance and challenged him to return to Procris in his new form and test her faithfulness. Cephalus did so. But this was an unfair test — for when Eos changed his appearance she had left him with his own personality. Procris, lonely, and confused by the disappearance of her lover, found herself mysteriously drawn to the young stranger, and declared her love for him. Thereupon, Eos allowed Cephalus to resume his own form and he accused Procris of unfaithfulness. The princess was devastated by these events. She ran off into the woods and joined the retinue of Artemis. The moon-goddess was delighted with her new recruit and gave her a spear that could not miss its mark. But Procris promptly took this spear as a love-offering to Cephalus, who was an ardent hunter. He was delighted with the spear; they became reconciled. After they were wed, however, Procris remained jealous of Eos, and suspected that her husband was trysting with the dawn-goddess. Finally her suspicions grew so intense that she followed him into the forest when he went out hunting. She spied on him from the underbrush and he, hearing the leaves rustle, whirled and threw his spear which could not miss. He went into the thicket and saw his wife lying on the ground, transfixed by the spear, bleeding to death. Wild with grief, he went into exile and never returned.

Cerberus (SIR bur us): The three-headed dog employed by Hades to guard the portals of death. One of the heads is turned toward Tartarus to watch that none of the dead escape. Another is turned outward to warn the living from the gates. And the third head is reserved for salvaging any of the dead who try to escape, or any of the living who try to trespass. Only twice has his vigilance been cheated. Once Orpheus lulled all three heads to sleep by playing beautiful lullabies on his lyre. Heracles overcame him more simply on his expedition into Tartarus. He throttled each of the three necks until the monster lost consciousness. Then, it is said, Heracles brought the dog back to King Eurystheus — for this was his twelfth labor, thus ending his servitude. But the king was appalled by the sight of Cerberus — as Heracles knew he would be — and hid in a ditch. He refused to come out until Heracles, in high glee, bore the beast back to Tartarus, collected a ransom from Hades, and planted Cerberus again before the gates.

Cercopes (sir KOH peez): Two dwarfish larcenous sons of Oceanus, who practiced every species of mischief. Once, coming across Heracles lying asleep, they gleefully began to steal the arrows from his quiver. However, he awoke and caught them. He tied them feet-first to a pole and carried them off, hanging head downward from his shoulder. They were so amused by their unusual posture that they burst out laughing. Heracles, amazed, asked them the cause of their mirth. Instead of answering, they laughed harder. Infected by their laughter, Heracles began to laugh and released them. However, they were audacious enough to practice some of their tricks on Zeus, who was not amused. He changed them into monkeys.

Cercyon (SUR sih uhn): A brutish king of Eleusis whose notion of hospitality was to challenge visitors to a wrestling match which would invariably end in their death. When Theseus visited Eleusis, however, there was a different outcome. For Theseus, who was small of stature, had perfected the art of turning an adversary's strength against him. The match ended when Theseus seized Cercyon by the ankles, whirled him off the ground, and dashed his brains out against a rock, to the delight of the entire countryside.

Ceres (SEE reez; SIHR eez): The Roman name for Demeter, goddess of the harvest. It is from her name that we derive our word, "cereal."

Cerynean Hind (sur ih NEE uhn HY'nd): Heracles' third labor was to capture this white stag, brother to the four stags employed by Artemis to draw her moonchariot. These were the most beautiful stags ever seen; they had golden horns and brass hooves. They ran more swiftly than the wind, these moon-stags, but swifter yet was their brother, the Cerynean Hind, the only one swift enough to escape Artemis when, in her girlhood, she had captured the other four. Heracles hunted this stag for an entire year, chasing him to the western rim of the world, then northward beyond the source of the snows, and back again. He was never able to catch him. Finally, he had to string the bow given him by Apollo, notch an arrow, and at more than a mile's distance, drive the shaft through the forelegs of the running stag, pinning the legs so that the beast could no longer flee, without otherwise harming itself. Then Heracles took the stag on his shoulders and bore it back to King Eurystheus. On the way, however, he was stopped by Artemis, who reproached him for injuring the marvelous stag. But Heracles promised he would return it unharmed, and that she would have it as a fifth stag for her moon-chariot. Whereupon she allowed him to go on his way.

Cestus (SEHSS tuhs): Aphrodite's girdle. A magical garment to which she was supposed to owe her irresistible attractiveness. However, most authorities agree that this girdle was a fiction concocted by other goddesses envious of Aphrodite's conquests, and that her only garment was her fleece of yellow hair. Certainly, all the male gods of the pantheon, scores of demigods, and dozens of heroic mortals were prepared to testify that the love-goddess needed no aid to her own charms.

Ceto (SEE toh): Daughter of the Titans, and mother of monsters. Her union with her brother, Phorcys, produced a frightful brood — including the haggish Graeae, the snake-haired Gorgons, the bat-winged Sirens, the dog-headed Scylla, and the huge-fanged serpent Ladon.

Charon (KAY run; KAHR uhn): The surly boatman who ferried the dead across the river Styx. The dead had to pay for this last ride; Charon demanded a silver coin in fee. That is why corpses in ancient Greece were buried with coins under their tongues. Those souls who could not pay, or whose bodies lay unburied, were condemned to wander the near shore of Styx for a hundred years — bewildered, lonely, hanging between death and life. Only after such time had passed would Charon consent to ferry them to their final exile in Tartarus. The living he refuses to ferry at all, for they are not allowed in Hades' kingdom. But there were three who crossed nevertheless: Orpheus charmed him with song; Heracles bullied him; and Odysseus tricked him. All three crossed the Styx into Tartarus, and crossed again coming back.

Charybdis (kuh RIB dihss): An underwater monster who had once been a greedy woman, so greedy she would steal the cattle of her neighbors and roast them for her dinner. Zeus, angered by this, hurled her into the sea, where she was transformed into the shape of her own greed; she became a whirlpool sucking down ships that passed too close by, and devouring their crews. She sat on one side of a narrow strait off the coast of Sicily. Opposite her squatted her partner in horror, the dog-headed Scylla. Between them they became the most fearsome perils to navigation along the coasts of the Inner Sea. Ships had to pass exactly in the middle of the strait between Scylla and Charybdis or risk being destroyed by one or the other.

Chione (KY oh nee): A princess of Thessaly who bore twin sons to different gods. One was sired by Hermes, the other by Apollo. Hermes' son was Autolycus, the master thief, whose descendant was Odysseus. His twin, sired by Apollo, was Philammon, a marvelous musician. But Chione coaxed Apollo to say that her beauty was greater than that of his sister, Artemis. The moon-goddess heard about this and was enraged. She killed Chione with one of her unerring silver arrows, but Apollo, intervening, turned the girl into a hawk.

Chiron (KY ruhn): Wisest of the Centaurs, and tutor to many heroes. He was expert in the arts of music, healing, archery, and the care of animals. Among his famous pupils were Heracles, Achilles, and Jason. He taught Peleus sword-play, and Asclepius a technique for setting bones.

Chrysaeor (kry SAY or): He was son of a monster and father of monsters, but he himself was a handsome warrior, known as the Chieftain of the Golden Spear. He was born from Medusa's blood when Perseus cut off her head. It was said that Poseidon had sired upon her this delayed offspring. Among the many monsters that Chrysaeor fathered was the three-bodied Geryon who enters the story of Heracles.

Chryseis (kry SEE uhs): A Trojan girl whose beauty plagued both Greek and Trojan armies. Captured and enslaved by Agamemnon, she prayed to Apollo whom her father served as priest. Apollo responded with pestilence, shooting fever-tipped arrows into the Greek tents. Nor was the plague lifted until Agamemnon released Chryseis. During her sojourn among the Greeks, however, she had fallen in love with Diomedes. Later, she betrayed her Trojan lover, Troilus, and brought secrets of the Trojan defenses to Diomedes as a love token. In medieval romances she is called "Cressida." The story of Troilus and Cressida provided a theme for both Chaucer and Shakespeare.

Cilissa (SY LIHSS uh): A minor character in the tragic story of the House of Atreus. When the usurper Aegisthus wanted to wipe out Agamemnon's line, he decided to murder the infant Orestes. But Cilissa, who was Orestes' nurse, put her own son in the prince's crib, and Aegisthus strangled him instead. Orestes lived to kill Aegisthus.

Circe (SUR see): A daughter of the sun's charioteer,

this beautiful demigoddess was skilled in magical spells and magical herbs. But even without the aid of magic, the sorcery of her singing voice and her physical beauty were enough to hold men enthralled. Many men loved her. When she tired of them, she did not dismiss them, but changed them into animals suggested by their personalities and appearances, and kept them as pets on her castle grounds. Her most famous encounter was with Odysseus. He had moored offshore, and sent part of his crew to explore the island. Circe received them royally — then, after she had wined and dined them, changed them into swine, knowing that their captain would come to rescue them; it was Odysseus who interested her. But when Odysseus arrived, he was armed with a counter-spell given him by Hermes, and was thus invulnerable to Circe's magic. He forced her to return his men to their own forms, and mastered her in every way. However, he too fell under her personal spell, remaining on the island for three years. During that time she bore him a son, Telegonus. Finally, however, his sea-fever returned and he resumed his voyage, but not before Circe had prophesied very accurately the terrible perils he would encounter before reaching his home.

Clio (KLY oh): The muse of history. She descended from Parnassus to visit certain men and fill them with a fever for delving into old manuscripts and searching out people who could tell them about times past. Then, under her patronage, these scholars would inscribe what they believed had happened.

Clotho (KLOH thoh): One of the Fates. She is the Sister of Spindle; youngest of the three. She spins the thread of life; Lacheis measures; Atropos cuts.

Clymene (KLIHM uh nee): A Nereid who was favored

40

by Zeus, and became the mother of Mnemosyne, goddess of memory.

Clytemnestra (kly tuhm NEHSS truh): Adulterous wife of Agamemnon, who murdered her husband when he returned from the Trojan War. She was a daughter of Leda; half-sister to Helen; mother of Orestes, Electra, and Iphigenia. She was killed by her son, Orestes, who thus avenged his father's murder.

Clytie (KLY tee): A daughter of Oceanus who was enamored of Apollo. She could not bear her loss when the god tired of her. She would arise early each morning and stand with her face upturned all day long watching the passage of his sun-chariot across the sky. She grew rooted to the spot, and was transformed into a flower which turns its face always to the sun, the heliotrope.

Comatas (koh MAY tuhss): A goat herd who glimpsed the Muses dancing on a slope of Mt. Helicon. He was so moved by the sight that he sacrified one of his master's goats. His master did not share his enthusiasm and shut him up in a box. But the Muses rescued him, and employed him thereafter to tend their flocks.

Copreus (KOH pree uhs): A herald of King Eurystheus, whose misfortune it was to carry the orders of the king to Heracles. Displeased by a really irksome assignment, Heracles flung him from the wall and killed him.

Corcyra (KOR sy ruh): A sickle-shaped island in the Ionian Sea. According to legend, it was formed when Cronus flung the sickle with which he had dismembered his father, Uranus, into the sea. Stained with the god's blood, it became a very fertile island, and gained its name from the nymph Corcyra; she was loved by Poseidon, who gave her the island as a dwelling place. It enters other legends. Odysseus' ship was wrecked upon its reef. Jason and Medea conducted their dark nuptials in one of its caves. This beautiful island is now known as Corfu.

Core (KOH ruh): Another name for Persephone, daughter of Demeter, and Queen of the Dead. "Core" means "maiden," and Persephone dropped this name after her abduction by Hades.

Cornucopia (kor noo KOH pih uh): The broken-off horn of the goat Amalthea, whose milk nourished the infant Zeus. To honor the goat, Zeus filled this horn with golden fruit and gave it the power to replenish itself when empty. The word "cornucopia" means "horn of plenty."

Coronis (kuh ROH nuhss): A princess of the Lapiths, who was loved by Apollo and became the mother of Asclepius. Apollo had forced his attentions upon Coronis. When pregnant with Asclepius, she rebelled, and returned to her first love, an Arcadian youth. Apollo's sister, Artemis, always watchful of his honor, was enraged by this and killed the girl with one of her silver arrows. Asclepius was born during her death throes. It is said that the infant — who was to become the father of medicine — watched the details of his own birth with profound attention, displaying a precocious talent for anatomy. Crows have always been associated with this legend, and take their Greek name from "Coronis." According to one tale, Coronis was turned into a crow after her death. In another version, Apollo appointed a crow to chaperone her; when the crow bungled its assignment, Apollo cursed all crows with a curse so terrible it scorched their white feathers. Since then, all crows have been black.

Corunetes (kor UHN uh teez): The cudgel-man. This brute used to prowl the roads of Epidaurus, waylaying travelers and crushing their skulls with a huge brass club. When Theseus traveled that road Corunetes tried to beat his brains out, but the lad seized the cudgel, and served the cudgeler as *he* had served so many others. Theseus kept the brass club as his own weapon.

Corybantes (kor ih BAHN teez): Sons of Apollo and Thalia; addicted to dance. Clad in full armor, they performed at the Winter Solstice, wearing crests of gorgeous feathers, clashing spear on shield to celebrate the mighty birth of Zeus.

Corythus (KOR uh thus): A son of Paris. His mother was the mountain-nymph, Oenone, who Paris deserted when he went in search of Helen. Oenone never forgave him, and tutored her son in the ways of vengeance. She sent Corythus to guide the Greeks past the Trojan defenses, into the city itself. While in Troy, however, preparing his treachery, the youth fell in love with Helen. Jealous Paris, not recognizing his son, killed him.

Creon (KREE uhn): The uncle of Oedipus, who took the throne of Thebes after Oedipus abdicated and Jocasta killed herself. Later, he played a villainous role in the episode of Antigone, ordering his niece to be buried alive because she had insisted on a decent burial for her brother, Polyneices. Creon was not a bad king and did many worthwhile things, but it is for this cruelty that he is remembered.

Cronus (KROH nuhs): Father of Zeus; son of Uranus and Gaia. Cronus was the father of the gods and gave his name to time. The youngest of the Titan brood, he married his sister, Rhea, and murdered his father, Uranus. He lived in fear of his father's last words which had predicted that Cronus would be as brutally dethroned by his own son. He was eager to disprove this prophecy, and swallowed his children one by one as soon as they were born. After losing five godlings in this way, his wife, Rhea, rebelled. She went off to have her sixth child in secret. Then she returned to Cronus carrying a stone swaddled in baby clothes, which he swallowed. Rhea named the infant god Zeus, and kept him hidden until he had grown into a radiant youth. Then she tutored him in ideas of vengeance, for she was weary of her all-devouring husband. Zeus ambushed Cronus when the old god was out hunting and kicked him suddenly in the belly. Whereupon he vomited forth first a stone, then the five children he had swallowed, still alive, still undigested — for they were destined to live as gods. Cronus fled through the grove and Zeus did not pursue. He was greeted by his brothers and sisters, who immediately named him their leader. Then he led them against the titanic forces of Cronus and a mighty battle raged across the floor of heaven. The young gods prevailed. Cronus disappeared, never to be seen again. Zeus remained master of the gods. Some say that Cronus and his Titans took refuge in the mountains and are heard there to this day, rumbling and spitting lava, and shaking the earth. Others say that Zeus caught Cronus and slew him according to prophecy, as Cronus had slain Uranus. Those who live near volcanoes believe the mountain tale. Those who live near the sea believe Cronus was slain and flung into the ocean-stream. They believe the ghosts of the slaughtered gods, Cronus and Uranus, wrangle underwater, and move the waters in those vast tantrums called tidal waves. In Roman mythology, Cronus was known as Saturn.

Cyclopes (SY klahps): Giant metal-workers, trained by Hephaestus to forge thunderbolts for Zeus and to do other fine work. They are distinguished by having but one eye each, which they wear in the middle of their foreheads. The most famous Cyclops in legend is Polyphemus, a ferocious specimen, who captured Odysseus' crew, and devoured many of them before Odysseus made him drunk and blinded his single eye. Homer described Polyphemus as being a son of Poseidon. After Odysseus blinded him, he prayed to his father for vengeance. The sea-god responded by hurling storms in Odysseus' path, wrecking his ships and drowning his sailors, thus delaying him for ten years in his return to Ithaca.

Cycnus (SIHK nuhs): A son of Poseidon, who was raised by a swan. Granted invulnerability by his father to spear-thrust and sword-cut, Cycnus became a very formidable warrior on the Trojan side. After slaying many Greeks, he finally encountered Achilles who recognized invincibility in no one but himself. However, Achilles could not wound Cycnus with spear or sword. Finally, Achilles hurled him to the ground and piled rocks on top of him until Cycnus was smothered. Cycnus' father did not allow him to die, however, but changed him into a swan. Since then, all swans have born his name.

Cyrene (sy REE nee): A Lapith maiden who loved to roam the mountain slopes, hunting deer and wrestling lions and bears. Apollo once reined up his sun-chariot to watch her wrestle a lion. He was so struck by her grace and strength that he abandoned the reins of his sun-stallions to his charioteer, Helios, and descended from the sky to begin an ardent courtship of Cyrene. She bore him two sons, Aristeus, founder of cities, and Idmon, wisest man of his time.

Dactyls (DAK tihlz): Ten demigods, children of Rhea or, some say, of Cybele. They were five males and five females who dwelt on Phrygia's Mt. Ida, and were so enormously skilled at metal work that the ten fingers were named for their deftness. They also acted as guides to the great Mysteries, initiating mortals into the secret rites of Cybele and Rhea. The Dactyls are associated in myth with the armored dancers, the Corybantes. Some tales hold that they are identical. Legends about them, though confused, seem to express the dawning wonder of ancient man in the increasing skill of his hands.

Daedalus (DEHD uh luhs): Master artificer, the greatest inventor of ancient times. He dwelt in Athens, and was particularly favored by Athena, who taught him mechanical principles never before divulged to man. Under her tutelage he invented the sail, the compass, the potter's wheel, and the axe. However, he grew jealous of his nephew, Talos, who worked as his apprentice and was displaying enormous talent. In a spasm of envy he killed Talos, thus forfeiting the favor of Athena and arousing the wrath of his neighbors. He was forced to flee Athens, and took refuge in Crete, where King Minos was happy to employ him, and where he quickly became embroiled in the intrigues of a corrupt court. He made marvelous toys for the little princesses, Ariadne and

Phaedra — parasols that opened by themselves when the sun hit them; tops that would spin in mid-air, and for Ariadne, a ball of thread that could unwind its full length, then reel itself up again. Especially attentive to him, though, was Queen Pasiphae, who desperately needed something that only he could provide. Cursed by Aphrodite, she had conceived a monstrous passion for a white bull of the royal herd. Daedalus contructed a handsome wooden cow for the queen, with glowing yellow eyes and ivory horns, and a musical moo. He hollowed it out so she could position herself inside, and tenderly upholstered it with leather for her comfort. Hidden in this wooden cow, she could approach the bull. Minos knew nothing of this until his queen gave birth to a little monster — half boy, half bull — which a jeering populace dubbed "Minotaur," meaning Minos' bull. The king ordered Daedalus to construct a novel open-air prison in his castle garden at Gnossos. It was a maze, full of winding paths that crossed and recrossed each other, dead ends, and hidden exits. It was impossible for anyone to find his way in or out. Here Minos imprisoned Pasiphae and the Minotaur. Daedalus and his son, Icarus, were also penned up in the labyrinth, for Minos had not forgiven the old craftsman who had made the wooden cow. Daedalus kept himself occupied in a workshop he set up in the labyrinth, and also studied the flight of birds. He was determined to understand why they could fly and man could not. Finally, at the urging of Icarus, he constructed two pairs of wings. And father and son flew out of the labyrinth. Icarus, however, perished on the journey. Daedalus, very much saddened, took refuge with a king of Sicily named Cocalus, for whom he built impregnable fortresses. The vengeful Minos came to Sicily with an invasion fleet demanding that Daedalus be surrendered to him. But the old artificer had endeared himself to the court, and Minos was killed by the daughters of Cocalus. Daedalus lived the rest of his life in Sicily, but was never quite the same. He missed his adventurous son, Icarus, and was eager to join him in death. Before he died, though, he invented the anchor-winch, the harpoon, and the pulley.

Danae (DAN ay ee): The mother of Perseus. Her father, Acrisius, king of Argos, had been warned by an oracle that he would meet his death at the hands of a grandson. Therefore, he was determined that his only child would bear no children. He imprisoned Danae in a brass tower with no doors and only a single arrow-slit for ventilation. But that arrow-slit was enough to admit a shaft of sunlight. And when Zeus determined to visit the beautiful princess in her cell he transformed himself into a shaft of sunlight, and slid in through the arrow-slit. When Acrisius found that his daughter had managed to become pregnant while in solitary confinement he knew that powerful and mischievous forces were at work. After she bore an infant son, he locked both of them in a wooden chest which he cast upon the sea. But the wooden chest floated like a boat to the island of Sephiros, where it was pulled ashore by a fisherman. The princess and her son were royally welcomed by the king of Sephiros. This king, Polydectes, fell in love with Danae, and tried to force her to marry him, but she resisted him. Later, when Perseus had gone on his wonderful adventures, and returned with the head of Medusa, he came to Sephiros just in time to interrupt the nuptials that Polydectes had finally forced upon Danae. He turned the king and all his wedding guests into stone, and bore his mother off to safety. Nor did his grandfather escape destiny: The prophecy came true. Perseus competed in a discus-throwing contest, and hurled the discus so far that it landed among the spectators, killing an elderly stranger — his grandfather, Acrisius. His daughter, Danae, did not mourn his death.

Daphne (DAF nee): A nymph who preferred to undergo transformation rather than suffer the embrace of Apollo. Pursued by the sun-god, she called upon her river-god father to help her. He changed her into a laurel tree. Apollo grieved, but honored the tree. He decreed that a wreath made of laurel leaves should be used to crown heroes, poets, and men who win games.

Daphnis (DAF nuhs): A son of Hermes by an unknown nymph. He inherited his father's talent for music, playing the pipes enchantingly, and composing the first song of the fields, called a pastoral. He was an ardent hunter also, and passionately devoted to the care of his hounds. According to legend, when five of his favorite hounds died suddenly of a mysterious ailment, he refused to eat, and grieved himself to death. Hades was moved to make special disposition of his case. He restored Daphnis' hounds to him, and allowed him to chase spectral deer forever over fields of asphodel in a part of Tartarus that abounds with game.

Deianeira (dee yuh NY ruh): Second wife of Heracles. She did what a generation of the most fearful giants and monsters failed to do — she killed him. She did not mean to kill him, but was used as a pawn by a vengeful centaur named Nessus. This centaur had attempted to assault Deianeira while ferrying her across a river. But Heracles, though half a mile downstream, made one of his famous long bowshots, and pierced Nessus with an arrow whose barb had been poisoned when Heracles had dipped it into the blood of the Hydra. The dying centaur told Deianeira that he repented of the insult he had offered her, and, in apology, offered her a vial of his blood, telling her that it would prove useful if she ever found that Heracles' affection for her was waning. All she would have to do then would be to dip one of Heracles' garments in this blood, and when her husband wore it he would resume all his old feeling for her. She took the vial of blood and Nessus died. Some time later, Deianeira became jealous of a maiden named Iole, in whom Heracles was displaying an interest. Deianeira dipped a shirt belonging to Heracles in the blood of Nessus. When Heracles put the shirt on he was seized with a terrible agony. It was a shirt of fire. When he tried to tear the garment off, strips of his flesh came off with it. He perished in utmost torment. But he did not fall into the clutches of Hades. For his father, Zeus, transported him to Olympus where he was received among the gods with great honor, and was granted immortality.

Deiphobus (dee IHF oh buhs): A prince of Troy, and Hector's favorite brother. He fought very bravely against the Greeks, and in recognition of his mighty deeds was awarded the custody of Helen after Paris was killed in the last month of the war. He married Helen against her will, but she soon made him pay for it. When the strategy of Odysseus succeeded, and the wooden horse was rolled inside the walls of Troy, Helen — knowing the Greeks — realized that the horse was hollow and that warriors were hidden inside its belly. Thereupon she stole all Deiphobus' weapons as he lay asleep. When the Greeks emerged from the horse in the middle of the night and began to sack the city they found Deiphobus unarmed, and were able to kill him easily. They also set his house on fire. Helen danced with joy when Deiphobus was slain. She danced by the light of the burning house hoping to win back Menelaus, the husband she had abandoned. She was successful.

Delphi (DEHL fy): The earth's navel — site of Apollo's temple, where the priestesses were noted for their gift of prophecy. Actually, Delphi is a system of caves opening out of Mt. Parnassus; the ancients believed it was the very center of the earth. Apollo pursued his mother's enemy, the Python, into one of these caves, and slew him there with his golden arrows. Priestesses of the sun-god were thereafter called Pythonesses in memory of that combat. These pythoness-oracles sat on three-legged stools straddling fissures in the cave floor which emitted gusts of steam. The oracles chewed laurel and went into a steamy trance — their famed prophetic sleep in which they uttered riddles. When solved, these riddles were supposed to contain secrets of the future... for those with sufficient piety who had paid an appropriate fee.

Demeter (duh MEE tuhr): Daughter of Cronus and Rhea; goddess of the harvest. This stately green-clad goddess strode up and down the land scattering seed and blessing the furrows. Crops were her concern. She presided over the sowing, the cultivation, and the harvest. She was beneficent but moody, and her moods were life and death to mankind. Her happiness was abundance; her wrath was famine. She was much occupied with her brothers. She favored Zeus, who was the father of her beloved flower-princess, Persephone. She never forgave her eldest brother, Hades, for abducting Persephone and forcing her to marry him. For that part of the year which Persephone must spend underground with her husband, Demeter forbade the earth to bear fruit. She also feuded with her brother, Poseidon, who, each springtime, used to swell mischievously, sending tides to flood her fields. But according to legend, they finally forgave each other. Their children, born where the land meets the sea, were the winged horse Arion, and the nymph Despoena. In Roman mythology, Demeter was known as Ceres.

Deucalion (duh KAY lih uhn): The Greek Noah, who survived the deluge Zeus sent upon earth to wipe out wicked mankind. Deucalion was the son of the generous Titan Prometheus, who had braved the everlasting displeasure of Zeus to give man the gift of fire. He inherited his father's nobility of soul, and was farsighted enough to build an ark before the deluge. When the flood came, Deucalion and his wife, Pyrra, sailed away on the ark, taking with them all the animals they could herd aboard. They floated on the raging flood-waters until, finally, the rains stopped, and the water subsided. They had run aground on the slope of a mountain which they later found to be Parnassus. Here were the caves of Delphi wherein dwelt the priestesses of Apollo. Deucalion consulted the oracle, who informed them that the race of mankind had been wiped out. Deucalion asked the Pythoness how man might be restored to earth. Out of her deep trance she answered, "Go with head averted, and throw behind you the bones of your mother." It was a typical riddle-answer of the oracle, and Deucalion and Pyrra spent the night trying to solve it. By morning they had hit upon an answer. Their mother, they decided, must be Mother Earth, and her bones must be the rocks. Thereupon, they walked the mountain slope with heads averted, casting stones behind them. Those that Deucalion cast became men. Those thrown by Pyrra became women. And these new beautiful men and women followed Deucalion and Pyrra in a joyous throng to begin the repopulation of the earth.

Diana (dy AN uh): Roman name for Artemis, goddess of the moon, and goddess of the chase.

Dido (DY doh): A princess of Tyre. She fled the city when her father died and her cruel brother succeeded to the throne. She led a band of Tyrrhian nobles to the north coast of Africa, where she contracted to purchase land, as much as could be covered by a bull's hide. But she tricked the seller by cutting the bull's hide into strips, and claiming enough land upon which to site a city. The Tyrrhians were bold and warlike, and Dido proved herself a resolute leader. The city she had founded became Carthage, capital of a powerful kingdom. Some years later, Aeneas landed there, the only Trojan prince to escape the sack of Troy. Dido welcomed him, and he spent long hours with the Queen, telling her about the war against the Greeks, and the mighty deeds performed before the walls of Troy. He told her of the battles and the deaths ... of Helen and Paris and Hector and Achilles, of Troilus and Chryseis, and Odysseus ... of women like Hecuba and Cassandra, and the noble Andromache ... of challenges and duels and deaths. Dido listened thirstily. She fell violently in love with Aeneas and he loved her in return. But Aeneas was destined to resume his journey to Italy, where he was to found a nation called Rome. Some say that Hermes came to him with a message from Zeus; others say that Zeus wrote his commandment in lightning on a stormy sky. At any rate, Aeneas obeyed the gods, and departed. Dido built an enormous pyre of wood, placed herself on top of it, and bade her slaves to set it afire. Aeneas, looking back from the deck of his ship, saw a pillar of smoke, and wondered about it briefly, then dismissed it from his mind, for the wind had changed and he had to shift sail. Dido perished in the flames of the pyre.

Diomedes (dy oh MEE deez): There are two mythological characters of this name. The earlier one was a son of the war-god Ares, and the lion-wrestling Cyrene, and he was worthy of such parents. He was a warlike brute, who kept a stable of man-eating mares. He cherished these swift beasts, and fed them lazy slaves, rebellious subjects, and prisoners of war. But then his kingdom was visited by Heracles, undertaking his eighth labor; his task was to yoke these same mares to a chariot and drive them back to King Eurystheus. Heracles informed Diomedes of his intention. Diomedes objected in very violent terms, whereupon Heracles fed him to his own mares, then drove them off in completion of his labor.

The second Diomedes was a figure of much more nobility. He was king of Aetolia, a leader of the Greek forces against Troy, and was counted one of the four best fighters among the invaders — the others being Ajax, Odysseus, and the matchless Achilles. In his most incredible feat, Diomedes encountered the war-god Ares, who had disguised himself and taken the field against the Greeks. Seized with battle-fury Diomedes wounded Ares with a spear-thrust and drove him from the field. He also wounded Aeneas, killed Rhesus, king of Thrace, and stole the Thracian horses of magical speed. Finally, he was one of those who hid in the belly of the Wooden Horse, to emerge at night and begin the last massacre of the Trojans. Between battles he found time to win the love of Chryseis, who brought him valuable secrets of the Trojan defenses. During the war, his exploits earned the favor of Athena, who was his protectress throughout — once even acting as his charioteer. But he earned the wrath of Aphrodite. Her anger was kindled against him on two counts: He had seriously wounded her son, Aeneas, and had scratched her own beautiful arm with his spear-point, causing her to flee, sobbing, from the field. She retaliated by teaching his wife to be unfaithful. So Diomedes left Aetolia and went into exile. In another legend, Diomedes was preparing to muster his forces against the journeying Aeneas, but Aphrodite foiled him by turning his warriors into birds. Later, it is said, he appeased the wrath of the goddess by naming his strongest city for her. After his death, he was made immortal by Athena.

Dione (dy OH nee): The oak-goddess. Her name crops up in the most ancient legends, those of the great mother-goddess who ruled under various names before invaders came out of the north with their array of patriarchal gods. Her key legend disputes Aphrodite's foam-birth. In this myth, Dione is the mother of Aphrodite; Zeus is her father.

Dionysus (dy uh NY sush; dy oh NIHSH ih uhs) : God of the vine, master of revels, bestower of ecstasy. This untamed, ivy-crowned youth was perhaps the most important of the nature gods, and his legends abound. It is agreed that Zeus is his father, but different stories give him different mothers. Demeter, queen of harvests, is one. The nymph Lethe, whose name means forgetfulness, is another. But in the tale most widely told Semele is his mother. She was a Phrygian princess, priestess of the new moon, whom Zeus courted, invisibly, as the night wind. Unfortunately, however, she suspected that he was other than he seemed, and coaxed him into dropping his disguise. He appeared to her in his own form; she was consumed by the divine fire upon which no mortal can look and live. Dying, she gave birth to Dionysus, who was born among fire. Ever afterward flame ran in his veins giving him his matchless radiance. Zeus wished to keep the infant hidden from the vengeful Hera, and gave him to mountain nymphs to raise. When half grown, the young god fell under the tutelage of Silenus, a shaggy, pot-bellied little woodland deity, said to be the son of Pan — very mischievous, and very wise. It was he who taught Dionysus the secret of the grape and the terrible enchantment cast by its fermented juice. Accompanied by Silenus, he wandered far, visiting all the kingdoms that border the Inner Sea, introducing men to vine-culture. He was followed by a troupe of dancing drunken worshippers — among them the sons of Silenus, the Sileni or Satyrs, and hordes of wild women, called Maenads, who revelled nightly under the moon. Once he was captured by pirates who took him on board their ship, thinking he was a prince they could hold for ransom. Suddenly the ship stopped, although it was sailing before the wind in deep water. The amazed pirates saw vines sprouting out of the ocean, climbing the hull, twining around the mast. And the oars of the galley slaves turned into sea serpents who wrenched themselves free and swam away. Where Dionysus had been sitting in the bow, a lion stood. The wind in the rigging became the sound of flutes, and the beautiful golden lion raised himself on his hind legs and danced. The terrified pirates jumped overboard and were turned into dolphins. It is told that Dionysus descended into Tartarus to rescue his mother, Semele. This was Hades' kingdom, the land beyond death, from which there is no return. But Dionysus brought a bouquet of flowers for Persephone that was so beautiful and whose fragrance was so intoxicating she could not refuse anything he asked. She permitted Semele to follow her son back to the land of the living. Dionysus then climbed Olympus and persuaded Zeus to make Semele a goddess. She became one of the moon deities. Zeus was so taken with his gorgeous son that he wished to enroll him among the Pantheon, which could not number more than twelve. But modest Hestia yielded her place to Dionysus. He was given a seat at the right hand of Zeus, and was honored among the gods. Nevertheless, he frequently descended from Olympus because of his love for mankind. And the festivals in his honor were so numerous and so joyous that the other gods often disguised themselves as mortals to join in the frolic. The grape, the ivy, and the rose were sacred to Dionysus; also panther, goat, and dolphin. One of his names is Lysios, the loosener, because his gift of wine unshackles men from the daily round, but, if taken in excess, foolishly loosens their tongues. Dionysus is loved beyond the other gods because he has taught men to escape the narrow bounds of their own personalities and yield to the ecstasy of natural forces, an ecstasy that permits them to know the gods in their deepest mystery.

Dodona (doh DOH nuh): A temple of Zeus in Epirus,

and dwelling place of his most ancient oracle. Here, under a giant oak tree, Zeus courted Dodona, the oak-goddess. And here, centuries later, Deucalion landed after the Deluge. In gratitude for his escape from the flood waters he built a temple and dedicated it to Zeus.

Doris (DOR ihs): A lovely green-haired ocean-goddess, who married Nereus, wise old man of the sea. They had fifty daughters, called the Nereids, who inherited their mother's beauty and became court attendants to the rulers of the sea, Poseidon and Amphitrite. The Nereids swam underwater, and broached like dolphins, swimming alongside ships, singing and calling sailors to drown. They emerged at dusk to dance upon the islands. Their lithe forms and sparkling eyes were the essence of the sea's beauty. They were courted by gods, demigods, and also mortals, and enter many legends.

Dorus (DOH ruhs): A grandson of Deucalion, who became an ancestor of the Hellenic tribe called Dorians. This warlike tribe invaded the Peloponnese from the north, overcoming the indigenous tribes who worshipped the mother-goddess, and imposing a patriarchal form of worship centering upon Zeus and the other Olympians.

Dryads (DRY uhdz): Wood-nymphs. These lovely fleet demigoddesses reigned over forest and glen, were custodians of wildlife, hunting companions of Artemis, and — above all — the titular deities of trees. Each dryad dwelt in a tree of her own and perished when that tree was destroyed. They ranged the forests, vigilantly guarding their trees and driving off anyone who carried an axe. In certain legends, they are most specifically associated with oak trees, the most sacred of all trees, that Zeus had adopted as his own.

Dryas (DRY uhs): Daughter of Pan. Unlike her sister

wood-nymphs, she was extremely shy and loathed the very idea of men. She fled whenever anything male approached, man or god. Finally, she entered her tree and never came out.

Dryope (DRY oh pee): A nymph on whose caprice the Argosy almost foundered. She inhabited a spring on the island of Pegae where Jason landed to take on water. While there, the beloved companion of Heracles, a youth named Hylas, wandered away, and knelt to drink of the spring. Dryope, lurking underwater, saw the lad, and fell in love with him. She pulled him into the spring, and never let him emerge. Heracles raged over the entire island, uprooting trees, and killing everything that crossed his path, man and beast. In his blood-lust, he was on the point of slaying all the Argonauts and smashing their ship. But Jason, using all his honeyed arts of persuasion, convinced him that Hylas must surely reappear if given time. Heracles grimly took up his post to wait for the lad — and the Argonauts sailed off, unharmed. But Heracles never saw Hylas again. In retaliation, according to one legend, Heracles rounded up the inhabitants of the island and took them to Delphi to be slaves.

Echidna (ee KID nuh): A monster, and mother of monsters. She was one of that fearful litter whose parents were Ceto and Phorcys. She coupled with the foul and gigantic dragon, known as Typhon, and bore a terrible brood, including Cerberus, the three-headed dog; the Chimera; and the cannibalistic Scylla. Echidna was half woman and half serpent. In some myths she is described as the mother of the hundred-headed Hydra, and the Sphinx. She was finally killed by another monster, who caught her asleep. Her murderer was the hundred-eyed Argus who never slept.

Echo (EHK oh): A tender-hearted nymph who helped Zeus escape the vigilance of Hera. The goddess learned of this, and punished Echo by wiping her lips of speech, permitting her only to repeat the last words of anyone who spoke to her. This hampered the nymph in her wooing of the handsome, vain Narcissus — who found her conversation boring. She grieved herself into invisibility, and is found now only in certain valleys and vaulted places, where she will answer if you call.

Eileithia (eye ly THY yuh): A minor goddess, who assisted Hestia, goddess of the hearth, and presided over childbirth. She enters the legend of Heracles at its very beginning. When Alcmene was about to give birth to

Heracles, who had been sired by Zeus, the jealous Hera sent Eileithia to delay this birth. She did this to thwart Zeus, who had declared that the first prince of the House of Perseus to be born that night should rule Mycenae. By the "first prince," Zeus meant Heracles, for his mother, Alcmene, was a granddaughter of Perseus. It was Hera's design to prevent the birth of Heracles, and allow a cousin of his to be born first that night, and inherit the throne of Mycenae. Therefore she instructed Eileithia to hamper Alcmene in her labor. Eileithia sat before Alcmene's door with crossed legs and crossed fingers. Alcmene labored but could not bear. Then, it is said, a servant of Alcmene, thinking Eileithia a witch who was casting a spell on her mistress, yelled suddenly — startling the goddess, who leaped up, uncrossing her legs and fingers. And Alcmene gave birth to Heracles . . . and to a twin, Iphicles, sired by her husband, Amphitryon. Eileithia punished the servant by changing her into a weasel.

Electra (ee LEHK truh): Daughter of Agamemnon and Clytemnestra, a key figure in the bloody tale of the House of Atreus. She loved her father very much, and vowed vengeance when he was murdered by Clytemnestra and Aegisthus. On the night of the murder she spirited her younger brother, Orestes, out of the castle, knowing that Aegisthus meant to murder him too. She left Orestes in a neighboring kingdom, and returned to Mycenae, where she pretended to be a dutiful daughter, dissembling her hatred of her mother and her mother's lover. Then, when Orestes had grown into a youth, she summoned him from exile, and inspired him with her own hatred. That night he entered the royal bedchamber with naked sword and killed his mother and Aegisthus. In the terrible time that followed, when Orestes was pursued by the Furies, and visited nightly by the howling ghost of his mother, Electra cared for him tenderly, and prevented him from taking his own life. Electra means amber, and amber was the color of her remarkable eyes. Our word "electricity" is derived from the name of this passionate girl, because the uncanny force was first summoned by rubbing amber with silk.

Electryon (ee LEHK trih uhn): Son of a hero, and grandfather of another. Perseus was his father, and Alcmene his daughter. After her encounter with Zeus, Alcmene bore Heracles. Electryon himself, though not of heroic stature, was a brave warrior, and a strong king who extended the frontiers of Mycenae.

Eleusinian Mysteries (ehl yu SINH ee uhn MIHSS tur eez): Annual rites performed by worshippers of Demeter, goddess of the harvest. They took place in Eleusis, a place sacred to her because she had been welcomed there with special reverence while on her heartbroken search for her abducted daughter, Persephone. A key ritual of these Mysteries was a dance-mime of Demeter's search, and of its conclusion: Persephone is brought back from the Underworld bringing flowers to the earth again.

Elysian Fields (ee LIHZ ih uhn FEELD'Z; ee LIHZ uhn FEELD'Z): That part of Tartarus which was the abode of the blessed. The weather was always fair, and spectral game abounded. There the heroes sojourned after death, as well as men and women of simple virtue. The Harpies and Furies and other demons of Hades were barred from these precincts.

Empusae (ehm PU see): A host of small demons who attended Hecate, queen of hags, as she went about her rounds in Tartarus, tormenting the shades. Each of these scurvy creatures had one donkey's hoof and one brass foot. Their hands were claws, and they had leathery wings. At night, they left Tartarus and flew to the upper world where they haunted the roads, bedeviling travelers. But, for such malicious creatures, they were oddly sensitive and fled before insult. That is why travelers were often heard speaking loudly and hurling abuse, especially at night.

Endymion (ehn DIHM ih uhn): A beautiful youth for whom Artemis broke her vows of maidenhood. She saw him asleep on a mountaintop, and reined up her moon-chariot in wonder. Then she climbed down from the sky and visited him in an amorous dream. Endymion took such pleasure in his dream that he begged Zeus for an eternity of restless sleep, and for eternal youth so that he might continue to enjoy his dreams. Zeus granted his request, and the youth slept through all the ages of mythology, visited every night by the moon-goddess, who bore him fifty daughters.

Eos (EE ohs): Goddess of the dawn. She had white wings and spread them over the sky when she judged that night had run its course . . . for the first light of the morning is white. Then this beautiful goddess tossed her flame-colored hair, a shimmering gold and red pelt that lit up the sky. Spreading her white wings, tossing her flame-colored hair, her rosy face beaming with smiles, she traveled from east to west to announce the coming of her brother, Helios, the sun-charioteer. Aphrodite, growing jealous of Eos because she was pursued by Ares, god of war, cursed the dawn-goddess with a preference for mortals. And so Eos flew to earth and spirited away various handsome young men whom she carried to her eastern palace in the sky. Being mortal, though, they grew old while she remained young — and she always lost her loves. This was the essence of Aphrodite's curse. She had five children — the four winds, and the Morning Star.

Epeus (ee PEE uhs): A Cycladean chieftain who fought against Troy. He was a formidable boxer, and very good with tools. It was he who actually built the Wooden Horse which Odysseus had designed. According to one legend he was shipwrecked in Sicily on his way home from Troy. The Trojan women he had taken captive burned his ship because they had heard tales of the murderous jealousy of his wife. Epeus, undismayed, stayed in Italy, journeying northward with his retinue to found the city of Pisa.

Epigoni (ee PIG oh ny): Name given to the sons of those warriors who besieged the city of Thebes in an effort to wrest the throne from Creon, and make Polynices king. They became known as the Seven Against Thebes. The Epigoni, vowing to avenge their fallen fathers, also attacked Thebes, and were successful. Thersander, son of Polynices, became king, occupying the throne of his grandfather, Oedipus.

Epimenides (ehp uh MEN uh deez): A Cretan shepherd who was fond of writing poetry. Often, he would sit down to scribble a verse — deaf to the barking of his sheep dogs, and to the piteous bleating of lambs being eaten by a wolf. Once he followed some strayed sheep into a cave, and was so pleased by the cool shade after the hot sun that he lay down and fell asleep, and slept for fifty-seven years. Epimenides belongs to a very ancient group of legends. In one of them he is named as the first to build an altar to the mother-goddess in Crete.

Epimetheus (ehp ih MEE thee us): Brother of Prometheus, and husband of Pandora. His gentleness, like his brother's nobility, was on a Titanic scale. After Pandora had indulged her curiosity, and loosed a box full of eternal trouble on mankind, he simply took the golden box from her, and comforted the sobbing girl.

Erectheus (eh REHK thee us): A king of Athens, who, in a war against the Eleusinians, was told by an oracle that his city could be saved only if he sacrificed his daughters. These daughters were remarkably courageous girls. Hearing of the prophecy, they decided to spare their father the pain of asking their death — and killed each other. The last one killed herself. The city was saved and the daughters of Erectheus were honored by Athenians forevermore.

Ericthonius (ur ihk THOH nih us): A son of Hephaestus; his mother is unknown. He became the fourth king of Athens. He was of noble character, but frightful appearance. Instead of legs, he was born with two serpent's-tails. However, he had inherited his father's skill with tools and designed the first chariot. Riding in the chariot he was able to conceal his serpentine legs. His image still abides among the stars as *Auriga*, the Charioteer.

Erinyes (ee RIHN ih eez): The Furies; three hell-hags with brass wings and brass claws. They pounced upon those who had offended the gods and harried them from place to place, never letting them rest — refusing to kill them but never ceasing their torment. They were held in such terrible fear that they were never referred to by their proper name, but were called the *Eumenides* or "kindly ones." In Roman mythology, Erinyes were known as Furiae.

Eris (AIR ihss; EE rihs): Daughter of Zeus and Hera; twin sister of Ares; queen of contention. She shared many of the amiable characteristics of her twin brother: riding beside him in his war-chariot, shrieking with glee at the sight of blood. War was her great festival, but she was addicted to strife in any form and ceaselessly fomented it — domestic quarrels, blood feuds, border skirmishes. She was detested by the other gods, but they tried to conceal their feelings, because her anger was deadly and she bore a grudge through eternity. In Roman mythology, Eris was known as Discordia.

Eros (EE rohs; AIR ohss): The archer of love. He is usually depicted as a slender winged youth bearing bow and arrows. These arrows are magical. Any man or woman pierced by a golden arrow fell passionately in love with whomever Eros designated; those pierced with a leaden arrow formed as violent a distaste. In most stories he is described as the son of Zeus and Aphrodite. But it is said that Zeus, fearing Hera's wrath, spread the rumor that Eros was born of Iris, the Rainbow, and that his father was the West Wind. Whatever the truth, he served Aphrodite with great devotion and skill and she used him as her agent for reward and reprisal. His well-aimed arrows made Helen fall in love with Paris, and Medea with Jason. He punished Princess Myrrh by instilling her with a passion for her own father and made Pasiphae conceive a monstrous yen for a Cretan bull. Only once did he disobey his mother, when he accidentally scratched himself with his own arrow and fell in love with Psyche, whom he wed despite Aphrodite's outraged protests. In Roman mythology, Eros was known as Cupid.

Erymanthian Boar (air ih MAN thih uhn BOHR): This huge savage beast roamed the slopes of Mt. Erymanthus in Arcadia, making life a misery to all who dwelt there. To capture this animal alive was Heracles' fourth labor. While pursuing the boar, Heracles was entertained by a centaur named Pholus. Suddenly they were attacked by a raging faction of centaurs who disliked Pholus and anyone they thought might be his friend. Pholus galloped away in terror but Heracles fought off the attack single-handed, killing many centaurs. Unfortunately, one of his arrows hit his old teacher, Chiron, in the knee. The wise old centaur later died of this wound. Thereafter Heracles, in a very bad temper, harried the boar out of his hiding place into a deep snow-drift. Heracles then leaped upon him, wrestled him to the ground, slung him over his shoulder, and returned to Eurystheus. Eurystheus, at the first sight of the boar, hid in a big jar and did not emerge until Heracles had taken the boar away and penned him up in a bronze cage.

Erysichthon (air ih SIHK thuhn): A brawling king of Thessaly, addicted to the battle-axe. In the irksome intervals of peace he would use his wild strength to cut down trees. Once he despoiled a stand of trees in a grove sacred to Demeter, arousing the implacable wrath of the goddess. Demeter summoned her servant, Famine, and bade her enter Erysicthon. Famine obeyed, and Erysicthon was seized by a raging unappeasable hunger. He ate all the food in the castle larder, then sent his servants to scour the countryside, bringing in all the cattle and all the grain they could lay hands on, which he promptly devoured. Finally, all of Thessaly was laid waste; the gluttonous king had eaten all the crops that grew, all the sheep and goats and beeves, and all the game that could be taken. Then he took his daughter and his axe and went to another land. There, when his gold ran out and he had nothing to buy food with, he sold his daughter to a wealthy merchant. The princess was trained to obey him and went off with her purchaser. But she prayed to Poseidon to grant her sea-change. Poseidon heeded her prayer and gave her the power of transforming herself. Before the merchant could touch her she changed into a gull and flew away. She returned to her father, who immediately sold her again. Again she changed her form and escaped ... and returned to her father, who sold her again! He kept selling her and buying food; she kept transforming herself and escaping. Finally, she met a young man who was unlike the other men. He matched her, transformation for transformation. When she changed into a cat he became a tom-cat, and kept courting her. He became a stag to her doe, and outraced her; a lion to her lioness, and wooed her thus. Finally, she changed back to her own form, and stayed with the young man, forgetting all about her father. Erysicthon waited for his daughter . . . waited and waited. She did not return. Now he had nothing to eat and no money to buy food. He had even sold his axe. He searched for his daughter along the edge of the sea, but did not find her. He shook his fist at the indifferent sky . . . and was attracted by the sight of his beefy paw. He gnawed at a knuckle, realized in horror what he was doing, but could not stop. He chewed off his hand, finger by finger. Then he ate his other hand. Hunger grew stronger with every bite; he ate one arm, then the other. He devoured himself completely, except for his lips, then swallowed them, and vanished altogether. After her vengeance was complete, Demeter's natural kindness asserted itself. She favored Erysicthon's daughter and her clever young husband and saw to it that their crops prospered and that their cattle grew sleek and fat.

Eteocles (ee TEE oh kleez): Son of Oedipus and Jocasta; briefly, king of Thebes. After Oedipus discovered that he had been committing incest all the years he had lived with Jocasta, he, in a spasm of horrified guilt, blinded himself. Jocasta, despairing, threw herself off the balcony to her death. Then Oedipus turned in wrath upon his twin sons, Eteocles and Polynices. He accused them of pride and heartlessness, claimed they had failed to support him and Jocasta during their terrible ordeal, and prophesied that they would die at each other's hands. Oedipus went into exile, leaving the throne vacant. The brothers agreed to share the throne, each ruling a year in turn. But Eteocles preferred to reign alone. He began to spread rumors about Polynices, defaming him and claiming that his murderous temper and general instablity made him unfit to rule. Eteocles gathered a faction about him and, when the end of his year came, refused to turn the throne over to his brother. Polynices, realizing that his life was in danger, fled the city and went into exile. He made his way to Argos, where he married, and with the help of his father-in-law, King Adrastus, forged alliances with powerful chieftains. After some years he marched against Thebes at the head of an army. Thus began the famous war known as the Seven Against Thebes. The invaders laid siege to Thebes, but the city held and there was great slaughter on both sides. Finally, Polynices challenged his brother, Eteocles, to single combat. Eteocles accepted the challenge and the brothers fought. They mortally wounded each other and died, according to their father's prophesy, at each other's hand. The invaders dispersed and Creon, brother of Jocasta, crafty uncle of the young kings, seized the throne of Oedipus.

Eumaeus (yoo MEE us): A swineherd of Ithaca, who remained loyal to Odysseus during the twenty years of his absence. He aided the wanderer when he returned, in disguise and in mortal danger from Penelope's rampaging suitors. It was the rude byre of the swineherd that Odysseus used as a hiding place, and where he summoned his son, Telemachus, for a rendezvous. It was here he polished the strategy that was to lead to the massacre of the suitors. Eumaeus aided him every step of the way.

Eumolpus (yoo MAHL puhs): A king of Eleusis and a favorite of Demeter, goddess of the harvest. Under her tutelage he instructed his subjects in vine-culture and animal husbandry. He formalized the worship of Demeter by establishing the Eleusinian Mysteries, those annual rites that celebrate the bounteous fertility of the goddess with dance, mime, and secret ritual.

Eumenides (yoo MEN uh deez): The word means "kindly ones"; applied to the Furies to divert the wrath of those ferocious hags, who were fond of flattery.

Euphemus (yoo FEE muhs): A son of Poseidon. It was said that he could run over the surface of the water without getting his feet wet, a useful talent in a sailor. And, indeed, he was a valued member of Jason's crew. He is the central figure in a curious tale of the Argonauts. A mighty storm swept the ship off the sea, hurling it into the middle of the Libyan desert. There they lay, helpless. Euphemus prayed to his father, Poseidon, who sent his half-brother, Triton, into the desert. Triton blew his curly horn and struck the sand with his staff. A channel appeared, leading to the sea, large enough to float the *Argo*. On parting, Triton gave Euphemus a clump of earth, instructing him to throw it into the sea, where, Triton said, it would grow into a habitation for the descendants of Euphemus. Euphemus threw the clod into the sea. It became the island, Calliste, and his descendants did dwell there and were great seafarers. It was they who colonized Thera, an island that became the capital of the last Atlantis.

Euphrosyne (yoo FRAHS uh nee): One of the Graces. Her name is variously translated as "Festivity" or "Joy." But legends agree that she was of joyous countenance and festivity followed her wherever she went.

Europa (yoo ROH puh): A princess of Phoenicia. She was a lovely, spirited, playful girl. She took enormous pride in being descended from mighty warriors. She loved tales of adventure and admired courage beyond all things. One morning, playing in the meadow with her maidens, she spied a huge handsome white bull browsing upon the grass. One of her companions dared her to ride the bull. Laughing with joy Europa leaped astride the bull and dug her heels into his side to make him gallop. He galloped. He galloped through the meadow, past the meadow, through fields and groves. Followed by a shrieking troop of maidens, the white bull raced onto the beach, and did not stop at the edge of the sea. Breasting the tide he swam away with Europa still clinging to his back. Bull and rider vanished over the horizon. Now, the bull was Zeus, who had transformed himself for the purpose of abducting the girl whom he had fallen in love with on first glimpsing her the day before. Europa stopped sobbing and began to enjoy the adventure. No girl, she thought to herself, had ever traveled so far, and no girl in the world would ever be able to match the tale she would have to tell when she finally returned to her father's court. But she never returned. Zeus changed into his own form, and took her to the cave where he had been born, an enormous dark pit gouged into the side of Crete's Mt. Ida. His daughters, the Hours, had hung it with rich tapestries, and carpeted it with flowers, making it a fragrant bridal chamber. There Zeus told Europa that he would honor her beyond all other mortal girls, that her descendants would people an entirely new part of the earth — to be named after her. And so the continent of Europe was named after the princess. She bore Zeus three sons — Minos, Rhadamanthus, and Sarpedon, all of whom became great kings. Under Minos, Crete prospered and became the most powerful empire in the world. And it was the abduction of Europa, and the attempt of her brother, Cadmus, to find her that led Cadmus on his journey through so many strange lands before he founded the kingdom of Thebes. Zeus always maintained a special affection for Europa. He hung a specially wrought chandelier of stars in the sky, naming it in honor of their courtship — the constellation called Taurus, the Bull.

Eurus (YOO ruhs): The East Wind. Like all the winds he was the son of Eos, goddess of the dawn, and the Titan, Aristeus. He was a surly, treacherous fellow, striking suddenly out of fair skies. He was a menace to shipping when his mood was foul and was much feared by mariners. He was especially violent and capricious in the springtime, and seamen were careful then to keep lee shores to the westward.

Eurydice (yoo RIHD ih see): Wife of Orpheus and a key figure in the great legend of a man's stubborn love and a god's treachery. Eurydice died young, bitten by a snake as she ran through a copse to avoid the embrace of Aristeus. Orpheus, greatest musician of his time, was devastated by her death and determined to retrieve her from the clutches of Hades. He made an incredible journey, doing what no other man had ever done — except Heracles, who was more god than man. Orpheus made his way to the brass gates which bar the entrance to Tartarus, and there was confronted by a hedge of evil teeth as Cerberus swung his three heads menacingly. Orpheus touched his lyre and sang a song of young dogs out hunting on a cool morning when the scent lies heavy on the ground. He sang so sweetly that Cerberus whined and crouched before the gates, weeping as no dog had wept before. And Orpheus passed, unharmed. Then, at the river Styx, the sullen boatman, Charon, refused to ferry him across. Orpheus touched his lyre and sang a boating song out of Charon's long-vanished youth, making him forget the inky Styx and his dismal freight, making him remember sparkling seas and bright skies and colored sails. Charon, weeping great tears, welcomed him aboard and rowed him across the Styx. And so, charming everyone with his lyre, Orpheus made his way through Tar-

71

tarus — into the black castle itself, past all the guards, into the throne-room of death, where Hades sat on an ivory and ebony throne, and Queen Proserpina sat next to him. Orpheus did not argue his case; he had made a ballad of it. He touched his lyre and sang of Eurydice's youth and innocence and astounding beauty. Of her flight from the ravisher, and of the indifferent brutishness of the serpent who had blotted her light. Finally, he sang of himself, the young husband, but one year wed, deprived forever. When he ended his song, Proserpina was sobbing and Hades scowling. For the king of the dead, who was an expert at remaining unmoved by piteous tales, knew that his wife would never forgive him if he refused Orpheus. Whereupon he pretended to relent and told Orpheus that he might lead his wife back to the land of the living on one condition: that he, Orpheus, must not look back at Eurydice during their journey through Tartarus. And he warned Orpheus that if he did look back for any reason at all, Eurydice would have to return to the death from which she had come. Orpheus joyfully assented. Eurydice was led out of the shadows and he began his journey back through Tartarus, followed by his beloved wife. Back he led her to the shore of the Styx, and across the dread river. They did not pass through the gates but followed an uphill route given to them by Hades which would lead them through the caves of Avernus. Orpheus walked on, never turning back. His keen musician's ear was tuned to his wife's light footfall and he knew she was following. But Hades had craftily directed them through a forest of pine where the pine needles lay thick, deadening footfall. Just as Orpheus was approaching the Avernian portals to the upper world, the sound of his wife's footsteps vanished. He strained his ears but could hear nothing. In wild fright he turned to look, and saw Eurydice. But even as he looked upon her she grew misty at the edges and hissed away like a plume of steam, never to be seen again.

Eurylochus (yoo RIHL uh kuhs): A cautious member of Odysseus' crew, the only one who refrained from drinking of Circe's enchanted cup — thus avoiding transformation into a pig. But his caution was overcome by hunger at a later stage of the voyage. When the starving voyagers made a landfall on the Isle of the Sun, Eurylochus was the first to kill and eat one of Apollo's sacred cattle, inspiring the rest of the crew to devour the herd. It was their last meal. The enraged Apollo wrecked their ship and drowned every man of them — except Odysseus, who had tried to prevent the sacrilege.

Eurynome (yoo RIHN uh mee): The moon. A startled light arose from the wastes of Chaos and became the goddess, Eurynome. She danced across the edge of nothingness and the path of her dancing became the margins of sea and sky. The North Wind pursued her as she fled, dancing. The West Wind and the South Wind and the East Wind joined the hunt; they surrounded her and became the coils of the Universal Serpent, Ophion. She was a prisoner of these coils and they closed about her. She turned herself into a white bird and flew away. She nested in the sky and laid a clutch of silver eggs ... which were the sun and the earth and the planets and all the stars that stud the sky. Upon the earth were trees, flowers, birds, beasts, and man. Eurynome means "far wanderer," the first name given to the moon. Ophion means "moon-serpent." And long before there were any gods, the ancient ones believed in the all-mother, the moongoddess.

Eurypylus (yoo RIHP uh luhs): A grandson of Heracles, who fought on the Trojan side, wreaking great havoc among the Greeks. However, he lost much sleep because of his hopeless love for Cassandra, who spurned all suitors, including Apollo. Finally, he was killed in battle by Neoptolemus, son of Achilles.

Eurystheus (yoo RIHS thee uhs; yoo RIHS thoos): King of Mycenae, appointed by Hera to preside over Heracles' twelve labors. Actually, Eurystheus was Heracles' cousin, a seven-month child whose birth had been hastened by Hera so that he might inherit the crown of Mycenae. Eurystheus is possibly the most cowardly king in all mythology — whose kings share every vice except cowardice. There is an irony about his legend. This man was frightened by the very idea of Heracles — so frightened that he never dared speak to him in person, but sent a herald to announce each new task. He invariably hid when the hero returned, dragging the carcass of a monster behind him, or carrying some huge beast on his shoulders. Yet this was the man who was Heracles' taskmaster. After the death of Heracles, he was emboldened to attempt the extermination of all the hero's children. But he was balked by their grandmother, Alcmene, whose courage matched her beauty. She spirited the children away to Athens. When Eurystheus led an army in pursuit she persuaded the Athenians to defend her grandchildren. Eurystheus was killed by Heracles' son, Hyllus.

Euterpe (yoo TUR pee): Muse of lyric poetry. She was a wild beautiful goddess addicted to word-juggling and the music of the flute. The distracted air worn by poets was caused by their straining to listen for the sound of her flute — which only they could hear.

Evander (ee VAN dur): An Arcadian son of Hermes, who settled in Italy before the Trojan Aeneas. Evander was a friend of Heracles and entertained him between labors when the hero's journeys took him to Italy. After Heracles' death he raised altars to the hero and organized cults of worship for this matchless son of Zeus. He welcomed Aeneas to Italy and helped him settle there. It was through Evander's teaching that Greek was introduced into this new land and became the father of Latin.

74

Fates (FAYT'S): Three dread sisters: Clotho, Lachesis, and Atropos, whom, it was said, even the gods must obey. They were the daughters of Themis, the goddess Necessity, and carried out her decrees in this manner; Clotho sat at her spindle spinning out the thread of each life (that is where we get the word "cloth"). Her sister, Lachesis, measured out what had been spun. But most terrible of the three was Atropos, who sat there with her shears, waiting, and snipped the thread when she thought it was long enough. Sometimes she cut it very short. It was the nature of gods and men to struggle against their fate, and this spectacle provided the sisters with much entertainment. In Roman Mythology, the Fates were known as Morae.

Furies (FU rihz): Hades' hell-hags. See *Erinyes*; *Eumenides.*

Gaia (JEE uh): Earth was the first mother, and her name was Gaia. She bore a son, Uranus, who had no father. Uranus preferred heights; he built a cloud castle which he set on top of a mountain. His beard was like cloud-fleece as he sat on the terrace of his castle brooding down upon his mother. So many clouds brought rain. Where the living rain fell, the earth put forth great meadows of grass and forests of trees. And birds and beasts were born from this first magical wetness. They lived among the groves and fields, and fish appeared to swim in the rivers and oceans formed by the overflowing rain. But not yet man. The first children of earth were giants taller than trees, each with a hundred hands. Next came the rude, twisted, one-eyed Cyclopes who were master-builders and whom earth bore to serve the gods who were not yet born. Then Mother Earth labored and bore the gods — a beautiful troublesome race. Then, finally, man was born — not quite so beautiful as the gods, but even more troublesome. In Roman mythology, Gaia was known as Earth.

Galanthis (guh LAN thuhs): A servant of Alcmene, who shortened the agonized birth-pangs of her mistress. She frightened Eileithia, goddess of childbirth, while she was in the process of knotting Alcmene's labors to delay the birth of Heracles. Galanthis screamed, startling

76

Eileithia, and Heracles was born. But Galanthis was turned into a weasel for her pains.

Galatea (gal uh TEE uh): The girl who began life as a statue and ended it as the sculptor's wife. Pygmalion, young artist of Cyprus, fell in love with the statue he had made and prayed to Aphrodite to give her life. The goddess was flattered by what she fancied was the statue's resemblance to herself, and granted the young man's request. The statue flushed with life and stepped off its pedestal into Pygmalion's arms. In gratitude, the sculptor carved marvelous wooden dolls of Aphrodite which, centuries later, were found at her altars.

Ganymede (GAN ih meed): Cup-bearer to Zeus. This beautiful lad was a prince of Troy, which was named after his father, King Tros. One morning, Eos, the yellow-robed, rosy-faced goddess of the dawn, peeked into the palace at Troy and saw the boy lying asleep. She snatched him up and bore him to Olympus. There he became a favorite of the gods, cup-bearer to Zeus himself. Now, the high honor of pouring wine for Zeus had belonged to Hera's daughter, Hebe. Hera fell into a rage and resolved to destroy the young Trojan. And Zeus, knowing the range of his wife's spite, thought it prudent to place the boy among the stars — where he still abides, under the name Aquarius. Since then, Dawn arises at midnight to give herself time to make a detour and visit this constellation before beginning her morning rounds.

Gemini (JEHM ih ny): The Twins, Castor and Polydeuces. Also called the *Dioscuri*. See *Castor and Polydeuces*.

Geryon (G'AIR ih uhn; JEE rih uhn): Antagonist in the tenth labor of Heracles. He was a truly monstrous figure, what might be called a Siamese triplet: three giant

77

bodies joined at the waist and all directed by a malevolent intelligence. His herds were famous — beautiful red cattle that grazed the plains at the western margin of the Inner Sea, the land now called Spain. It was Heracles' task to fetch these cattle, drive them back to Mycenae, and add them to the herds of King Eurystheus. Heracles traveled overland for part of this journey, crossing the Libyan desert. There he became angered at the sun for shining too hotly and unslung his bow, preparing to shoot Helios, the sun's charioteer, out of his chariot. But Helios appeased the hero by offering him a golden goblet — more seaworthy, he claimed, than any ship. Heracles embarked in this goblet and sailed from North Africa to Spain, where he found Geryon tending his flocks. He was immediately attacked by Geryon's dog, a huge and savage two-headed beast. Heracles killed the dog with his club, smashing both heads. Then, deciding that to wrestle the three-bodied giant would be a cumbersome task, he unslung his bow again and shot Geryon dead, using three arrows. But his troubles were not over. Driving the herd eastward, he was deviled by Hera who sent her gadfly, Brize, to sting the cattle, making them stampede. Heracles finally chased the gadfly, rounded up the cattle, and resumed his journey to Mycenae. Eurystheus was very disappointed at the successful conclusion of this tenth labor. He had been assured by Hera that Heracles would be killed by Geryon. Now, Heracles had originally been assigned only ten labors, and considered this raid upon Geryon his last. When Eurystheus hastily disqualified two of the labors — the Hydra and the Augean Stables — and imposed two other labors in their place, making twelve in all, Heracles flew into a rage. He killed the herald who brought him this news and rampaged over Mycenae, searching for Eurystheus, who was keeping himself well-hidden. But Heracles remembered that he had been forbidden by Zeus to kill Eurystheus, and submitted in time to the two additional labors.

Glaucus (GLAH kuhs): There are several figures of this name in mythology. Perhaps the two most interesting are: (1) A Boetian fisherman who discovered an herb that kept fish alive after he caught them. Thinking such a talent would prove useful in his domain, Poseidon spirited Glaucus away to the depths of the sea and gave him the task of healing wounded fish. Glaucus was very successful at this. Poseidon's flocks prospered. In return, he made Glaucus a minor sea-diety, and gave him immortality. (2) A king of Corinth, father of the hero Bellerephon. This Glaucus was extremely proud of his royal stables where he kept the finest racing mares in all the Peloponnese. So that they might not be distracted by maternity from their business of running faster than other horses, he forbade them to breed. The mares grew furious at this deprivation, stampeded into the stable-yard and battered the king to death with their hooves.

Golden Fleece (GOHL duhn FLEES): This was the pelt which had become a holy relic in Colchis and the object of the Argonauts' quest. Legends as to its origin vary greatly. According to one, when Zeus was young a great golden ram dwelt among the crags of Mt. Ida. He was the last of that breed of ram worshipped as gods in the mist of time. The young Zeus hunted the ram up and down the mountain and finally slew him. But, before he could take his pelt, he was distracted by a mountain nymph, whom he pursued, leaving the carcass of the ram on the ground. It was found by a shepherd, who skinned it, and kept the golden fleecy pelt for himself. Dancing in it, he found he could call down rain in a dry season. Armed with this power, he made himself king, and his descendants reigned for hundreds of years. Each of these kings dressed the altar of his holiest temple with this fleece. Another legend speaks of a golden-fleeced winged ram sent by Poseidon to rescue the children of Nephele who were being menaced by the jealousy of their step-mother, Ino. The children climbed on the back of the ram, who flew to Colchis. On the way, however, the young boy, who was named Helle, fell off the ram and was drowned — giving that part of the sea the name Hellespont. His sister arrived safely and was welcomed by Aeetes, king of Colchis, father of Medea. It was from Aeetes that Jason stole the fleece.

Gordius (GOR dih uhs): A ploughman of Phrygia in its earliest days. An eagle perched on his plough one day and remained there while Gordius ploughed the field. Greatly puzzled, he consulted an oracle as to the meaning of this sign. For the people of Phrygia believed that their gods were in constant communication with them through cryptic signs and riddling wonders, which had to be unraveled by their oracles, who were young priestesses. The oracle told Gordius that the eagle connoted royalty and that the special attentions of this eagle meant undoubtedly that a son of Gordius would be king of Phrygia. Gordius was so excited by this prophecy that he offered to marry the girl, and was accepted. They had a son named Midas. But the family seemed very far from royal estate and Gordius began to train his son for the plough. Some years later Phrygia was torn by internal strife. The leaders consulted an oracle who told them that their king would come on a wagon. They emerged from the temple, discussing the prophecy, to see a wagon draw up. In it were Gordius and his wife and the young Midas, a stalwart handsome youth. Awe-struck by the speed with which the prophecy was fulfilling itself, they immediately offered the kingship to the young man. He became a very powerful ruler. He ran into some difficulties himself, later, in the matter of the famous "golden touch." His father, Gordius, who as a member of the royal family could not be allowed to work as a ploughman, found himself with too much time on his hands. He spent the time concocting puzzles and solving them.

Once he tied a knot with concealed ends. Neither he nor anyone else could untie it. The knot was a wonder to the court. In the Phrygian manner, Midas immediately consulted an oracle, who declared that he who finally untied this knot would be Lord of Asia. The legend persisted and the knot was kept in a guarded place. Centuries later, when Alexander came there, he was told of the prophecy. Unable to untie the knot, he drew his sword and cut through it. This was the famous episode of the "Gordian Knot," after which Alexander proceeded to conquer Asia.

Gorgons (GOR guhnz): Three monstrous sisters who figure in the tale of Perseus. They were once beautiful maidens, but the youngest of them, Medusa, was courted by Poseidon, thus arousing the jealousy of Athena, who changed Medusa into the ugliest creature imaginable. She had a scaly body, bulging red eyes, brass wings and claws, and every hair on her head became a hissing snake. So dreadful was her aspect that anyone who looked upon her was turned to stone. When her sisters protested, Athena changed them into similar monsters. Medusa was finally decapitated by Perseus, who used her head to turn his enemies to stone.

Graces (GRAYS uhz): These gentle radiant daughters of Zeus and Euphrosyne went about among mankind spreading joy and peace. They taught women those amiable arts which, alone, kept men from lapsing into savagery. They were beloved of the gods as well, and together with their beautiful sisters, the Hours, and their talented half-sisters, the Muses, ornamented every gathering on Olympus. Their names were Aglaia (Splendor), Euphrosyne (Festivity), and Thalia (Rejoicing). In Roman mythology, the Graces were known as Charites.

Graeae (GREE ee; GRAY yee): Their name means

"old woman." Some say they were sisters of the Gorgons, born old. They had but one eye and one tooth among them, which they passed from one to another. They were forced by Perseus to disclose the secret hiding place of the Gorgons. They refused to tell him until he had kidnapped their eye and ransomed it for their secret.

Griffins (GRIHF ihnz): Winged lions, but their heads were eagle's heads. They lived north of the North Wind where the Hyperboreans dwelt, and there guarded a legendary trove of gold hidden under the snow. They had to keep constant vigil, for their neighbors were the one-eyed Arismapsi, the most thievish folk in the entire world, north or south, and who never stopped trying to steal this gold. In another legend the Griffins' dwelling place is the northern desert of India, where they spent their time clawing up gold dust. Their neighbors here, however, were more successful at theft. They spread delicious food for the Griffins and, while the monsters were feeding, they filled their sacks full of gold-dust.

Gyges (JY jeez): A Libyan shepherd who found a magic ring which allowed him to become invisible at will. He recognized how useful invisibility might be in a political career and immediately abandoned his flocks and set off for the royal palace. Making himself vanish, he passed the sentries without challenge, entered the throne-room, and declared himself a candidate by killing the king. He married the queen, and became king himself. Despite his abrupt tactics, he proved a better ruler than the one he had supplanted. His descendant, also named Gyges, was the great monarch of Libya, whose armies were victorious everywhere, and who made his kingdom great among the nations.

Hades (HAY deez): Son of Cronus and Rhea; ruler of the underworld; king of the dead. This eldest brother of Zeus was well-cast to rule the dead. He was somber, loathed change, and was given to slow black rage. He was a very jealous, very thrifty god. He sought always to enlarge his kingdom and forbade his subjects ever to leave his realm. Only Heracles — whose deeds were always unique — was ever able to rescue anyone who had fallen under Hades' rule. Tartarus was the name of his kingdom; it lay far underneath the earth and was girded by black rivers. Its gates were guarded by a three-headed dog named Cerberus, trained to keep the living out and the dead in. It was only rarely that Hades left his domain. Then he drove a golden chariot drawn by four black horses. He attended only the most important tribunals upon Olympus, but when he came he brought rich gifts — for great troves of gems and precious metals lay in his kingdom. What he liked best was to sit on his ebony throne with his beautiful queen, Persephone, at his side, listening to the twittering petitions of the drifting dead (which he always ignored). Cerberus barked in the distance, herding ghosts, and those brass-clawed hags, the Furies, flew overhead; the chiming of the Furies' brass wings was pleasant to him. He valued only death. The bright bustle of life offended him. The weeping of mourners was song to Hades; he drank tears like wine.

He was so loathed and feared by mankind that no one ever referred to him by his right name, but spoke indirectly of him, using a good name to deflect his course. They called him "Pluton," or the "rich one." But he was patient, the most patient of gods. He outwaited all strategies and, finally, always caught the one he was waiting for. In Roman mythology, Hades was known as Pluto.

Haemon (HEE muhn): Courageous suitor of Antigone. He was ordered by his father, Creon, for whom young love was distinctly subordinate to affairs of state, to bury Antigone alive — because she had defined Creon's order against burying her brother, Polynices, who had fallen in an attempt to claim the kingship of Thebes. At the risk of his life, Haemon too defied his father, and spirited Antigone out of the country and made her his wife. According to another legend Antigone was immured alive in a stone tomb and Haemon killed himself. The latter tale seems more in the spirit of that tragic Theban court, stained by incest, and bloodied by feud.

Halirrhothius (hal uh ROH thih uhs): A son of Poseidon who assaulted a daughter of Ares and was killed by the angry god. Poseidon, who stood high in Olympian councils, protested to the other gods, and they called Ares before a court of judgment in the world's first murder trial. A hill was raised in Athens to be used by the gods as a judgment seat; it was called Areopagus, or Hill of Ares. Poseidon was eloquent at the trial, heaping scorn upon Ares, calling him hypocrite. He cited the wargod's innumerable assaults upon goddess, demi-goddess, nereid, nymph, and mortal woman, and accused him of using any excuse at all to indulge his taste for homicide. But Ares responded by pleading the immortal right of a father to kill his daughter's ravisher. The gods inclined toward Poseidon's view of the case. But the goddesses voted unanimously for Ares. Since Poseidon was disqualified from voting the gods were outnumbered and Ares was acquitted. For centuries afterward, the Areopagus was used for trying important murder cases. Orestes stood trial there for the murder of Clytemnestra.

Halitherses (hal uh THAIR seez): A gentle Ithacan who had learned the language of birds and spent hours chatting with them. Birds are great travelers, especially the gull family, and they brought him much information. He knew before anyone else that Odysseus was on his way home to Ithaca. He hastened to warn the suitors that they had better cease their depredations before the king returned. But his advice was ignored. And long after the suitors had been killed by the avenging Odysseus, old Halitherses limped among the trees of Ithaca, happily gossiping with the birds.

Hamadryads (ham uh DRY uhdz): A type of wood-nymph. All dryads are concerned with trees and live in them when they are not roaming the forest — but each hamadryad is the spirit of a particular tree. She lives always in this tree and speaks out to warn woodman away when they try to set an axe to her tree. When the tree dies, she dies too.

Harmonia (hahr MOH nih uh): Wife of Cadmus, the founder of Thebes. She was a goddess, the daughter of Ares and Aphrodite, but her husband, Cadmus, had certain godlike propensities too, and they were well-matched. The necklace of Harmonia, centuries later, was used as a bribe in one of the plots that surrounded the war of the Seven Against Thebes. She was the mother of sons and daughters who later distinguished themselves in various ways: Agave, Autonoe, Ino, Polydorus, and Semele. The name of another Harmonia occurs in early legends. Her pedigree is vague. According to some accounts, she was the mother of the Amazons, who were sired by Ares.

Harpalyce (hahr PAHL uh see): A princess of Thrace who was an insatiable huntress. When game was scarce she hunted whatever else she could find — travelers, shepherds, ploughmen, almost anything that moved. Finally, the Thracian folk decided she was going too far, even for a princess. They caught her in a net and beat her to death with sticks.

Harpies (HAHR pihz): They are variously described but a sense of dread and loathing permeates all the descriptions. They seem to have been winged women of beautiful form and ravaged face. They had talons like an eagle and were extremely ill-tempered. Their chief employer was Hades who sent them to bear away by force and bring to Tartarus those who were unwilling to die. But they also did vengeful errands for the other gods. In a famous Argonaut story they tormented a king named Phineus who had incurred the wrath of a god. They swooped down at his table and snatched his food before he could eat it; they defecated in his plate. Phineus would have starved to death or killed himself but he was rescued by the Argonauts Zetes and Calais, who drove away the Harpies and, some say, killed them. There were three Harpy sisters. Various names are given to them, but the most noted one is Podarge, who, despite her appearance, attracted the notice of Boreas, the North Wind. She bore him a pair of beautiful colts, Xanthus and Balius, who became the fabulous stallions of Achilles.

Hebe (HEE bee): Daughter of Zeus and Hera; cup-bearer to the gods. She poured their nectar from a golden goblet and summoned the servants to bring them ambrosia. She was a mistress of rejuvenation and, when properly approached, granted eternal youth to a protégé of a god or goddess. She was often a scapegoat, however, for the wrath of Zeus. When he installed Ganymede as his cup-bearer, he discharged her from her duties, causing her much anguish and moving her mother, Hera, to vengeful intention. At another time, enraged because Hera had tricked him by delaying the birth of Heracles, Zeus seized Hebe by the hair and flung her from heaven. However, she seems to have been remarkably resilient. She always returned to her pleasant duties as cup-bearer and, as befitting an expert at rejuvenation, grew younger and lovelier each year. When Heracles was accepted into the company of the Olympians, he married Hebe.

Hecate (HECK uh tee): A goddess of the underworld. Some say she was an aspect of Persephone, Hades' queen, in her most deadly phase. But she is usually depicted as a self-sufficient deity, very ancient, very cruel . . . a torturer of ghosts and mistress of the brass-winged, brass-clawed Furies, whose task it is to torment those who have offended the gods. She was known also as queen of the roads, because, in ancient times, the dead were taken beyond the city walls and buried along the side of the roads. Hecate's cult outlived those of all the other Greek gods. She was adopted by the medieval witch covens as their patroness and was worshipped in their secret rites.

Hecatomb (HEHK uh tahm; HEHK uh toom): A sacrifice of special magnitude to the gods. The word literally means "killing of a hundred," usually a hundred cattle, but sometimes a hundred slaves or prisoners.

Hector (HEHK tur): Son of Priam and Hecuba; crown-prince of Troy. Priam was too old to lead the Trojan forces, so Hector assumed command. He was the natural choice, far and away the mightiest warrior among the Trojans — indeed, mightier than any among the Greeks except for Achilles. His wife was Andromache, a beautiful, loyal, intelligent princess who, throughout the war, did everything possible to help and inspire her husband. Actually, Hector had been a voice of moderation in Trojan councils, and had done his best to avoid war with the Greeks, advising Paris to return Helen. But when war did come, he was fearless and deadly on the field. It is estimated that he killed more than thirty Greeks in single combat. He fought to a draw in a day-long battle with the gigantic Ajax. While Achilles was sulking in his tent after his quarrel with Agamemnon, Hector led an irresistible charge that broke the Greek line. He had begun to set the invaders' ships afire when Poseidon arose from the sea to drive the Trojans back. But his final victory was to lead to his death, for Patroclus, beloved friend of Achilles, had donned the hero's armor so that the Trojans might think that Achilles had taken the field. This was a plan of Odysseus to blunt the Trojan's relentless attack. But Hector sought Patroclus out in battle and killed him. Maddened with grief, Achilles returned to the war. The night before, Andromache had pleaded with Hector to refrain from battle the next day — the first time she had ever done so. For the first time in his life, he refused her request. For he had been told by an oracle that if he died by the hand of Achilles, his slayer would not outlive him by three days. In the nobility of his soul he was willing to trade his life for the life of so terrible a foe of the Trojans. The next day, he met Achilles in single combat. Achilles fought like a demon. He was completely the master and cut Hector to the ground. Then he tied Hector's heels to his chariot-axle and drove seven times around the walls of Troy, trailing the dead body in the dust, taunting the Trojans who lined the walls, weeping at the sight. But Apollo, who favored the Trojans, cast a spell upon the body so that it remained intact. That night

Priam came to Achilles' tent and pleaded for the return of his son's body. At first Achilles refused, but becoming touched by the old man's tears, relented. Hector was burned with great pomp on a funeral pyre. Later, it is said, his bones were taken to Thebes because the Thebans had been promised prosperity if they maintained those mighty remains as holy relics. Hector was ultimately a loser, but he is an enormously attractive figure in mythology and is remembered with greater affection than the victor, Achilles.

Hecuba (HEHK yoo buh): Wife of Priam; queen of Troy. She bore Priam fifty sons and twelve daughters — among them such noted ones as Hector, Paris, and Cassandra. Her mood was extremely bitter during the war. She seemed to know that all her children would be killed or enslaved. According to one legend, she was given as a slave to Odysseus after the fall of Troy. But there is no mention of her on his voyages. Indeed, it is unlikely that the canny Odysseus would have encumbered himself with the sullen old queen on his voyage home. As it turned out, he ran into sufficient difficulties without her. It is told that she raged and snarled at the victorious Greeks until, by pure power of association, she was transformed into a brindle bitch who ran howling into the hills.

Helen (HEHL uhn): Daughter of Zeus and Leda; queen of Sparta; and known as Helen of Troy. Zeus had courted Leda in the form of a swan, and their daughter, Helen, had the stature of a goddess, the radiant complexion and suave muscularity of a swan, and her mother's enormous blue eyes. Her beauty was matchless. In the words of Christopher Marlowe, hers was "the face that launched a thousand ships." She began her career of being abducted at the precocious age of twelve, when the elderly but inflammable Theseus bore her off to Attica. They were followed by Helen's formidable brothers, Castor and Polydeuces, recognized as the best boxer and the best wrestler in the entire world. This combination tended to make even heroes like Theseus a bit cautious and he allowed Helen to return to Sparta with them. She proved nothing but trouble, however, to her foster-father, King Tyndareus, whose court was thronged with brawling chieftains from every part of the Peloponnese and beyond, each demanding Helen's hand, and eager to fight for it. Tyndareus feared to make a choice; he knew that the rejected suitors would declare war on him and waste his kingdom. Therefore, he heeded the counsel of Odysseus, one of the suitors, who drew up this agreement: Tyndareus would choose one of their number to be Helen's husband — all of them having pledged beforehand to abide by the choice, to keep the peace, and to unite against anyone who might seek to take Helen from her husband. The suitors agreed, and Tyndareus chose Menelaus, an unremarkable fellow, but his brother was Agamemnon, most powerful warlord in the Peloponnese. Tyndareus made him heir to the throne of Sparta and Menelaus was a contented husband until Paris came. Now Helen had been prepared for the Trojan prince and his rich embassy. Aphrodite visited her in a dream and told her she had been promised to Paris in return for his wise bestowal of the golden apple. Then the goddess schooled Helen in the ultimate refinements of love — those arts which Aphrodite alone knew the secret of, and which she had been careful not to teach anyone else. When added to the already extensive repertoire of the world's most beautiful woman, the result was devastating. After Paris had taken Helen to Troy, it was recognized by all at Priam's court that the result would be war with an extremely powerful enemy. However, by the time the High Council sat, forty-eight of Paris' forty-nine brothers had fallen in love with Helen and they refused to consider giving her up. The only exception was Hector, whose love for Andromache could withstand even Helen's beauty. After the fall of Troy, Helen was reclaimed by Menelaus, who had vowed to kill her. But his resolution melted before her beauty and he took her back to reign again as queen of Sparta. There she was forgiven, one by one, by those of her former suitors who had survived the bloody fighting under the walls of Troy. According to one legend, however, Helen was killed by Orestes, who held her responsible for causing the war that had kept his father away from Mycenae for ten years and led his mother into adultery and murder.

Helenus (HEHL uh nuhs): Prince of Troy; Cassandra's twin. She taught him to read the future, as Apollo had taught her, but without the curse that Apollo had attached to the gift: that is, the prophecies of Helenus were believed. He fought well against the Greeks but turned traitor in the last days of the war. Some say that he was embittered when, after the death of Paris, Helen had been given in marriage to his brother, Deiphobus, instead of to himself. Whatever the cause, he imparted to the Greeks certain secret options of destiny which led to their capture of Troy. He told them that the Palladium should be stolen from Troy, that the inheritor of Heracles' arrows, the archer Philoctetes, should be brought to the battleground. And according to some legends, it was Helenus who gave Odysseus the idea of building a wooden horse. His treachery served him well. The Greeks spared his life during the sack of Troy. He was the only one of Priam's sons to escape the massacre. Afterwards, he married his widowed sister-in-law, Andromache, and they ruled over Epirus.

Heliades (hee LY uh deez): Daughters of Apollo by the nymph Clymene. These beautiful gentle girls took care of the infant Dionysus, at the request of his father, Zeus, and adopted many clever stratagems to protect him from the raging jealousy of Hera. They had a brother, Phaeton, whom they adored. This was the lad who insisted on driving his father's sun-chariot and drove it so heedlessly that he scorched the earth, and startled Zeus, who looked down and saw forests burning and seas drying. Zeus killed Phaeton with a thunderbolt, and his sisters, the Heliades, grieved so that Apollo turned them into poplar trees — which still drop tears of amber sap.

Helicon (HEHL uh kuhn): There were two mountains sacred to Apollo — Helicon and Parnassus. He sported with the Muses on both mountains, according to the season, but on Helicon the Muses were joined by their beautiful sisters, the Graces and the Hours. Apollo's sister, Artemis, preferred Helicon too, and often stopped her moon-chariot there — unyoked her white stags and let them pasture on the lush grass of that enchanted mountain and drink from the delicious spring called Hippocrene. It is said that shepherds who drink of Hippocrene often find themselves babbling verse, abandon their flocks to the wolves, and wander off, talking to themselves in rhyme and hoping that someone will overhear.

Helios (HEE lih ohs): Son of Hyperion and Thia. His sisters were Semele, the moon, and Eos, the dawn. He himself is variously described as the sun-god, the sun itself, and the Charioteer — who, at Apollo's direction, drove the golden-spoked chariot of the sun across the blue meadows of the sky. After he drove his chariot from east to west, it is said, he embarked in a golden goblet and sailed all night from west to east to prepare for the next day's journey. In one legend, Zeus gave him an island for his own to be called the Isle of the Sun. But Helios named the island after a nymph he had loved there, called Rhodus, and the island today is still known as Rhodes. The Colossus of Rhodes, one of the seven wonders of the world, was a seventy-foot statue of Helios carved by the Rhodian sculptor, Chares. In all his various personifications as solar deities of one degree or another, Helios was much beloved. One of his names was *Terpsimbrotos*, "he who brings joy to mankind." But he produced some wicked female descendants: Circe and Pasiphae were his daughters; his granddaughter was Medea.

Hellen (HEHL luhn): Son of Deucalion and Pyrrha; first child to be born in the unpeopled world after the deluge. He ruled Phthia, a region including Mt. Parnassus, where Deucalion's ark had landed. His three sons, Aeolus, Dorus, and Xuthus, became the fathers of those tribes which made up the Greek nation. The land that Aeolus ruled was called Aeolia; his descendants were called Aeolians. Dorus joined forces with the sons of Heracles and conquered the Peloponnese. The sons of the third son, Xuthus, were named Ione and Acheus; their descendants were the Ionians and Acheans. The ancient Greeks did not call themselves "Greeks." They called themselves, collectively, "Hellenes" after Hellen, or "Acheans," or, sometimes, "Argives." That is how Homer refers to them, as do most of the other ancient chroniclers. The name "Greek" occurred later. It apparently arose out of confused legends about the earliest migrations and intermixing of peoples in which some racial memory asserts itself centering on the rituals of the matriarchal tribes antedating the Hellenes. "Greek" was derived from a word meaning "Worshippers of the Gray One." ("Gray One" meaning the Arch-Crone, or the primal moon-goddess in her waning stage.)

Hemera (HEHM ur uh): The Day. A deity out of the earliest creation myths. Hemera and Aether, meaning light, were the two radiant children of Erebus and Nyx, or darkness and light. They dethroned their parents and brightened the skies in celebration. The attibutes of Hemera were later absorbed by Eos, goddess of the dawn.

Hephaestus (hee FEHS tus): Son of Zeus and Hera; the smith-god. Lord of artificers, patron of crafts. This most industrious of the gods had a troubled childhood. He was born twisted and ugly and Hera hated him on sight. She flung him from Olympus; he broke both legs in the fall and forever afterwards was lame. A sea-goddess, Thetis, found the crippled infant on the beach and took him to her underwater grotto where she raised him as her own. He contrived beautiful ornaments of coral and pearl for his foster-mother and entertained her by setting living jewels to swim in the warm waters; we know them now as tropical fish. Nevertheless, he fretted in exile and resolved to take his rightful place among the gods. He won back his birth-right by a clever ruse. He built a golden throne and sent it to Hera as a gift. She sat upon it, its golden arms clamped about her and she could not rise. She remained a prisoner of the throne until Hephaestus had extracted a promise from the gods that he would be accepted into the Pantheon. Hera avenged herself upon him by marrying him to Aphrodite, who tormented him with her infidelity. However, Hephaestus loved his wife so much that he found happiness despite his mother's evil design. But he did not spend much time on Olympus; he preferred his workshop in the crater of Mt. Aetna in Sicily. There he stood at a mightly anvil, forging thunderbolts for Zeus and weapons for special heroes. His apprentices were the one-eyed Cyclopes, whom he kept teaching new skills even though they had been born skillful. He patched up his quarrel with his mother and made her many marvelous gifts, among them a table that ran about by itself serving food and drink. Despite his grimy appearance and modest manner, Hephaestus was much revered among mankind. For, in ancient times, the smith was considered a potent sorcerer who could lend magical properties to the tools and weapons he forged. In Roman mythology, Hephaestus was known as Vulcan.

Hera (HEE ruh; HUR uh): Daughter of Cronus and Rhea; sister and wife to Zeus; queen of the gods. Hera's jealousy had such dramatic consequences, so many of the tales of gods and heroes pivot on her spite, that her own legend has become somewhat obscured. But there was much more to Hera than jealousy. She was a beautiful, majestic goddess, chosen wife of Zeus — who had the whole world to choose from — to whom he always returned. Hera's most famous grudge, the one most productive of legend, was aimed at Alcmene, mother of Heracles. Of all mortal women, Alcmene, Lady of the Light Footsteps, was the most beautiful, and the most wise — and Hera hated her beyond measure. Her loathing extended to the son of Zeus and Alcmene, Heracles. Through his entire career Heracles was tormented by Hera's venomous wrath. His enslavement by the wicked king Eurystheus, and the ordeal of the Twelve Labors were all imposed by Hera. But it was the accomplishment of these labors that kindled his immortal fame. Hera's vengeance became his glory. In fact, the name "Heracles" means "Hera's glory." In the mighty metaphor of Hellenic belief each god plays a unique role, and Hera's envious nature is a most significant theme. Her hostility to the hero-brood of Zeus symbolized the hostility of nature itself. And the heroism of heroes was precisely defined by the dimensions of their troubles and by their ability to surmount disaster. As for Hera herself, queen of the gods, she held an invincible advantage over her rivals. Every springtime she bathed in a spring called Canathus; its crystal waters washed away age and fretfulness. She became a young maiden again, lovely as in the dawn of time when Zeus courted her as rain cloud and cuckoo, lovelier by far than any goddess, nymph, or mortal. Then Zeus courted her again. He raised a golden cloud for their privacy and the flowers of earth sent forth an overpowering fragrance. In Roman mythology, Hera was known as Juno.

Heracles (HUR uh kleez): Son of Zeus and Alcmene; greatest of the legendary heroes; and the strongest man who ever lived. Heracles occupies a unique place in mythology. Many of his exploits resemble those of other heroes, but other of his deeds transcend mortal possibility and signify godlike powers. Indeed, he was the favorite son of Zeus, who took special measures in his procreation so that he might be the mightiest hero of all. Zeus intended that this son be more than a hero; he was to be a god who would spend his life among mortals, much of it in servitude, thus gaining special insight into the human condition. Then, when he finally joined the Olympians, he would bring with him a knowledge of the real world that would aid the gods in their councils. All his life, Heracles was pursued by the venegful wrath of Hera. It was she who drove him mad in his young manhood, making him mistake a group of his sons for a raiding party of enemies and killing them all with his arrows. It was for this crime that he was sentenced to hard labor — the famous Twelve Labors — at the court of his cousin, King Eurystheus. The Twelve Labors are described elsewhere in these pages under the names of his central adversaries in each labor, but this is a list of his tasks: (1) Kill the Nemean Lion; (2) Kill the Hydra; (3) Capture the Cerynean Stag; (4) Cage the Erymanthian Boar; (5) Clean the Augean Stables; (6) Kill the Stymphalian Birds; (7) Claim the Mares of Diomedes; (8) Pen the Cretan Bull; (9) Seize the girdle of the Amazon Hippolyte; (10) Take Geryon's Cattle; (11) Fetch the golden apples of the Hesperides; (12) Impound Cerberus, hound of hell. Any one of these labors — except the last — might have been performed by Perseus or Theseus, or any of those wonderfully powerful mortals known as heroes. But other of Heracles' deeds belong to godhead. He offered to shoot Helios out of his sun-chariot and refrained only when given the Charioteer's golden boat. At the age of eight months he strangled two huge blue serpents introduced into his crib by Hera. He attempted to seize the Delphic temple from Apollo and fought the sun-god on equal terms until Zeus parted them with a thunderbolt. He also met Poseidon and Ares in single combat and bested them both, wounding Ares severely. In another episode out of his infancy, Hera was tricked into offering him her breast. Recognizing him, she dashed him to the ground. Whereupon he spewed forth the milk and it spattered across the night sky, forming the Milky Way. All these are the acts of a god, not a man. And the Milky Way story belongs to pure creation myth, in which Heracles is identified with some earlier universe-shaping deity. Indeed, after his death, Zeus summoned him to Olympus where he was received by the Olympians and given immortality. Hera objected at first but was persuaded by Zeus to drop her enmity and to adopt Heracles as her own son. He soon became her son-in-law also for he married her daughter, Hebe. Altars to Heracles were raised in every Hellenic land, and indeed, in all the lands of the Inner Sea which he had visited on his adventures. He was worshipped as a god. In fact, through the cult of Heracles men were brought into more intimate connection with the immortal gods because Heracles had lived among them as a man and suffered among them. And this too was part of Zeus' plan. In Roman mythology, Heracles was known as Hercules.

Hermaphroditus (hur maf ruh DY tuhs): Son of Hermes and Aphrodite, as his name implies. He was a beautiful modest lad who fled the embraces of a nymph named Salmacis. Inflamed beyond reason by his reluctance, she prayed to the gods that her body be eternally united to his. For some reason, this request was granted. Thereafter, they existed as one organism, named Hermaphroditus, sharing attributes of male and female . . . to the dismay of his parents, who preferred him as he had been, despite his newly found self-sufficiency.

Hermes (HUR meez): Son of Zeus and Maia; god of commerce; patron of liars, gamblers, and thieves; protector of travelers. Before Hermes was half a day old he had climbed out of his cradle and stolen a herd of cattle belonging to Apollo. Confronted by the angry sun-god, the infant Hermes appeased his wrath by teaching him to play the lyre — which he had found time to invent before he was two days old. Apollo took the precocious babe to Olympus where he endeared himself to Zeus. He was appointed Herald God and charged with the duty of conducting the dead to Hades. It is said that Hermes invented dice, astronomy, taught the gods the use of the fire-stick, and developed the first system of weights and measures. He was the wittiest of the gods by far, and very good company. Zeus used him exclusively on confidential errands and invariably chose him as a companion for his nocturnal adventures, when he would disguise himself as a mortal and descend from Olympus to mingle among earthlings. Hermes is depicted as a slender beardless young god, wearing a pot-shaped hat and winged sandals, and carrying a herald staff. In Roman mythology, Hermes was known as Mercury.

Hermione (hur MY oh nee): Princess of Mycenae; daughter of Helen and Menelaus. It is said that her father first affianced her to Orestes, but later, when Orestes fell into disrepute, quickly married her to Neoptolemus, son of Achilles. According to some legends, this was one of the reasons for Orestes' subsequent murder of Helen.

Hero and Leander (HEE roh) (lee AN dur): Hero was a priestess of Aphrodite who lived on a windy island called Sestos. Across the Hellespont was another wind-battered island, named Abydos, where dwelt her suitor Leander. Their love had to be kept secret because priestesses were not allowed to marry. Every night Hero lighted a torch in her tower, and Leander, guiding himself by the light, swam the turbulent Hellespont to visit his beloved. With every visit their love increased. They had met in the summertime; by winter they could not do without each other. Despite the vicious winds that piled up mountainous breakers on the waters of the Hellespont, Leander continued to swim across every night. One night, the wind blew out the light. Leander lost his way in the howling darkness, and drowned. His body was washed onto the beach at Sestos, and Hero discovered it. She hanged herself.

Hesione (hee SY oh nee): A daughter of Laomedon, an early king of Troy who was very reluctant to pay his debts. He cheated Poseidon once, and the sea-god sent a monster to ravage the shores of Troy. The king was informed by an oracle that he would have to sacrifice his daughter to the monster if he wished to save his country. The beautiful Hesione was bound naked to a rock. But Heracles happened along at the time and promised to deliver Hesione if Laomedon would give him the two marvelous stallions which had been given by the gods to Tros, first king of Troy, to compensate him for the abduction of Ganymede. Laomedon promised. Thereupon Heracles dived into the sea, allowed himself to be swallowed by the monster, and proved his utter indigestibility by systematically disemboweling the beast. However, after the monster was killed, Laomedon refused to pay. Heracles then seized Hesione, whom he later married to his friend, Telamon. Laomedon was not to escape so cheaply, however. Heracles attacked Troy with a handful of troops, defeated the Trojans, and sacked the city. This was a full generation and a half before the famous Trojan War. The name Hesione crops up again in connection with that later war. It was allegedly to reclaim his aunt that Paris went to Greece. But this, of course, was only a pretext for his detour to Sparta, where he won the confidence of Menelaus and the love of Helen, preparing the way for the most costly elopement on record.

Hesperides (hehs PAIR uh deez): Nymphs of the west; sometimes called the Apple-nymphs. They were three, these lovely daughters of Atlas, and they lived in the garden at the far western rim of the world where their father stood holding the edge of the sky on his shoulders. It was their task to guard the golden apples that grew on Hera's tree — transplanted to this far garden to keep the apples from Zeus, who used to distribute them as love-tokens. It was lonely there at the western margin of the earth and the Hesperides greeted their rare visitors with great joy. They enter the stories of Heracles and Perseus.

Hesperus (HEHS pur uhs): Son of Atlas; brother of the Apple-nymphs. He was an exceedingly wise and kindly Titan — so beloved by mankind that he aroused the envy of a powerful god — no one knows which one. This envious god sent a mighty wind to whirl Hesperus away while he was out mountain-climbing. He would have been dashed to pieces on the rocks below, but Zeus took pity on him and lifted him into the sky. There he abides, scattering sheaves of light over the night sky — Hespersus, the Evening Star, most beautiful of the firmament.

100

Hestia (HEHS tih uh): Goddess of the hearth. Cronus and Rhea produced six divine children — Hestia, Demeter, Hera, Poseidon, Hades, and Zeus — but Hestia, the eldest sister, was very different from the rest of her family. She never took part in any of the conspiracies that simmered on Olympus and always shunned the battlefield, striving to act as peacemaker among gods and men. She was a gentle, benevolent goddess — queen of the homestead, patroness of marriage, and instigator of domestic joys. She never took a husband herself nor bore any children of her own, but was guardian to all orphans and lost children. She was worshipped with a multitude of small fires; in her honor no hearth was allowed to grow cold.

Hippe (HIHP pee): Lovely coltish daughter of the wise old Centaur, Cheiron. She was courted by Aeolus, an early Hellenic chieftain, and bore him a daughter named Melanippe. However, she knew that the clannish Centaurs would kill her if they knew that she had consorted with a mortal. She prayed to Artemis for help, and the moon-goddess responded, placing her among the stars as the constellation of the Horse.

Hippodameia (hihp oh duh MY uh): A princess of Pisa, who married Pelops, and became mother of the bloody-chronicled House of Atreus. Indeed, the details of her courtship were steeped in crime. Her father, Oenomaus, a masterful charioteer, challenged each of her suitors to a chariot race, promising her in marriage to anyone who might beat him, but demanding the suitor's head if he should lose. Thirteen young men raced him; thirteen lost their heads. Finally, one came along who struck Hippodameia's fancy: Pelops, young king of Phrygia. Determined that Pelops should win this race, the girl bribed her father's stableman to saw half-through the axle of the royal chariot. During the race, a wheel fell off and Pelops won. He killed Hippodameia's father, and then, so there should be no witnesses to the affair, killed the stableman. Pelops married Hippodameia and they became the parents of Thyestes and Atreus whose bloody feuding compounded the family curse and flowered into a multitude of murders.

Hippolyta (hih PAWL uh tuh): Queen of the Amazons, whom Heracles subdued in his ninth labor, and whose girdle he took in completion of his task. Some legends say he subdued her in single combat with sword and spear. Others say he out-wrestled her. In another legend, Hippolyta falls in love with Heracles and gives him her girdle as a love-token. In still another tale, she becomes the wife of Theseus and mother of the woman-hating, horse-taming Hippolytus. In this last legend her identity seems to have been confused with that of her sister, Antiope — also cited as wife of Theseus and mother of Hippolytus.

Hippolytus (hih PAWL uh tuhs): Son of Theseus and the Amazon queen, Antiope. He was a solitary young man; his passions were chariot-racing and the training of horses. But then Phaedra came into his life. She was the young wife of his aging father and a hot-blooded Cretan princess. She could not tolerate her handsome step-son's preference for horses and did her best to persuade him toward other pleasures. But he spurned her. In a rage she went to Theseus and accused Hippolytus of assaulting her. Theseus fell into the trap. Without giving his son a chance to exculpate himself, he stabbed the boy to death with his sword. Or, some say, he upbraided him so violently that Hippolytus went storming off in his chariot, which overturned, sending the horses into panic. They turned on their master and killed him. In any case, the boy was dead. Phaedra, belatedly repentant, hanged herself.

Hippomenes (hih PAHM uh neez): The mild-mannered suitor who succeeded with Atalanta where so many more aggressive young men had failed. Instead of trying to outrace her, he prayed to Aphrodite for help. The goddess of love responded by giving him three golden apples. He dropped them one by one during the race, thus distracting Atalanta. He won the race and a difficult bride.

Hours (OW urz): Daughters of Zeus and Themis, half-sisters to the Fates, but of more pleasing aspect than those stern spinsters. There were three: Eunomia (Harmony), Dyke (Justice), and Eirene (Peace). They regulated the seasons, assuring that summer followed spring, and autumn, summer, in their appointed course ... that trees and flowers bloomed in their season. Each year on Judgment Day, Dyke sat at the left hand of Zeus and heard the appeals of those who felt that they had been accused of crimes they did not commit. Zeus trusted her to sentence the guilty, acquit the innocent, and punish judges who had taken bribes. In Roman mythology, The Hours were known as Horae.

Hyachinthus (hy uh SIHN thuhs): A lad whose beauty caused a feud between Apollo and Boreas. But the boy preferred the radiant sun-god, and Boreas, who was the North Wind, went into a fit of jealous sulks. One day, when Apollo was hurling the discus, Boreas puffed spitefully — blowing the discus out of its course. It struck Hyachinthus on the head, killing him instantly. Apollo did not allow Hades to claim the beloved boy, but changed him into a purple flower, the hyacinth, that blooms early in the spring. He also decreed that the people of Sparta celebrate his memory with a spring festival called the Hyacinthia. It became so sacred a ritual the warlike Spartans always suspended hostilities in April so that they might conduct the Hyacinthia.

Hyades (HY uh deez): Seven daughters of Atlas; their mother was Aethra, whose name means light. They had one brother, Hyas, an ardent hunter, whom they loved very much. Hyas was killed by a savage boar and the sisters mourned themselves to death. Now, they were held in high esteem by Zeus, because they had cared for his son Dionysus in his infancy and had adopted many stratagems to hide the godling from the murderous wrath of Hera. Zeus showed his appreciation by setting the seven sisters high among the stars — a wreath of seven bright stars, the constellation called Hyades.

Hydra (HY druh): A hundred-headed monster; hunted by Heracles in his second labor. The hundred heads actually do not express the ferocity of this creature — for when any head was cut off, two new ones sprouted in its place. At first Heracles struggled in vain against the monster. Its serpentine body enwrapped him; two heads sprouted for each one he cut off. Heads were coming at him from all directions, burying their teeth in his flesh. Finally, he instructed his nephew, Ioleus, to set fire to a tree. He uprooted the burning tree and used it as a torch, searing the stump of each neck so that no new heads could grow. Then he cut off the central head and buried it under a rock. Thus the Hydra was rendered lifeless, despite the belated appearance of a giant crab Hera had sent to aid the Hydra, which Heracles crushed under his heel. The Hydra's hundred heads became a hundred underground springs which ran pure water and gave water its name. As for the crab, Hera was grateful to it despite the failure of its mission. She changed it into a star and hung it in the sky, where it still hangs as the constellation Cancer — the Crab. Killing the Hydra was one of Heracles' most difficult tasks. He was enraged all the more when Eurystheus disallowed it because he had been helped by his nephew, Ioleus!

Hylas (HY luhs): A favorite of Heracles and his companion on the Argosy. He was kidnapped by the Nymphs of the Spring and was never found despite a frantic search by Heracles. See *Dryope*.

Hymenaeus (hy men NEE us): A poor lad of Athens who played the lyre and sang very sweetly. However, he was forbidden to marry the girl he loved because her father wanted a rich husband for her. Then the girl was captured by pirates in a sudden raid. They also took Hymenaeus whose delicate features convinced them he was a girl. But Hymenaeus had his lyre with him. He sat on deck and played so enchantingly that the pirates fell asleep. Whereupon he tumbled them overboard and sailed the ship back to Athens. Hailed as a hero, he married the girl and sang at his own wedding — singing so beautifully that the nuptial song was thereafter called a "hymenael." In another, lesser legend, he is the son of Dionysus and Aphrodite, a minor deity presiding over marriage.

Hyperboreans (hy pur BOH ree uhnz): Those who dwelt in a place beyond the North Wind, perhaps Britain. Apollo sought refuge among the Hyperboreans when he was exiled from Olympus for slaying the Cyclopes. He thereafter returned for a few days every winter to display his affection for those who had welcomed him so warmly. His annual return is still awaited with great eagerness by those who dwell among the mist and cold.

Hyperion (hy PEER ih uhn): First son of Uranus and Gaia, he was the eldest Titan whose name means "the one above." He married the Titaness Theia, whose radiance, it is said, first inspired men with their love of gold. They became the parents of Helios, Semele, and Eos — or the sun, the moon, and the dawn.

Hypnos (HIP nuhs): The god of sleep. He was the son of Night, little brother of Death, and the father of Dreams. He dwelt in a cave on the island of Lemnos with his wife, Aglaia, most brilliant of the Graces. Outside the cave was a garden of herbs where the poppy grew, and the lotus, and other flowers which help men sleep. Hypnos was also known as Lord of the Two Gates, these being the Gates of Ivory and the Gates of Horn. Through the Gates of Ivory thronged those false visions which teased folk at night, tempting them into foolish ways. Through the Gates of Horn flew forth true dreams of prophecy and inspiration. In Roman mythology, Hypnos was known as Somnus.

Hypsipyle (hip SIP uh lee): Queen of Lemnos. The Lemnians had been in the habit of raiding Thrace and bringing home Thracian girls whom they preferred to their wives. Finally, the wives lost patience and killed every man on the island, living husbandless for many years. The Argonauts landed there and were tumultuously welcomed. Every woman had a child by an Argonaut. Hypsipyle, who had chosen Jason, bore him twin sons, but he had departed by then and never saw them.

I

Iapetus (eye AP ee tus): Son of Uranus and Gaia; one of the primal Titan brood, elder brothers of the gods. He was married to Themis and produced a mighty progeny: Atlas, who bore the sky on his shoulders; Prometheus, who gave fire to mankind; and Epimetheus, husband of Pandora.

Iasion (eye AY zih uhn): A son of Zeus and one of the Pleides. Iasion was a very handsome demigod and Demeter fell in love with him at the wedding of Cadmus and Harmonia. They lay all one night on a thrice ploughed field on the island of Crete — which, thereafter, Demeter blessed with fertility. But Zeus was seized by a jealous rage when he learned of this encounter and killed Iasion with a thunderbolt. Demeter sped to Olympus and pled so eloquently that Zeus forbade Hades to take Iasion and granted his son immortality, ranking him among the lesser deities. However, Zeus always bore a grudge against him and never allowed him into the higher councils. There was a cult of Iasion in Arcadia, where, inspired by Demeter, he had taught the Arcadians advanced methods of agriculture.

Icarius (eye KAH rih us): Central figure in a curious legend of Dionysus. Icarius was an Attic ploughman. He and his daughter, Erigone, were the first to welcome the radiant young god when he came to Attica. They celebrated his advent with a joyous festival. Dionysus was grateful and taught Icarius secrets of vine-culture, how to press wine out of grapes, and how to age the wine. After Dionysus had departed, Icarius followed his instructions and made vats of wine which he shared with his neighbors. The neighbors, however, drank too much, and became drunk. Never having done so before, they thought Icarius had poisoned them. They murdered him and hid his body. Erigone went out with her keen-scented dog, Maera, in search of her father, and the dog found the hole where the man lay buried. When Erigone realized what had happened, she hanged herself. Dionysus learned of this and punished the people of Attica — laying a drought upon the land and filling the women with crazed spite so that they tormented their husbands. Then Dionysus set his friends in a special place among the stars. Icarius became that constellation called the Ploughman and Erigone's constellation was called Virgo. Nor did the god forget the dog, which he placed at the heels of the Ploughman as the dog-star, Sirius.

Icarus (IHK uh ruhs; EYE kuh ruhs): Son of Daedalus, he persuaded his father to make wings so that they might escape from the prison-maze at Gnossos, called the Labyrinth. The great artificer yielded to his son's demands, made the wings, and they flew away. But Icarus, whose imagination always out-leaped his capacities, was so intoxicated by flight that he disregarded his father's warning and flew too near the sun. The wax of his wings melted and the boy plunged into the sea, thereafter called the Icarian Sea. We derive our own word "Icarian" from him; it means "of bold vaunting imagination."

Icelos (YS uh luhs; IHSS uh luhs): A son of Hypnos; god of sleep. He changed himself into a different animal every night. There are those who say he was one of Hypnos' dream-brood—the kind of furry dream with bright bestial eyes that prowls the margins of night.

Idas and Lyncaeus (EYE duhs) (Lihn sooss): A pair of fabulous twins, the only pair to rival the immortal Castor and Polydeuces. Some say that Poseidon fathered one of both of these twins. In any case, they were marvelous warriors. Idas was a master spearman and Lyncaeus had eyes sharper than an eagle's. After their return from the Argosy, Idas fell in love with a princess named Marpessa. Now, anyone who courted her had to submit to a chariot-race with her father—the loser to lose his life also. Dozens of young men had perished in this way, for Evenus, her father, owned the swiftest stallions in that part of the world. But Idas asked Poseidon for aid and received a chariot drawn by winged horses. So equipped, he easily outraced Evenus, who then hanged himself. Idas married Marpessa and they lived happily together until Apollo took a fancy to the beautiful girl and abducted her. But Idas followed swiftly in his winged chariot and was bold enough to challenge the god, one of the few mortals ever to do so. They fought a duel with bows and arrows. But Zeus parted them, declaring that Marpessa should decide for herself whom she wished to live with. Unhesitatingly, she chose her husband. In an earlier legend, the twins joined those other twins, Castor and Polydeuces, on a cattle raid. But they quarreled over the spoils and the quarrel developed into a bloody brawl. Castor killed Lyncaeus, Idas killed Castor, and Polydeuces finished off Idas. Only Polydeuces survived and he was unable to live without his beloved twin. Nor did Marpessa wish to live without her husband and she too killed herself.

Idomoneus (eye DAHM ee nooss; eye doh mee NEE us): Son of Deucalion; king of Crete. He led a great expedi-

109

tionary force against Troy and shared the supreme command with Agamemnon. He fought well during the war and was an exceedingly effective leader. While refusing to dispute Agamemnon's rash decisions, he was always admired for his quietly successful generalship. Sailing homeward from Troy, his fleet ran into a violent tempest. Idomoneus, desperate to save his booty-laden ships and the lives of his men, vowed to Poseidon that if he were allowed to reach Crete he would sacrifice to the sea-god the first living thing he saw. The winds fell and he was able to bring his ships safely home. Upon disembarking, the first person he saw was his own son running joyfully to greet him. Legends differ at this point. Some say that Idomoneus kept his vow and sacrificed his son to Poseidon. Others say that he intended to keep his vow but that Zeus by this time had grown weary of human sacrifice and decided to put an end to the custom. He sent a pestilence down upon Crete — a swift deadly plague that cut men down where they stood. Idomoneus was forced to abandon the ceremony of sacrifice. He consulted an oracle who told him that he must spare his son and that he would be forgiven by all the gods, including Poseidon, who would accept a ram instead.

Iliad (IHL ih uhd): Homer's tremendous epic which pivots upon two months in the tenth year of the Trojan War. Achilles and Hector are the central characters but there is a cast of thousands. Homer is loosely credited with all the tales surrounding the Greek invasion of Troy and those who fought on both sides. Actually, most of the accounts of the events leading up to the war, the first nine years of the war, and the events following the sack of Troy, are non-Homeric. But, unlike the other tales and fragments of tales from antiquity, the *Iliad* and the *Odyssey* are integrated, beautifully structured narratives, written in poetry and stamped uniquely by one man's genius. They are thronged with marvelously developed human beings who are sometimes godlike and with gods who are all too often too human.

Ilium (IHL ih uhm): An ancient name for Troy after its fourth king, Ilus. "Iliad" means "story of Ilium."

Ilus (EYE luhs): Early king of Troy who actually built most of the first city. His grandfather, Dardanus, had settled the great sea-washed plain and had begun to build a nation. But for three generations no city had been built; the Trojans — not yet called the Trojans, but Dardanians — had been too busy fighting their enemies and extending the boundaries of their new land. According to legend, Ilus, the fourth king, was told by an oracle to follow a cow which had been given to him by a Phrygian king whom he had defeated in a wrestling match. He was to follow that cow until it lay down, and there build his city. He followed it across the Dardanian plain to the hill of Ate, where the cow rested. There he built his city, which was named after him. But it was also called *Tros* in honor of another early king, sometimes described as the grandfather of Ilus, sometimes as his nephew.

Ino (EYE noh): A daughter of Cadmus and Harmonia, she led a very eventful and tragic life. She become the second wife of Athamas, king of Boetia, who had discarded his first wife for her sake. Now, this first wife, named Nephele, was a curious phantom goddess who irritated Hera by prowling the garden of Olympus, sobbing out her troubles and disturbing the festive mood of Hera's soirées. Hera, therefore, cursed Athamas for returning Nephele to Olympus and cursed his house for generations to come. It is told that Ino hated the sons of Nephele, Phrixus and Helle, and evolved a plot to rid herself of them. She secretly advised the women of

Boetia to parch the seed-grain before sowing it. This, of course, meant that the seed did not grow and famine struck the land. Athamas, thereupon, consulted the oracles at Delphi, as was the custom. But Ino, as part of her plot, had bribed certain of these oracles, who informed the king that the famine would be lifted only if he sacrificed his sons to Demeter, goddess of the harvest. But Nephele, aware of this, cornered Zeus in the garden, and besought his aid. Whereupon, he sent a winged golden ram to carry Nephele's sons away from Boetia. Hera sent a dream to Athamas, informing him of Ino's plot. Enraged, he killed his son by Ino, a boy named Melicertes, and pursued Ino, intending to kill her also. But she leaped into the sea and Zeus — who had always been partial to Ino because, long before, she had helped care for his infant son Dionysus — changed her into a sea-deity. He changed her name also to Leucothea, meaning the white goddess. She wore a magic white veil that conferred immunity against drowning on anyone who wore it. It was Leucothea who came to the aid of Odysseus when the voyager was swept off his raft by one of Poseidon's spiteful squalls. Ino wrapped him in her magic white veil and he was able to float safely to the island of Drypane where he was welcomed by the lovely Nausicaa.

Io (EYE oh): A princess of Argos; loved by Zeus and loathed by Hera. Zeus knew that Hera had sent her hundred-eyed servant, Argus, to spy upon his meetings with Io. To escape this multiple vigilance he changed Io into a cow — a beautiful black and white heifer with great black eyes and polished horns. Hera, seeing through the disguise immediately, pretended innocence and asked Zeus to make her a gift of the heifer. He could not refuse. She then sent Argus to watch the cow day and night so that Zeus could not change the cow back to her own form. Thereupon, Zeus entrusted the matter to the infinitely witty and resourceful Hermes. The messenger god sped to the meadow where the unhappy Io was tethered and there found the hundred-eyed Argus watching her with all his eyes. Hermes was god of thieves and supernaturally thievish, but, with a hundred eyes watching, he knew that even he could not escape detection. He began to pipe upon his flute, playing sleepy tunes. The sun was hot and the flute sounded now like bees buzzing in the clover, now like the far sound of cowbells, now like the small wind seething in the grass. One by one, the eyes of Argus closed, until all hundred were closed and Argus lay fast asleep. Then Hermes rose softly, drew his sword, and cut off the head of Hera's sentry. He untethered Io and she wandered off. But Hera had other resources. She sent her demonish servant, Brize, to torment the cow. Brize was an enormous gadfly with a sting as long as a dagger. She flew about Io night and day, savagely stinging her. The anguished heifer rushed across meadow and field and plunged into the sea, which thereafter bore her name — the Ionian Sea. By this time, Hermes had flown to the scene with a golden net. He netted the gadfly and drowned it. Io swam across the sea to Egypt, where, finally, Zeus was able to hide her from Hera. He returned the girl to her own shape. She bore him a son named Epaphus, who become king of Egypt and father of Libya. It is said that the cult of cow-worship began in those lands upon the arrival of the black and white heifer. Hera, mourning the lost Argus, removed the hundred brilliant eyes from his head and set them on the tail of the peacock, thus making it the most ornamental bird in the world.

Iole (EYE oh lee): A beautiful girl who figured in the mighty legend of Heracles. The hero become interested in her at one point, arousing the jealousy of his wife, Deianeira, who, in an effort to win back his love, dipped his shirt in the poison blood of Nessus, which had been recommended to her as a love-philtre. The shirt of Nessus clung to Heracles, burning like fire; when he pulled it off he pulled away his flesh and died.

Iphicles (IF uh kleez): Son of Amphitryon and Alcmene; Heracles' half-brother, and his twin. Iphicles was a modest honest man who lived for years in the mighty shadow of his brother, doing everything he could to help the hero in his tormented labors and performing many courageous deeds. He was the father of Ioleus, Heracles' favorite nephew, who also attempted to aid the hero in his labors and was of particular help during Heracles' battle with the Hydra. Iphicles was killed during Augeas' treacherous attack on Heracles and was mourned throughout Mycenae.

Iphigenia (if uh jee NY uh): Eldest daughter of Agamemnon and Clytemnestra. When the Greek forces were gathered at Aulis, preparing to embark for Troy, Agamemnon went hunting and killed a white stag belonging to Artemis, which she had unyoked briefly from her moon-chariot. Artemis, enraged, summoned Aeolus and asked him to whistle up the North Wind. The wind blew, and blew directly into the harbor, and the ships could not sail. Agamemnon consulted the soothsayer Calchas, who killed a bird and from its entrails read the wrath of Artemis and the meaning of the tempest. He informed the king that he must sacrifice the most beautiful of his daughters to Artemis if he wished to appease her wrath and calm the tempest. Agamemnon thereupon led his eldest daughter, Iphigenia, to the altar and cut her throat with his own hands. The winds fell and the fleet sailed for Troy. In a more cosmetic version of this myth the sacrifice is prevented at the last moment when Artemis sends another white stag to take the girl's place. But the first version is the one most widely told. The sacrifice of Iphigenia is cited as one of the reasons Clytemnestra, her mother, conceived hatred for Agamemnon and later murdered him.

Iphis (EYE fuss): A warmhearted youth who lived in Salamis and fell in love with a girl named Anaxerete. But he aroused no response in her at all. One night he went to her house and hanged himself from the lintel of her doorway. The next morning she saw him hanging there, but still displayed no emotion. This stony-heartedness displeased Aphrodite who changed her completely into a stone.

Iris (EYE rus): The rainbow-goddess, and Hera's messenger. She flew about on Hera's errands very much as Hermes did for Zeus. However, she was of dazzling good nature and carried messages for other gods as well. She was a natural peacemaker. After a violent storm she sent a many-colored streamer arching across the sky to gladden men's hearts with a promise of fair weather. Her amiability was such that she never raised a word of objection when Zeus, wishing to conceal his dalliance with Aphrodite, spread the rumor that their son, Eros, was in reality the son of Iris and the West Wind. Hera was not deceived by this and savagely upbraided Iris for allowing such a story to be told. Iris did not defend herself. First she wept softly, then smiled at Hera. And that smile, gleaming through tears like the rainbow flashing through storm clouds, was so enchanting that Hera stopped scolding — for the first time in the annals of Olympus.

Ismene (ihss MEE nee): Sister of Antigone; daughter of Oedipus and Jocasta. Although not so well-known as her courageous sister, Ismene was of the heroic mold too. For when Creon sought to punish Antigone's disobedience by ordering her buried alive, Ismene declared that she shared her sister's guilt and wished to share her punishment. However, Antigone, wishing to save her sister, denied every statement she made.

Itylus (IT uh lus; EYE tih lus): Victimized child in a bloody tale of jealousy and revenge. See *Philomela and Procne*.

Ixion (IHK sy uhn; IHK sih uhn): A king of Thessaly whose audacity was immortal and punishment eternal. He actually tried to cuckold Zeus and abduct Hera. Zeus, in one of his complex and puzzling ruses, molded a cloud into the stately form of his wife. He named this cloud Nephele and endowed it with a kind of low-grade vitality. Ixion, deceived, abducted Nephele, who became the mother of the Centaurs — those creatures who are half horse and half man, and gallop through fables, sometimes brutal, sometimes wise. Then Zeus struck with his thunderbolt. He killed Ixion and had Hades prepare him a special punishment after death. Ixion was bound to the spokes of a flaming wheel; as he turns and burns, demons flog him with whips made of serpents. Nephele continued to float mournfully about, sometimes courted by others, but always finally abandoned.

Jason (JAY sun): Leader of the Argonauts in their search for the Golden Fleece. Jason had a valid claim to the throne of Iolchus, a situation which the usurping king, his uncle, Pelias, found intolerable. The yellow-haired prince was very popular and Pelias did not dare to kill him but did the next best thing. He sent him on a mission which had always proved fatal — to retrieve the Golden Fleece from the savage king Aeetes, of Colchis, and his even more dangerous daughter, the witch-princess Medea. Jason, however, was attracted by danger and sent heralds to proclaim his quest throughout the lands of the Inner Sea. The table of their names is the most illustrious roll-call of heroes ever assembled in one spot. Peleus was there, greatest warrior of his time; the invincible twins, Castor and Polydeuces. Atalanta, fleet-footed huntress; and some forty other battle chiefs, the noblest and bravest of their day. Orpheus came to sing his songs and fill their hearts with hope. And Argos, the master shipwright, built them a ship called the *Argo* which gave its name to their quest. Before launching the ship they sacrificed to all the gods. Jason aimed an especially fervent prayer at Aphrodite who had always been his favorite among the Olympians. She resolved to help him by lighting torches of desire in his path, and this incendiary aid was to have very mixed consequences. It was a long hard voyage. They encountered storms, pirates, man-eating birds, wild women, rocks that pursued them trying to grind their hull to bits, and a tribe of six-handed giants. They were able to beat off their enemies with the formidable assistance of Heracles, who had joined them briefly. But he left the expedition in mid-voyage, to the unspoken relief of his shipmates, who knew that his smoldering temper and wild strength made him almost as dangerous a friend as a foe. When they reached Colchis, Jason with two companions tried a swift night raid on the shrine of the Fleece. But they were captured and condemned to the Ordeal of the Plow — which meant yoking up two bulls and ploughing a field. The bulls were not ordinary, but huge fire-breathing beasts with brass horns and brass hooves. No one had ever lived through the first minutes of this test. Now it was that Aphrodite took a hand. She dispatched her son, Eros, archer of love, to shoot his sweetly en-venomed arrows into the heart of Medea, daughter of Aeetes and a high-priestess of Hecate, a powerful sor-ceress. Driven half mad by her newly aroused passion, she decided to betray her father and use all her demonish knowledge to save the handsome young prisoner. Visiting him secretly in his cell, she made him promise to love her and in return anointed him with a magical oil which would protect him against the flaming breath of the bulls. The next day, made invulnerable by Medea's oint-ment and using some potent incantations she had taught him, Jason subdued the brass bulls and ploughed the field. While he was taming the bulls and astounding the court, Medea went to the shrine of Hecate where a great dragon guarded the Fleece. She sang a sorcerous lullaby, casting the dragon into a deep sleep, stole the Fleece, and brought it as her dowery to Jason, who had been freed by Aeetes according to the terms of the Ordeal. The Colchian fleet gave chase but the Argo was too swift. Jason, Medea, and the Argonauts scudded safely homeward with the Golden Fleece nailed to the mast.

Then Jason, with the help of Medea and his hero-crew, deposed Pelias and seized the throne of Iolchus. But the end of the story was tragic. Jason tired of Medea, and she — mad with rage and jealousy — murdered their two sons. Jason reigned for many years; he had other wives and other sons. And Medea continued her career elsewhere.

Jocasta (joh KASS tuh): Queen of Thebes; wife of Laius; mother and wife of Oedipus. See *Oedipus.*

Judgment of Paris: See *Apple of Discord.*

Juno (JOO noh): Roman name for Hera, queen of the gods. See *Hera.*

Jupiter (JOO puh tur): Roman name for Zeus, king of the gods. This transformation of name from its Greek to its Latin form provides a good example of how one language developed into the other. "Jupiter" is a corruption of the words "Zeus pater," Father Zeus.

Lachesis (LAK ee sihs): Middle sister of the Fates. She measured out the thread of life which Clotho had spun, then gave it to Atropos, sister of the shears, who cut the thread when she thought it was long enough.

Ladon (LAY duhn): A serpent stationed by Hera in the Garden of the Hesperides to guard her golden apples. He was a special serpent designed for dread. There was no distinction between head and body; his jaws were hinged at the tail. In other words, he was a half mile of living gullet, lined with teeth — each one longer than an elephant's tusk and sharper than the sharpest sword. When Heracles came to the Garden of the Hesperides to fetch the golden apples for the completion of his eleventh labor, he first had to contend with Ladon. The sight of those murderous jaws made even Heracles hesitate. He did not wish to get close enough to use sword or spear, and the serpent's leather hide, he knew, was proof against arrow-shot. He went into the forest; there he sought dead trees where bees like to build their hives. He hung the buzzing hives from his belt and approached Ladon. First, he tossed honey combs to the monster, who snapped them up greedily. Then, Heracles took the hives themselves, full of angry bees, and hurled them one by one into the gaping gullet. The bees swarmed furiously, stinging Ladon in the only part of him that was vulnerable — his tongue and the inner membranes of his throat. The serpent was stung to death, but in his flailing agonies wasted the orchard — all except Hera's tree of golden apples, which Heracles then picked.

Laelaps (LEE laps): Matchless hunting hound which Artemis gave to Procris. This lithe beautiful dog never lost a scent and would run any game to the ground and hold the beast at bay, no matter how large and fierce it was, until the hunter arrived. Procris gave this dog to her husband, Cephalus. And Laelaps was with Cephalus on that fatal hunt when he accidentally killed his wife. It is said that the dog remained in one spot, howling with dismay, refusing to eat or drink, until Artemis came to reclaim him. See *Cephalus*.

Laertes (lay UR teez): King of Ithaca, and supposed father of Odysseus. Actually, he was the hero's foster father. He knew that the boy had been begotten by Autolycus, son of Hermes and master thief, who often stole wives from husbands. However, Laertes forgave his wife, Anticlea, and was a good father to Odysseus, recognizing that the thievish craftiness of Autolycus had been transmuted into incredible shrewdness and resourcefulness in his son, and that the boy would be a hero and a great king.

Laestrygones (less TRIG oh neez): Giants who inhabited an island off Sicily and whose favorite food was human flesh. The sight of this island bewildered sailors, for the sun chased the moon across the sky like a hound chasing a deer, and night followed day and day followed night in a matter of minutes. This swift alternation of light and shade confused helmsmen and led to many shipwrecks — which delighted the giant cannibals. Odysseus, unfortunately, chose that island for a landfall. The giants attacked. They stamped two of his beached ships to splinters and ate the crews alive. When Odysseus finally managed to escape with one ship and a battered crew, he was more disheartened than at any other stage of his journey.

Laius (LAY uhs; LAY us): King of Thebes; husband of Jocasta; father of Oedipus. He was killed by his son, Oedipus, in fulfillment of a prophecy that the youth was attempting to flee. Oedipus subsequently married his mother, completing the circle of murder and incest. This myth has echoed down the ages and given its name to the central theme of Freudian psychology. See *Oedipus*.

Lamia (LAY mih uh): A monster; half woman, half serpent. Once she had been all woman, and a beautiful one, but Zeus had loved her and Hera had retaliated. The goddess transformed Lamia into a hideous creature whose disposition matched her appearance. She lurked along roads at night, it is said, snatching up travelers and devouring them.

Lampetia (lam PEE shih uh): A demigoddess; daughter of Apollo. She was appointed by her father to guard his golden sun-cattle on the island of Thrinacia. Odysseus and his starving crew landed on this island. Odysseus recognized the beeves as sacred and warned his men not to touch them. But hunger was stronger than obedience. They slaughtered the cattle and began to roast them. The hides of the slaughtered cattle arose and began to move about, lowing piteously, attracting the attention of Lampetia who had been on another part of the island. Lampetia immediately sped to Olympus to inform her father. Apollo hurled a vicious squall at the island, wrecking the ship and drowning its sailors as they put out of the harbor. Odysseus alone was spared because he had not eaten of the sacred beef and had tried to restrain his men. He clung to a broken mast, half drowning, and drifted for days until he was swept ashore on Calypso's island.

Laocoon (lay AHK oh uhn): Son of Priam and Hecuba. He was no warrior, but a priest — and a very wise and courageous man. He mistrusted the Wooden Horse on sight, saying, "I fear the Greeks, even bearing gifts." And he tried to prevent the Trojans from rolling the horse within the gates. But Poseidon, who favored the Greek cause, wished Odysseus' ruse to succeed and wanted the hollow wooden horse with its belly full of armed men to enter the gates. Therefore, Poseidon sent two huge sea-serpents onto the beach at Troy. They seized Laocoon's two young sons and began to devour them. Without hesitation, Laocoon flung himself upon the serpents and wrestled them with wild unnatural strength. But they wrapped themselves about his body and slowly crushed him to death. The Trojans took this as a sign that Laocoon had been uttering sacrilege and that indeed the wooden horse was a sacred tribute to the gods as well as a great prize. They rolled the horse into Troy. And all of them died that night when the armed Greeks came out of its belly.

Laomedon (lay AHM ee duhn): Fifth king of Troy; father of Priam; and a man very reluctant to pay his debts. Since he tended to have formidable creditors like Poseidon and Heracles, the consequences were painful. See *Hesione*.

Latinus (luh TY nuhs): A son of Circe and Odysseus. He settled in Italy where he carved out a territory for himself and defended it very ably. When Aeneas landed in Italy after the sack of Troy, Latinus welcomed him and allowed him to marry his daughter, Lavinia. Aeneas succeeded Latinus as king of Latium; later their descendants founded Rome. The name Latinus became immortalized by becoming the name of a people and their language — Latin.

Laurel (LOH rehl; LOR uhl): The name given to Daphne after she was turned into a tree while fleeing the embrace of Apollo. The tree became sacred to the sun-god; he made wreaths of its leaves to crown victors, and his priestesses at Delphi chewed laurel leaves to induce a prophetic trance.

Leda (LEE duh): Paramour of Zeus; mother of Helen, Castor, Polydeuces, and Clytemnestra. Zeus put on the form of a white swan to woo this beautiful young queen of Sparta. She gave birth to quadruplets — Helen and Polydeuces sired by Zeus; Clytemnestra and Castor, whose father was her husband, Tyndareus. Her husband learned this but did not dare complain. Indeed, he took great pride in the exploits of his foster children. All four of Leda's children led extremely eventful lives and had a certain aptitude for involving innocent bystanders in the consequences of their deeds.

Lethe (LEE thee): A river in Tartarus whose waters were oblivion. It took its name from the nymph Lethe, whose name means forgetfulness. She was the daughter of Eris, which means discord. This beautiful sparkling stream was the one first encountered by the dead entering their place of eternal exile. Parched by their long journey, they stooped and drank from this spring. They drank forgetfulness. All memory of their past life fell away. They forgot those they had loved and had left behind on earth. They forgot triumphs and crimes, friends and enemies. Here, at the entrance to Tartarus, at the very threshold of their eternal banishment, on the banks of this sparkling stream, they encountered a first and last kindness. For by forgetting the events of their mortal life they were able to accept death without rancor or rebellion.

Leto (LEE toh): Zeus loved this maiden, who was known as Leto of the Dark Robe. She bore him two children, the most radiant ever born. Hera flew into a furious jealous tantrum, worse than any she had ever displayed before, because it had been foretold that these twins would outshine all her own children. She had known this even before they were born and had cursed Leto's labors, forbidding her to give birth anywhere the sun had ever shone. Leto wandered the earth looking for a place where the sun had never shone so that she might bear her children but she could find nothing. Finally, Zeus raised an island which had been floating undersea — the island of Delos. Zeus raised it to the surface and anchored it there. Since the sun had never yet shone on Delos it could not be touched by Hera's curse and Leto was able to begin her labors. She bore Artemis and Apollo, who became the gods of the moon and the sun, greater by far than any of Hera's children.

Leucippos (loo SIPH us): A grandson of Perseus who loved the nymph Daphne, also loved by Apollo. The lad put on girl's clothes and joined Daphne's attendants so that he might bathe with her in the river. But his ruse was discovered by Apollo who shot him full of arrows and left him dead in the river.

Leucothea (loo KATH ee uh): Name of the sea-deity who had formerly been the tragic princess, Ino. See *Ino*. Leucothea ordered a great pit dug near Epidaurus and filled it with prophetic waters. It became a sacred lake. There folk threw barely cakes to test their luck. If the cake sank, it meant good luck. If it floated, luck would be bad. The women of Epidaurus, it is said, developed a heavy hand with pastry.

Libya (LIHB ih uh): Granddaughter of Io; grandmother of Europa. She ruled a large area in North Africa and part of that coast still bears her name. Libya means "falling rain," and in that dry part of the world, the queen-priestess presided over rain-making rituals — the most significant ceremonies of the year.

Lichas (LY kuhs): A servant of Heracles who brought him the shirt which had been dipped into the poison blood of Nessus. In his death-throes, Heracles seized Lichas by the leg and hurled him off the cliff. But Zeus took pity and arrested the fall, turning him into a rock — which then fell to the beach. For centuries afterward, this rock was seen on the shore of Euboea and was a famous landmark because of its manlike shape.

Linus (LY nuhs): Brother of Orpheus, and also a great musician. He was of mournful bent; his specialty was composing songs of lament for dead heroes, thereafter, called "linus-songs." In one legend, he was given the task of teaching Heracles the lyre and reprimanded the hulking lad whose fingers were clumsy on the strings. Heracles responded by smashing the lyre over his teacher's head, but struck too hard, killing Linus. Then his brother, Orpheus, sang a linus-song at his funeral pyre. The departing shade was so gladdened by the pride of authorship, it is said, that he changed his mode in Tartarus and began to sing joyous songs — the only happy sounds to be heard in those gloomy precincts.

Lityerses (liht ih UR seez): A wicked king of Phrygia who would challenge visitors to use one of his enormous scythes in a winnowing contest. When the stranger lost, as he always did, the king cut off his head. However, one of these strangers was Heracles, who hefted the huge sickle, and scythed an entire field with one sweep of his arms; on the back-stroke, he cut off the king's head.

Lotus-eaters (LOH tuhs EE turz): They dwelt upon an elbow of the Libyan coast where the lotus-flower grew, casting sleep upon all who breathed its fragrance or tasted its honeyed blossoms. The folk here ate of this flower and slept, and woke only to eat again, and fall again into a deep sleep laced with mild dreams. Odysseus almost lost the crews of his three ships when he landed in this place. The men ate of the lotus, fell asleep, and awoke only to reach out for the flowers and cram their mouths full, then fall asleep again. Odysseus himself ate of the lotus. But when he awoke, he realized what was happening, and refrained from eating again. Struggling against sleep, he propped his eyelids open with little splinters of wood. Then he staggered from beach to ship, carrying his sailors aboard one by one. He lashed the three ships together and all alone maneuvered out of the harbor into the open sea while the sailors still slept. When they awoke, the coast of Libya was only a shadow in the distance and they thought it had all been a dream.

Lycaon (ly KAY uhn): A king of Arcadia in very ancient times. The Arcadians worshipped a wolf-god and offered him human sacrifice, usually a child. Participants in these rites could eat of the sacrifice too. It was believed that any man who ate human flesh would turn into a wolf. If, during his incarnation as a wolf, he refrained from eating human flesh, he was transformed into a man again. According to one legend, Zeus visited Arcadia disguised as a mortal. But Lycaon knew who he was and, loath to change gods, challenged the divinity of Zeus. He set before his guest a roasted haunch of child, claiming it was a joint of beef. Whereupon, Zeus dropped his mortal guise and hurled his thunderbolt, killing Lycaon and all his sons, except the youngest, to whom he gave the throne of Arcadia on condition that no human being would ever be sacrificed to the gods.

127

Lycomedes (ly koh MEE deez): A king of Scyros who harbored the youthful Achilles at the request of Thetis, who was trying to hide the lad from Odysseus and others recruiting for the Trojan War. The sea-goddess Thetis, with her prophetic powers, knew that her beautiful son would never return from the war if he went and she was determined that he would not go. This was at a time when Achilles was still young enough to obey his parents and he remained in Scyros dressed as a girl among the playful daughters of Lycomedes. However, Odysseus came for him, disguised as an old peddler. He displayed his wares in the chamber of the king's daughters — who all fell gleefully upon the bolts of colored cloth and flasks of perfume and heaps of jewelry. All except Achilles. Still dressed as a girl, he pounced with a shout of joy on a sword that the crafty Odysseus had put among his other wares. Thus, Achilles revealed his irrespressible warlike instincts and Odysseus claimed him for the Trojan campaign ... from which he never returned. However, he left Lycomedes a little grandson, born after Achilles' departure, much to the king's surprise. This was Neoptolemus who later joined his father on the Trojan field.

Lycurgus (ly KUR guhs): A king of Thrace who refused to let Dionysus and his followers enter the kingdom. Dionysus, lord of the vine, cast a vegetable madness upon the impious king. Lycurgus imagined himself being overgrown by vines. He seized his axe and cut down the nearest vine, but it was his son, Dryas. His madness deepened. He thought that his own legs were stalks of some menacing plant and cut them off at the knee and died. A new king took the throne. Dionysus and his revelers returned to Thrace.

Lycus (LY kuhs): There are several of this name in mythology. Perhaps the most interesting is Lycus, king of Euboea who, driven from his throne by an ambitious brother, turned from politics to religion. He studied the mysteries of the Great Goddess and was visited by her in dreams. She instructed him in many of her secrets and made him promise to write them down for the enlightenment of generations to come ... when men would weary of the brutal Olympians and return to the goddess. He wrote her secrets on a sheet of copper and buried it in a brass urn among a grove of myrtle trees. He was also a soothsayer, and much beloved. Aegeus, king of Athens, grew jealous of this old sage who was gaining so much influence among the people and expelled him from the land. Lycus, thereupon, made his way to Asia Minor where he found a people who revered wisdom. They made him their king and thereafter called themselves Lycians. But the Athenians did not forget him. They raised a temple of Apollo at the place where Lycus had done much of his healing and named it in his honor — the Lyceum.

Lymnades (lihm NAY deez): Water-demons who inhabited lakes, streams, and marshes — hated humans, and had a fatal gift of mimicry. When a traveler approached they would call for help in the voice of the one dearest to him. When he ran to the water's edge, they would pull him in and drown him.

Machaon (muh KAY uhn): Son of Asclepius. He and his brother, Podilarius, inherited their father's talent for healing and were rigorously schooled by him. Machaon became a master surgeon; Podilarius was more inclined toward the diagnosis and cure of disease. The brothers joined the Greek expeditionary force against Troy and performed nobly, saving many lives. Machaon gained greater fame because the brutal injuries of warfare call more upon surgery than diagnostics. He was killed by Penthesilea, an Amazon princess who fought on the Trojan side. It is said that the arrow she sent winging toward Machaon killed a thousand and one men — Machaon himself and the thousand wounded men who would have survived had he been there to tend them.

Maenads (MEE nahdz): Women intoxicated by the radiance of the vine-god, Dionysus. They traveled in his train and reveled at night beneath the moon. They were also called *Bacchantes*.

Maia (MAY yuh; MAY uh): Beautiful daughter of Atlas who was loved by Zeus and became the mother of Hermes. She was one of the Pleiades, those whom Zeus placed among the stars after their death.

Maron (MAIR uhn): A grandson of Dionysus. He ruled the Ciconians, whose cities Odysseus raided on the first leg of his fateful voyage from Troy. The Ciconians defended themselves fiercely and the Greeks had to retreat. At one stage of the campaign Odysseus captured Maron in his castle, but impressed by his captive's descent from Dionysus, god of the vine, spared his life. Maron responded graciously, giving Odysseus a skin of wine said to have been pressed by Dionysus himself. This wine-skin later saved Odysseus' life in the Cyclops' cave. The one-eyed giant heretofore had drunk only ox-blood and goat's milk. After Odysseus had given him undiluted wine to drink the monster went into a deep sleep, allowing Odysseus the chance to blind him and lead his men to safety.

Mars (MAHRZ): Roman name for Ares, god of war. See *Ares*.

Marsyas (MAHR sih uhs): A satyr who played the flute more beautifully than anyone since Pan. His melodies enchanted the forest-folk. Fauns and satyrs and dryads gathered to listen as he sat on a rock, piping, under the first stars of evening. The birds and the beasts gathered too. Wolf stood next to deer, listening . . . and did not attack. Nor did hawk stoop upon field-mouse as Marsyas played. His listeners praised him to the skies, not realizing how jealous the gods could be, and what terrible forms their jealousy could take. They said that Marsyas played more beautifully than Apollo, the god of music. When Apollo heard about this he was determined upon vengeance. He challenged Marsyas to a contest. They played on a slope of Mt. Helicon and the Muses sat in judgment. Marsyas played the flute and Apollo played the lyre. A hush fell over the land; only the sound of the flute was heard, then the sound of the lyre. Then Apollo sprang his trap. He turned his lyre upside down and played it that way, singing as he played, and challenged Marsyas to do likewise. Of course, it is impossible to play the flute upside down or to sing while playing it. Apollo declared himself the winner and the Muses were forced to assent. Thereupon Apollo decreed a terrible penalty for the loser. Marsyas was bound upside down to a tree and the skin was flayed from his bones. The dead satyr was mourned by all who loved him. Fauns and satyrs and dryads gathered at the spot and wept... and the birds and the beasts came and wept too. They wept so copiously that their tears became a river and the river was called Marsyas. And, it is said, the sound of its waters is more musical than any other river or stream.

Medea (mee DEE uh): Princess of Colchis; priestess of Hecate; Jason's wife. She had been tutored in the use of spells, incantations, and magic potions by her aunt, Circe, the island sorceress. When she fell in love with Jason, who had come to Colchis seeking the Golden Fleece, she spread a magic unguent over him, making him invulnerable to the fiery breath of the brass bulls he had been condemned to fight, allowing him to overcome these bulls. She helped him steal the Fleece, then eloped with him. She helped him kill his usurping uncle and reclaim the throne of his native land. However, she was just as passionate in her hatred as she was in her love. When Jason deserted her, she murdered their two children, then made her way to Athens, where she married the aged Aegeus and caused much mischief in that court until expelled by Theseus. See *Jason*.

Medusa (muh DOO suh): Youngest of the Gorgons. Cutting off her snake-haired head was the climax of Perseus' hero-task. See *Gorgons; Perseus*.

Megaera (muh JEE ruh): Princess of Thebes; Heracles' first wife. They lived happily together and she bore him three sons. But then Hera, who had been biding her time allowing her vengeance to ripen, suddenly drove Heracles mad. She deranged his vision so that he mistook Megaera and his three children for a raiding party of enemies and slew them all. It was for this crime that Zeus sentenced him to serve Eurystheus and perform any ten labors the diabolical wits of the king might devise. The ten labors became twelve. There are some clues to certain puzzling elements in the enormous body of legend surrounding Heracles. One of these concerns the killing of his sons in the fit of madness sent upon him by Hera. Madness was a classic alibi in ancient times for child sacrifice. This episode indicates that some of the tales of Heracles come from the earliest rudest times before such sacrifice was prohibited.

Melampus (mee LAM puhs): A wise man and healer of Argos. He had always loved animals. Once he discovered a brood of young snakes whose parents had been killed. He took them home and raised them, feeding them milk out of a dish as if they were kittens. One night, as he lay asleep, they came and licked his ears. When he awoke he understood the language of animals. Conversing with animals, he learned many secrets. He learned to read the future by signs that other men disregarded. He learned the medicinal properties of herbs and how to cure ailments that had seemed incurable. He was particularly skillful in curing impotence in men and sterility in women. Once, the daughters of King Proetus mocked at a weather-beaten wooden image of Hera, a very ancient one turned up by a farmer's plough, and the goddess made them go mad. Melampus cured them by secluding them in a temple of Artemis and persuading them to undergo a period of self-examination and meditation. During this time he administered a broth of herbs to strengthen their bodies. They were

133

cured and Proetus rewarded the old seer with a third of his kingdom.

Melanippe (mehl uh NIHP ee): A daughter of Hippe and Aeolus. See *Hippe*.

Melanippus (mehl uh NIHP uhs): One of the descendants of those men who sprang from the dragon's teeth sowed by Cadmus. Melanippus was one of Thebes' greatest warriors and fought bravely against the armies of the invading Seven. He killed two of their greatest chiefs and was finally killed himself by Amphiaraus.

Meleager (mehl ee AY jur): Prince of Calydon; Argonaut; lover of Atalanta. All the mightiest hunters and fighters of the age were mustered for the Calydonian Boar Hunt and Meleager was its leading spirit. An enormous savage boar had been sent by Artemis to ravage Calydonia for a fancied affront and, in truth, Meleager welcomed the occasion to hunt so fearsome a beast. Ordinary game no longer offered a challenge to him. For he was a marvelous hunter himself, and with the bold, fleet-footed Atalanta as his hunting partner, he scoured forest and mountain slope for game worthy of his skill. The prince loved this mountain girl passionately and was determined to make her his wife despite the viperish hostility of his mother, Altheae. The arrogant queen of Calydonia hated the long-legged Atalanta who could outrace a deer and liked to wrestle bears. In the first blush of his love, and in the vigor of his young manhood, Meleager knew that this hunt for the great boar would be a mighty occasion. Heroes assembled for the hunt: Jason, Theseus, Castor and Polydeuces, Peleus — most of those bold chieftains who later joined Jason on the Argosy ... as well as Meleager's two uncles, sour cautious men. It was an arduous hunt. The boar refused to be cornered. It killed many dogs and savaged many hunters. Finally, Meleager and Atalanta, working in tandem, maneuvered the huge beast into a pocket of rock. Atalanta, in a reckless charge, ducked under its horns and cut the tendons of its back legs. The boar whirled and pinned her under him. But then Meleager leaped in, and with a mighty heave of his shoulders, thrust his spear into the boar's heart. The heroes celebrated the death of the beast and Meleager awarded the hunt trophies to Atalanta — the hide and tusks of the boar. His uncles objected. These tusks were solid ivory; the hide was so tough and so flexible that it would make the best armor ever worn. They scolded Meleager savagely for awarding such a prize to an unknown waif from the hills. They continued to revile Atalanta until Meleager, afire with wrath, stepped between them, whirled his sword, and beheaded them both with a single stroke. Now, these uncles were the favorite brothers of Altheae. When she heard the news of their death, she opened a secret compartment in her chamber wall and drew forth a half-charred pine branch. She had kept this branch in its secret place for twenty-five years — since the day of Meleager's birth. For on that day the Fates appeared in a vision to Altheae and told her that her son would live only so long as the branch burning in the fireplace would be unconsumed. Altheae immediately stuck her hand into the fire, pulled out the branch, and hid it away so no one would find it. Now, crazed by anger, she placed the branch carefully on the fire and watched it as it burned. At that moment, Atalanta, sitting on the edge of a windy cliff with her beloved Meleager, saw his flesh begin to char. A smell of burning meat arose. Horrified, she saw him writhing in agony as he was consumed by some internal fire. She had no way of easing his pain; she could only watch him die. She ran off into the hills, vowing never to marry. Only a ruse of Aphrodite's made her break that vow. See *Atalanta; Hippomenes; Calydonian Boar Hunt.*

Melissa (meh LIHS uh): A mountain-nymph who cared for the infant Zeus and hid him from his father, Cronus, who was intent on devouring his progeny. It was she who milked the goat Amalthea, and fed the milk to the child. Wishing to vary his diet, she plundered bees' hives — giving him a permanent taste for honey — which, when he ruled Olympus, he decreed should be fermented to make nectar. But Cronus became aware of the nymph's role in thwarting his murderous design and changed her into an earthworm. Zeus, however, transformed the worm into a splendid queen bee, forevermore to be concerned with honey. *Melissa,* in Greek, means honey.

Melpomene (mehl PAHM ee nee): Muse of tragedy. Her spirit informs those who write the noble cadences of tragic plays and those who speak such lines with sonorous voice and classic gesture.

Memnon (MEHM nuhn): King of Ethiopia and Priam's ally against the Greeks. He was a fierce warrior and had killed Antilochus, son of Nestor. The indomitable old chieftain, Nestor, older by a generation than any other warrior on either side, challenged his son's slayer to single combat, a challenge which Memnon courteously declined because of Nestor's age. He offered, however, to fight any other Greek who would take up the old man's challenge. Unfortunately it was Achilles who took up the challenge. Like everyone else who fought Achilles, Memnon was killed.

Menalippe (men uh LIHP ee): Beautiful daughter of Cheiron who was assaulted by Aeolus, king of Aeolia. Her father, the wise old centaur, decided that in a world inhabited by such brutal men it would be better for his daughter to drop her half-share of human form. Therefore, he changed her into a mare and she dwelt happily among horses — who are much stronger than men, but much more gentle.

Menelaus (men uh LAY us): King of Sparta; Helen's husband, and Agamemnon's brother. He lived in the shadow of two stronger personalities and his reputation was defined by the amorousness of his wife and the belligerence of his brother. Nevertheless, in his stubborn plodding way, he managed to assert himself very strongly. He was a kind husband, a brave fighter, and a just king. He bested Paris in single combat and would have killed him had not Aphrodite intervened. Battered by storm and menaced by monster on a journey reminiscent of the Odyssey, he proved himself an indomitable captain, and brought his men safely home from Troy. And — not the least of his exploits — he obeyed the best instincts of his nature, forgave Helen, and reinstated her as Queen, braving the disdain of those who called him arch-cuckold. He defied public opinion on another occasion when he offered shelter to his nephew Orestes, who was fleeing the curse of matricide. He outlived both Helen and Agamemnon, as well as most of his contemporaries. When he died, it is told, Hades reunited him with Helen in the Elysian Fields.

Menoeceus (mee NEE sooss): Prince of Thebes; son of Creon, and a great improvement on his cruel and cowardly father. In the war of the Seven Against Thebes, when the city was besieged by superior forces, an oracle spoke, prophesying that Thebes could be saved only if a descendant of the "sown men" would sacrifice his life for the city. These sown men were those who had sprung from the dragon's seed sowed by Cadmus centuries before. Their descendants were the nobility of Thebes. Unhesitatingly, Menoeceus went to the highest point of the wall and flung himself off in full sight of the enemy. The invaders were driven off and Thebes was saved.

Mentor (MEN tor): A wise Ithacan; trusted counselor of Odysseus. Before embarking for Troy, Odysseus placed Mentor in charge of his affairs. He entrusted the education of his young son, Telemachus, to him, and certain other confidential matters, requiring judgment and acumen. Mentor performed his duties well. Under his tutelage, Telemachus grew into a fine, noble-hearted, clear-thinking young man. He also advised Penelope in the difficult matter of her suitors. According to one legend, it was he who counseled her to delay matters by claiming she could not choose among the suitors until she had finished a sacred task of weaving an altar cloth she had promised to Artemis. Then, following his counsel, each night she would unravel what she had woven that day. Thus the altar cloth remained unfinished and the suitors were delayed until the return of Odysseus. In the course of the Odyssey, Athena, who had guided the fortunes of Odysseus throughout, often assumed the form of Mentor to counsel him and Telemachus. The word "mentor" has come to mean wise tutor or guide.

Mercury (MUR ku ree): Roman name for Hermes, the messenger god. See *Hermes*. In its Roman form his name was given to that quick elusive metal. Our word "mercurial" derives from it, meaning "of swiftly changing mood or disposition," and expresses both the qualities of the god and the metal.

Merope (MAIR oh pee): The lost Pleiad. At first she shared a place in the skies with her six sisters who, after their death, had undergone a radiant transformation into stars. But Merope, filled with unquenchable shame because her husband, Sisyphus, had so gravely offended the gods and had been condemned to so terrible a punishment, withdrew from the constellation and lost herself in the shadows beyond the stars.

Metis (MEE tihs): A Titaness who was courted by Zeus but displeased him when she became pregnant. He devoured her and was forced to give birth to the daughter of Metis, suffering a skull-cracking headache in the process. For what issued from these cerebral birth-pangs was no naked infant, but a tall maiden, clad in armor and wielding a spear. She was Athena, goddess of wisdom. See *Athena*.

Metra (MEE truh): Daughter of Erysichthon. Her father had offended Demeter and was punished with ceaseless hunger. Metra received the gift of sea-change from Poseidon. When her father sold her for food she was able to transform herself into bird or animal and escape her purchaser. She then returned to her father, who sold her again. Finally, however, she met a young man whom she wished to remain sold to and her father, unable to find other food, ate himself. See *Erysicthon*.

Midas (MY duhs): A king of Phrygia who loved gold with so avid a passion that he publicly assailed Apollo for the spendthrift way the sun-god would scatter sheaves of golden light. Apollo punished him with a gift. He appeared to Midas in a dream and offered him his choice of magical aptitudes. Midas requested the power to turn anything he touched to gold. Apollo assented. When Midas awoke, he immediately tested the dream by touching everything within reach. Bedpost, wall, pillow — they all turned to gold. He walked in the garden turning the flowers to gold. They lost their scent and tinkled in the wind. And the plundering bees turned to gold. His little daughter, who was playing in the garden, came running to him. She leaped into her father's arms and he held a heavy little golden statue. He was very hungry from his morning labors. But when he began to eat, the food turned to gold as soon as it touched his lips. He was tormented by hunger; even worse was thirst. For wine and water turned to gold. Finally, starved and parched, he prayed to Apollo to take back his gift. The god appeared then in the full fire of his wrath and released Midas from the terrible gift of the golden touch. But he punished the king for his foolish avarice and impiety by pinning on him a pair of donkey's ears. The vain king let his hair grow long to conceal the ears. No one in the court knew about them until a servant trimmed his hair and discovered what the king wore under his long locks. The king warned the servant on pain of death not to disclose the secret. But the servant could not contain the news. He did not dare tell anyone. He dug a hole and whispered the secret into it. But the breeze snatched up his words and whispered them through the trees. And birds repeated them. Soon the whole country was buzzing with the rumor... "Donkey's ears... the king has donkey's ears..." When Midas heard this, he knew who had told, and ordered the servant put to death. But the man pleaded and the king relented. Then Apollo appeared again to Midas to inform him that since he had learned compassion, he would be relieved of his donkey's ears.

Minerva (mih NUR vuh): Roman name for Athena, goddess of wisdom. See *Athena*.

Minos (MY nohss): Son of Zeus and Europa; king of Crete. Legends about Minos bear such different character that it has been claimed there were two Cretan kings of the same name. According to this theory, the first Minos, the son of Zeus and Europa, united Crete, extended its borders, defeated its enemies, and instituted very wise laws. So wise was he, indeed, that after his death he was appointed by Hades to sit as one of the great judges of Tartarus. It was his task to evaluate the quality of the life which had been led by each of the dead and assign punishment or reward. The second

Minos would have been a descendant of the first — husband of Pasiphae, father of Ariadne and Phaedra. This Minos was a cruel and vengeful king who shut his adulterous wife and her monstrous son in the labyrinth built by Daedalus, and imprisoned Daedalus in the prison maze also. This would have been the Minos who defeated Athens and demanded a yearly tribute of twelve of its most beautiful youths and maidens — all of whom were placed in the labyrinth to be devoured by the Minotaur. He persisted in this cruel exaction until Theseus, coming to Crete as one of the Athenian youths, killed the Minotaur, and broke the power of Crete forever. Other authorities claim, however, that the same Minos is the central character in all these tales — and that it is entirely consistent with the nature of power for an all-powerful king to allow his wisdom to erode through self-indulgence, and to become suspicious, cruel, and vengeful.

Minotaur (MIHN oh tor): Monstrous son of Pasiphae and a prize bull. He is usually described as half bull and half man, but this does not convey what Theseus saw in the labyrinth. He was shaped like a man, but an incredibly huge and brutally muscular man covered with short, dense brown fur. He had a man's face, but a squashed bestialized one, with poisonous red eyes, great buck teeth, and leathery lips. Sprouting out of his head were two long, polished horns. His feet were hooves, razor-sharp. His hands were a man's hand, but much larger, and hard as horn. When he clenched them they were great fists of bone. This was the monster imprisoned by Minos who howled in a maze of shadows and waited for his meal of human flesh. But Theseus managed to kill him and find his way out of the labyrinth. See *Theseus; Minos; Daedalus.*

Minthe (MIHN thee): A nymph pursued by Hades.

The lord of the dead, for all his somber preoccupations, was capable of lighter moments. In one of these he courted the lovely meadow-nymph Minthe. But Persephone, his queen, who was well aware of her husband's skill at abduction, distracted him from his pursuit, then changed Minthe into a flowering herb with a spicy scent, which we call "mint."

Mnemosyne (nee MAHS ih nee): A goddess whose name means "memory." She was the mother of the nine Muses, of whom Zeus was the father. The Greeks, who understood the artistic process very well, were apt at describing it as springing from a union between creative thrusting nature and fertile memory.

Moira (MOH'EE ruh): A goddess out of the oldest legends who seems to have combined the attributes of all three Fates and who, by her own caprice, directed the destiny of mankind. In later legends her powers are divided among the three sister Fates: Clotho, Lachesis, and Atropos. Indeed, another name for the Fates was *Moirae.*

Mopsus (MAHP suhs): The most remarkable soothsayer of his age. He is the one who defeated Calchas in a fortune-reading contest. See *Calchas.* Mopsus had shared the rule of a country called Mallus with his friend, Amphilocus. But they each desired sole sovereignty. They quarreled, fought a duel, and killed each other. The funeral pyres were set close together. Their ghosts arose out of the flame and, forgetting the dispute, remembering only past friendship, tenderly embraced each other and resolved on a common enterprise. They founded an oracle which rivaled that of Delphi. The ghosts spoke through the mouths of the priestesses and were infallible in their reading of the future. Sometimes, however, in response to written questions, they did not answer with words, but appeared in the seeker's dreams.

Morpheus (MOR fuhs; MOR fee uhs): A variant name for Hypnos, god of sleep. See *Hypnos*.

Muses (MUZ): Daughters of Zeus and Mnemosyne; nine beautiful goddesses who governed the various arts that ornamented man's hours, quickened his perceptions, and deepened his understanding. They were associated with Apollo, god of the sun, of music, and of healing — and preferred to sojourn on either of his sacred mountains, Parnassus or Helicon. These were their names and realms: Calliope, epic poetry; Clio, history; Melpomene, tragedy; Euterpe, lyric poetry; Erato, love lyrics; Terpsichore, dance; Urania, astronomy and astrology; Thalia, comedy; Polyhymnia, music and geometry. (See each of them listed separately under their names).

Myrmidons (MUR mih duhnz): Warriors whom Achilles led to Troy, and who fought with deadly skill under his leadership. According to legend, they were descended from ants. Achilles' grandfather was the demigod Aecus, son of Zeus and the nymph Aegina. Zeus, to escape Hera's vigilance, had transported Aegina to an uninhabited island protected by rocks and reefs. Aecus, thus king of an empty island, asked his father, Zeus, for company. Zeus sent Hermes with a deed of transformation. Hermes visited every ant-hill on the island and the ants became men. They were fierce, tireless, disciplined fighters, who preferred brown armor. Aecus was the father of Peleus, who became the father of Achilles. When Achilles sailed for Troy, it was these island warriors, the Myrmidons, who sailed with him.

Naiads (NAY uh deez): Nymphs of those waters which were not the sea. They inhabited rivers, lakes, streams, fountains, and springs. They were the spirits of these places and brought the bounty of their waters to trees and plants. Because of this, they were considered harbingers of fertility, and it was an ancient custom to sprinkle the bridal bed with spring water to ensure a large crop of children. Usually identified as daughters of the local river-god, they are invariably described as beautiful. They abided underwater by day and were rarely seen by mortals. But sometimes, on special nights, they arose from moon-dappled waters to trouble men's dreams. Naiads were believed to have special powers of healing, which they bestowed upon those waters called curative springs.

Narcissus (nahr SIHSS uhs): A youth so vain that he spurned the beautiful nymph Echo in favor of his own reflection. Aphrodite was enraged by this insult to love and rooted him to the river bank where he sat admiring his face in the water — and transformed him into a yellow and white flower which still likes to bow to its image in pool and stream and is still called narcissus.

Nauplius (NAH plih uhs): Son of Poseidon; an Argonaut. He was regarded by Jason as perhaps the most valuable member of the crew because his father, the sea-god, had taught him secrets of wind and current and he had become a remarkable helmsman.

Nausicaa (nah SIHK ay uh): Central figure in Odysseus' last adventure before reaching Ithaca. She was daughter of the king of Phaeacia, a fleet-footed fanciful girl whose beauty drew many suitors to the island. Though many of them were handsome and all were brave, she refused them all. She wanted a man whose wit was as quick as hers and who would have her same vivid response to things that others overlooked. She persuaded her father she was still too young to marry and remained happily on her island, roaming its beaches, swimming in the sea, playing the lyre, and singing songs she had made up herself. One day she and her maidens were at play on the beach, flinging a leather ball to each other. One of them ran after the ball and shrank back, shrieking; a bloody naked man was crawling out from behind a rock. It was Odysseus, just awaking from a swoon after being hurled battered and half dead upon the rocky shore. Ino's veil had kept him afloat but could not protect him against the rocks. Among the shrieking girls, Nausicaa alone was unafraid. She commanded them to silence and approached the man. Although he barely had strength enough to speak, Odysseus had wit enough to address her as the goddess Artemis, and thank her for taking him to one of her moon-shoals after his death, instead of letting Hades claim him. Nausicaa was much pleased by this. She commanded her maids to bring the stranger clean raiment. Then she bound up his wounds with her own hands and led him back to the castle as an honored guest. Her parents were not pleased. For just that morning, as it happened, an oracle had warned the king against shipwrecks, strangers, and storytellers. Then Nausicaa came to the king, aglow with excitement, telling him of the shipwrecked stranger who had been astounding her with tales of people who ate flowers and fell asleep, of one-eyed giants, of cannibals as tall as trees, and sorceresses who turned people to pigs. The king knew that this newcomer combined all that the oracle had warned against, a shipwrecked stranger telling wild tales, and he resolved that the man should die. The laws of hospitality forbade the king to kill a guest, no matter how unwelcome, but there was nothing to stop him from dropping an unspoken hint to his young courtiers. The young men invited the stranger to enter their games, planning that some mis-thrown discus or spear would rid them of the fellow — who stubbornly refused to tell his name — while preserving the appearance of accident. However, Odysseus was an old hand at such tactics. When one of the young men threw a discus, and challenged him to throw farther, he picked up a chariot wheel and hurled it against the castle wall, breaching the rampart. Then he invited any of them who wished to fight him with spear, sword, or simply to wrestle. They were prudent enough to decline. Displeased to find his guest still alive, the king was constrained, nevertheless, to give a banquet in his honor. After the feasting, Nausicaa, who had been trying to unriddle the stranger's identity, took the harp from the minstrel's hand and sang a song that she made up as she went along. She sang of heroes, of Jason and his Argonauts, of the Seven Against Thebes, of those at the Calydonian Boar Hunt. She sang of such famous exploits, watching Odysseus narrowly all the while. She sang of Troy, and of its heroes on both sides, and of Odysseus, king of Ithaca, who so many times had taken over the leadership from Agamemnon and kept the Greek army together in face of defeat. She sang of how Odysseus had persuaded Achilles to enter the fray and defeat Hector. Finally, she sang of the great ruse of the Wooden Horse and of the men who hid in its belly. Now the guests were amazed to see the hard-bitten sailor put his head in his arms and weep. He raised his streaming face and said, "Pardon, oh king, this unseemly display, but I am Odysseus of whom your lovely daughter sings." Then there was a great shout of welcome, for no name in all the world shone more brightly than that of Odysseus. Nevertheless, the king and queen were determined that this honored guest make a speedy departure. They feared their daughter was falling in love with him and they knew he had a wife in Ithaca. They showered gifts upon him and hurried him aboard a vessel already rigged for sailing. Nausicaa watched from the beach until the sail disappeared. But of all the beautiful Titanesses and nymphs and naiads that Odysseus met on his voyage, and who attempted to enchant him away from thoughts of home, none, it is said, affected him so deeply as this black-eyed girl who ran so swiftly along the beach and sang so wonderfully songs of her own making. As for Nausicaa, one legend says she never married, but became the first woman minstrel, traveling from court to court singing hero songs, especially songs of Odysseus and his adventures among the terrible islands of the Middle Sea. Some say she finally came to the court of Ithaca and married Odysseus' son, Telemachus. Others say she fell in with a blind poet who took all her songs and wove them into one huge tapestry of song. Whatever the case, she had a special place in the weather-beaten heart of the great voyager.

Neleus (NEE loos): A king of Megara. He refused to administer rites of purification to Heracles, who wished to expiate a hasty murder. Enraged by the king's refusal, Heracles lengthened his list of homicides by killing Neleus and twelve of his sons, sparing only Nestor, who became the most venerable chieftain in the Trojan War.

Nemean Lion (NEE mee uhn LY uhn): Heracles' first labor was to kill this dread beast. This lion was as large as an elephant, its teeth were ivory daggers, its claws like razor-sharp baling hooks, and its hide could not be pierced by sword, spear, or arrow. Its favorite prey was man. It roamed the Nemea mountains feasting unchallenged upon goats and sheep and cattle. At night it entered the villages to devour whoever dared leave his house. Heracles was ordered by Eurystheus to kill this lion and bring its carcass home to Mycenae. He had no need to track the lion for it was always ready for combat. Heracles found it waiting upon a mountain trail. He unslung his bow to notch an arrow. As fast as he could pull arrow from quiver he launched the bolts against the lion. These were shafts with barbed heads which Heracles could drive through a stone wall three feet thick. They bounced harmlessly off the animal and clattered harmlessly to the ground. Heracles hurled his great spear. It glanced off the beast's shoulder and hit an ash tree which it split in two. The lion yawned and prowled closer. Heracles raised his club, which was a single uprooted oak tree with the twigs trimmed off, and smote the lion wih all his might. The club shattered; the lion shook his head. Now, it was very close. Heracles knew he had only one chance against this monster. He closed with the lion, wrapped one mighty arm around its head in a wrestler's grip, braced his legs, and twisted. Now in actual contact with the enemy, Heracles' blood boiled with the joy of close combat. He felt the voltage of the thunderbolt brandished by his father, Zeus, coursing through him as he twisted and strained. He felt the head turn in his grip. The lion sank to its knees. He swiftly shifted his grip and wrapped both arms around the lion's neck. His flesh was shredded where he had been raked by the terrible claws, but he ignored his wounds, and squeezing harder, strangled the beast. Its hide had been invulnerable to weapons, but no bone or sinew could withstand that unearthly pressure. Heracles broke off one of the lion's claws and skinned the animal, for no other blade could cut that hide. Then, wearing the skin as an armor, and the great skull as a helmet, Heracles strode back toward Mycenae with the flayed carcass over his shoulders, while the people came out of the villages rejoicing and strewing flowers in his path. When Eurystheus, who was watching from the sentinel tower of Mycenae, saw what looked like a two-legged lion approach with a bloody bundle on its back, he fled into the city, leaped into a brass jar, and hid there until Heracles had gone on his way. Eurystheus was in such terror of Heracles that he had his men bury that brass jar in a pit. And every time Heracles came near, he would hide in the jar, relaying his orders through a herald. After that, Heracles wore his lion-skin armor on special occasions. He made ivory daggers of its teeth which he gave to his friends, and he used its claws for arrowheads.

Nemesis (NEHM uh sihs): A sister of the Fates. Two younger daughters of Necessity helped the Fates maintain control over human destiny. They were Nemesis and Tyche. Tyche's job was to distribute luck, but she was a tricky irresponsible wench who acted only according to her own strong preferences. When she liked someone she heaped him with good fortune; those she disliked did not seem to prosper, no matter how able, industrious, or virtuous. But Tyche's caprice was countered by the divine sense of justice which moved her sister, Nemesis. For if anyone favored by Tyche bragged too loudly of his accomplishments, or refused to share his fortune with others, then Nemesis intervened and cast this man down from the heights. Sometimes, too, she would seek out a gifted person whom Tyche had condemned to obscurity and humiliation. Nemesis inspired him with an unearthly energy which allowed the unfortunate to break the shackles of misfortune and rise to the eminence he deserved. This beautiful daughter of

Themis carried a wheel made of applewood to signify turning, and wore a whip at her belt to scourge the arrogant. Those who had suffered at her hands tended to identify her as the goddess of vengeance, but this was a coarse and partial view. She was a divine arbiter of justice, distributing both rewards and penalties.

Neoptolemus (nee ahp TAHL ee mus): Son of Achilles. He arrived in Troy one day after his father had fallen to the arrow of Paris. Now, since he was begotten at the court of Scyros where the young Achilles had been hidden by his mother, Thetis, and since the infant's mother Deidama, daughter of the king, did not give birth until after Achilles had departed, and since Achilles was killed in the tenth year of the war, Neoptolemus could have been only ten years old when he came to Troy. Nevertheless, he is depicted as a fearsome fighting man, very much his father's son. However, time tends to be elastic in myths and whatever the timing of it, Neoptolemus did come to Troy, and did avenge his father's death in a number of ways. He killed Priam, king of Troy, with his own hands. He snatched Astyanax, son of Hector, from his mother's arms, and hurled him from the wall. Then he enslaved the mother Andromache, and took her back to Greece, where she bore him three sons. Later he married Andromache off to her brother-in-law, Helenus, the soothsayer who had predicted that Troy would not fall until Neoptolemus appeared on the field. He then married Hermione, daughter of Helen and Menelaus. This, however, according to one legend, led to his death. For Hermione had been promised first to her cousin, Orestes. Neoptolemus was challenged to single combat by Orestes and fell before that avenging sword which had already tasted the blood of Clytemnestra and Helen.

Nepenthe (nee PEHN thee): A magic potion made by

adding one drop of Lethe water to a cup of nectar. It eased fatigue and pain and made the drinker forget his troubles ... for a while. Helen of Troy learned the recipe from the queen of Egypt when she and Menelaus were stranded there and she was riven by grief for all the men whose deaths she had caused. She kept the recipe. And when young Telemachus, searching for his father, Odysseus, came to her court in Sparta, she brewed him a cup. He drank it, was eased of his grief for a space, and was able to learn of his father's deeds before the walls of Troy.

Nephele (NEHF uh lee): Counterfeit Hera whom Zeus carved out of a cloud. See *Ixion*; *Ino*.

Neptune (NEHP toon): Roman name for Poseidon, god of the sea. See *Poseidon*.

Nereids (nee REE uh deez): Sea-nymphs who took their name from their father, an old sea-deity. He fathered fifty daughters upon Doris, a lovely nymph, and the daughters were as beautiful as their mother. They were mermaids who swam in flashing shoals underwater and served as ladies-in-waiting to their sister, the sea-queen Amphitrite.

Nereus (NEE ruhs): Son of Oceanus and Gaia, or the sea and the earth; called the wise old man of the sea; husband of Doris; and father of the Nereids. He was reputed to know all secrets, all hiding places, and was constrained by destiny always to speak the truth when questioned. Thus, he was always being hunted in the depths of the sea by those who wished to learn secrets. The only way he could defend his privacy was to change nis shape, which he did with enormous skill. He enters the legend of Heracles because he was the only one who knew where Hera had planted her tree of golden apples.

When Heracles came seeking him he transformed himself into one sea-shape after another ... eel, seal, shark, gull. But Heracles followed Nereus through these changes and the old man of the sea was finally obliged to resume his own form and tell Heracles what he wanted to know.

Nessus (NEHS uhs): The vengeful centaur killed by Heracles, whose posthumous ruse caused the death of the hero. See *Deineira*.

Nestor (NEHS tur): Son of Neleus; only one of the family to survive the wrath of Heracles. Later he fought in the Trojan War, eldest of all the chieftains on both sides. He was much beloved among the Greeks because of his fair-mindedness and knowledge of human nature. He took part in the highest councils. Although his companions were often irked by his long-windedness they generally heeded what he had to say.

Nicippe (NY sihp ee): Queen of Mycenae, who owns the dubious distinction of producing the most cowardly son in all mythology ... Eurystheus, king of Mycenae and the small-minded taskmaster of Heracles.

Nike (NY kee): Called Bestower of Victory. She was a winged goddess who flew about the battlefield choosing the winners and rewarding them with glory and the chance for further battle. However, it is claimed that she did not actually bestow victory herself, since this critical decision was made by the Fates and by the more powerful gods. But she was a swift messenger of destiny and her winged form was the last thing a loser saw through his bloody haze and the first sight that fledged itself out of the winner's joy. Her body was like alabaster, her wings white as snow, and her hair of fiery gold. In both death and glory she was a beautiful apparition.

Niobe (NY oh bee): Daughter of Tantalus and granddaughter of Atlas. She was queen of Thebes; mother of seven beautiful sons and seven beautiful daughters. She was very proud of her children and boasted that she was more fortunate than Leto, mother of Apollo and Artemis, because Leto had only two children, not fourteen, and that each of her fourteen was more radiantly beautiful than either of Leto's two — although they happened to be sun-god and moon-goddess. This was the kind of remark calculated to evoke prompt and cruel reprisal, and it did. Apollo and Artemis flew to Thebes. Apollo took seven golden arrows from his quiver and slew the seven sons of Niobe. Artemis drew seven silver arrows from her quiver and slew the seven daughters. Niobe began to weep and never stopped. Leto, still angry, but somewhat repentant, changed Niobe into a rock whose tears became a sparkling spring which still flows near Thebes.

Nisus (NY suhs): King of Egypt and father of a daughter named Scylla — not the infamous sea-monster, but sufficiently monstrous in her own way. She fell in love with King Minos, who was besieging Nisus' capitol. Knowing that her father was protected by the Fates as long as a lock of his red hair went uncut, she decided to offer her father's life as a love-token to Minos. She crept into his chamber as he lay asleep, cut off the lock of red hair, and brought it to Minos — who then led a charge that breached the walls of the city. He found Nisus and killed him. Afterwards, Minos deserted Scylla and sailed for Crete. She leaped into the sea to swim after his ship, whereupon Aphrodite, in pity, changed her into a gull.

Notus (NOH tuhs): The South Wind. It blows warmly at times. At other times it brings pestilence and the destruction of crops, especially in autumn when it carries rain and savage hail that can scythe down a field of grain in a single night.

Nymphs (NIHM' fs): Daughters of the gods; eternally young and eternally beautiful. There are many kinds of nymphs: Dryads, or wood-nymphs; naiads, or river-nymphs; nereids, or sea-nymphs. There are the Nyseides who sported with Dionysus; and the Oreades who ran with Artemis. Flowers twined in their hair, they race through legend after legend, pursued by god, satyr, and demigod, encountering mortals in grotto, copse, and lake, bringing unique pagan color and fragrance to the Greek myths, and becoming mothers of gods, demigods, and heroes. Identified as they are with field, stream, forest, and sea, they personify in a larger sense the natural sensual joys — not shameful furtive pleasures, but parts of the great rhythm of nature. In Greek the word *nymph* originally meant "bride," but was extended to mean "young girl."

Nyx (nihks): Darkness; mother of light. She was described as the dark-robed goddess of night; a daughter of Chaos. While her nature was gloomy and violent, she had changes of mood. Sleep traveled in her train and brought an interval of rest to man's care.

Oceanus (oh SEE uh nuhs): The eldest Titan; son of Uranus and Gaia. He came to personify that unimaginably vast stream of water which, according to ancient belief, girdled the disk earth. He married his sister, Tethys, who bore three thousand daughters, the Oceanids — all of them minor goddesses, some of them giving their names to land masses and rivers like Asia and Styx.

Odysseus (oh DIHS uhs; oh DISH ee uhs): King of Ithaca; son of Sisyphus; grandson of Autolycus, thus great-grandson of Hermes. He was the wisest strategist among all the Greek chieftains who fought against Troy; the most indomitable voyager of all time; and, possibly, the most interesting single personality, god or mortal, to emerge from Greek mythology. After spending ten years fighting at Troy, he spent another ten years trying to get home. Poseidon, who in general had favored the Greeks, took an intense dislike to Odysseus and plagued him throughout his voyage with every variety of maritime disaster in the enormous repertoire of a sea-god's malice. Each of these adventures is briefly described in these pages under the name of its chief actor — Circe, Calypso, Cyclops, Sirens, etc. But there are many marvelous legends about Odysseus that are not related in Homer's *Odyssey*, nor in the *Iliad*, where Odysseus figures as the most important character next to Achilles. He was a remarkably complex personality for an age in which heroes tended to be simple and single-minded. He could be treacherous and cruel as well as noble and brave. His treatment of Palamedes and Ajax reveals the grasping dark side of his nature. See *Ajax*; *Palamedes*. In appearance too, he was unlike the ideal hero, being described as short-legged and red-headed. Perhaps what makes him unique in mythology, however, is that he survived his terrible ordeals, overcoming formidable monsters, and thwarting deadly conspiracies not so much through physical strength, magically bequeathed, as through intellectual superiority. In Roman mythology, Odysseus was known as Ulysses.

Odyssey (AHD ih see): Literally "story of Odysseus," Homer's great epic that is a companion-piece to the *Iliad*. It relates the wanderings of Ulysses on his homeward journey from Troy to Ithaca. See *Odysseus*. It has been called "the first novel ever written, and perhaps the best."

Oeax (EE ax): Brother of Palamedes, the Greek chieftain who was killed because of a plot organized against him by Odysseus. Oeax vowed vengeance against all the leaders who had abetted the conspiracy, and his father, Nauplius, joined him in that vow. They lighted signal fires among the rocky reefs of the Peloponnesian coast so that returning ships might be tempted too close to the rocks and be wrecked. But Oeax engaged in more specific mischief. He visited all the wives he could of the Greek chieftains and informed them that their husbands had taken captive scores of beautiful Trojan maidens whom they had forced into concubinage. Many of these wives were inflamed by this tale; many of them took lovers, others swore reprisal against their husbands. Among them, it is said, was Clytemnestra, who added this to her many other grudges against Agamemnon, whom she eventually murdered.

Oedipus (EHD uh puhs): A king of Thebes who murdered his father and married his mother. Warned by an oracle that he would be killed by his son, Laius, king of Thebes, snatched his newly born child from its mother, Jocasta, drove a nail through the infant's feet, and ordered that it be exposed on a mountain. But the crippled child was found by a shepherd who took him home and raised him as his own, naming him Oedipus, or "swollen-foot." Later, the youth made his way to Corinth where King Polybus reigned. King and Queen were struck by the young man's beauty and, being childless, adopted him and made him heir to their throne. However, on a visit to the Delphic Oracle, Oedipus was told that he would murder his father and marry his mother. Thinking that he was being warned about his adopted parents, for he had never known any other, he refused to return to Corinth, where he had been so happy, and became an exile and a wanderer. Leaving Delphi by a narrow mountain road, he found his way blocked by the chariot of King Laius. The king, in a rage, ordered his charioteer to run the traveler down. But Oedipus avoided the rush of the horses and killed both charioteer and king. The young traveler proceeded toward Thebes, ignorant not only that he had killed its king, but that that king was his real father. On the way he encountered a monster called the Sphinx — a daughter of the Chimaera, even more terrible than her mother — part woman, part lion, part serpent, and part eagle. The monster lay astride the road to Thebes devouring everyone who could not answer her riddle. But Oedipus guessed the riddle, killed the monster, and was acclaimed king of Thebes by a grateful populace. Since he was now king, the widowed Queen Jocasta became his wife. They lived very happily for some years until a pestilence descended on the land. Oedipus, determined to cleanse Thebes of this plague, consulted an oracle who told him that he himself was the cause — that Apollo had shot fever-tipped plague arrows into Thebes because he, Oedipus, the king, had broken the oldest taboos by murdering his father and marrying his mother. When he learned the truth the horrified Oedipus tore out his eyes and left Thebes to become a homeless beggar blindly wandering the roads. But his loving daughter, Antigone, followed him, though he wanted no company, and led her blind father to a grove called Collonus, near Athens, where he finally died. He was buried by Theseus with great honor.

Oenone (ee NOH nee): A fountain-nymph and daughter of a river-god; she owned prophetic powers, and knew that her love for Paris, son of Priam, would lead to great misery. But passion overcame prophecy and she pursued Paris, a simple shepherd, on the slopes of Phrygia's Mt. Ida before the lad was recognized as a Trojan prince. After Paris had been appointed judge in the tricky affair of the golden apple, and had awarded the prize to Aphrodite, receiving in return her promise of the most beautiful woman in the world for his lover, Oenone prophesied again, telling him that if he claimed Helen, he would lose his life. His father and his forty-nine brothers would also lose their lives, thousands of others would be slain, and Troy would burn. Nevertheless, this prophecy too was ignored and Paris went off in search of Helen. Later, Oenone tutored her son, Corythus, in vengeance and sent him to lead the Greeks by secret ways into Troy, a plot that failed. See *Corythus*.

Oenopion (ee NOH pih uhn): A son of Dionysus and Ariadne. He was taught vine-culture by his father; his name means "rich vintner." He was king of Chios and had a beautiful daughter named Merope. Now,

Merope was courted by a gigantic handsome son of Poseidon, named Orion, greatest hunter of his age. Oenopion did not wish to give up his daughter. Seeking a pretext, he informed Orion that he could wed Merope only if he first killed all the wild beasts that infested Chios. This seemed to be an impossible job, for wolves, lions, bears, and huge serpents abounded. Nevertheless, Orion went hunting and killed every one of the wild beasts or drove them into the sea. Fishermen, tacking around Chios, were amazed by the sight of bears and lions swimming straight out to sea. Orion then claimed his bride. Oenopion pretended to comply and gave him a nuptial cup of undiluted wine, the most potent ever brewed. Orion fell asleep, Oenonion put out his eyes, and had him carried out of the castle onto the beach. The blinded giant, thrashing about bewildered, was told by an oracular gull that he could regain his eyesight if he traveled to the east and turned his sightless sockets upon the sun rising naked and blazing from its eastern couch. He did so. Sight was restored in a joyous blaze of color. He came raging back to Chios to avenge himself upon the treacherous Oenopion. However, this king had prepared himself for Orion's recovery. He had built himself an underground burrow, luxuriously furnished, and dwelt there comfortably until Orion, unable to find him, had taken Merope and left the island. See *Orion*.

Olympus (oh LIHM puhs): Dwelling place of the great gods whose king was Zeus. It is a mountain in northern Greece, the highest in that part of the world.

Omphale (AHM fuh lee): Queen of Lydia whom Heracles was condemned to serve as a slave to expiate the murder of Iphitus. Omphale was a masterful mistress. It is said she compelled him to wear women's clothes and do women's work, while she strutted about in his lionskin and staggered under the weight of his club. He kept a leash on his terrible temper, for the decree of servitude imposed by Zeus had been absolute. He wore his gauzy robes uncomplainingly and wielded spindle and distaff with his huge hands. Soon, however, Omphale had to call on his masculine attributes. A powerful cabal of enemies had been planning to take her throne. Raiding parties struck out of the forest, making off with cattle and killing her men. Heracles donned his lion-skin, took his club, and went into the forest. In a matter of days he swept the kingdom of her enemies. Whereupon Omphale decided she preferred him in that role and drafted him as her consort. Legend says she bore him three sons.

Ophion (oh FY uhn): The universal serpent. In the beginning was a storm of nothingness which clotted into the form of the serpent, Ophion, who had no eyes because there was nothing to see. Yet he slithered this way and that among the vast rubble of space, called Chaos, searching for something that was not there. And the rage of his blind searching moved invisibly as wind. The pack of searching winds coursed like hounds and blew so hotly that they kindled a corner of Chaos and set it aflame. From this flame was born the moon-goddess, Eurynome, upon whom Ophion sired sun, earth, stars, and all living creatures.

Orestes (oh REHS teez): Son of Agamemnon and Clytemnestra; prince of Mycenae. The curse which had been fastened upon the House of Atreus for so many generations came to crisis and conclusion in the fury-wracked career of Orestes. On that terrible night when his mother and her lover murdered his father, Orestes was spirited out of the castle by his sister, Electra, who knew that Aegisthus would seek to kill off every male member of the royal house so that he could take the throne. See *Electra; Aegisthus*. Electra took him to the court of his uncle in Phocis, where he lived like a brother with his cousin, Pylades. They never altered in their friendship for each other through every species of disaster. But all through his boyhood Orestes kept his father's murder in the front of his consciousness and never abandoned the vengeance he had vowed when he was ten years old. When he had grown enough to handle weapons, he and Pylades made their way back to Mycenae disguised as beggars. With Electra's aid they were introduced into the castle. Orestes drew his sword from under his rags and slew first Aegisthus, then Clytemnestra — who recognized her son, and pleaded for her life, but fell before his sword nonetheless. Now, Orestes had been encouraged in his vengeance by Apollo, whose oracles had told him that he must kill those who had killed his father. But even Apollo's patronage was not enough to protect Orestes from the bat-winged, brass-clawed Furies who flew ravening out of the shadows to tear at his flesh and to scourge him with their barbed whips. Although they flogged him until the flesh hung in strips from his bones, the physical agony was not the worst. For, as they tormented his body, they shrieked, "Matricide! Matricide! You killed the mother who gave you life. You shall be tortured through eternity!" Only Electra, his sister, and Pylades, his friend, were able to afford him comfort. They did their best to ward off the terrible hags. They bound his wounds and anointed him with oil. They kept him alive, but they could not keep him sane. The Furies finally drove him mad. He raced about from place to place performing ancient rites of purification. He drank pig's blood, washed in running water, and shaved his head. But still the Furies hunted him and his madness deepened. Then Electra appeared with a bow of horn given to her by Apollo. With this horn bow, Apollo had told her, the youth would be able to beat off the Furies or at least thwart their worst attacks. He was able to try it that very night when the hags screeched down at him again. He did beat them off, but not without suffering fresh

161

wounds. However, his madness had burned itself out. The deep tenderness and understanding shown by Electra and Pylades finally soothed his flayed nerves and reason returned. But a new trial was approaching, a formal one. He was summoned before the Judgment Seat of the gods at the Areopagus to stand trial for matricide. The gods were evenly divided. Clytemnestra's crime was recognized but matricide was a primal taboo. However, Apollo acted as counsel for the defense. And Athena, who had been born from her father's head and had little instinct for motherhood, argued eloquently for Orestes. They swayed the judges and Orestes was acquitted. In his new-found legitimacy he decided to settle some old scores. He killed Helen, his aunt by marriage, because he blamed her for causing the war that had taken his father from Mycenae. Then, he killed Achilles' son, Neoptolemus, who had married Hermione, daughter of Helen and Menalaus, a lovely girl who had been Orestes' childhood sweetheart. He married Hermione, then returned to Mycenae and reclaimed his throne. After his grandfather's death he also became king of Sparta. To his great joy, Electra and Pylades married each other. And the family curse, which had begun with Tantalus, seemed to have become a cinder of memory and the stuff of legend.

Orion (oh RY uhn): Giant son of Poseidon; said to have been the handsomest man alive. He was a great hunter, not only of animals, but of women. Mortal women, goddesses, demigoddesses, nymphs and Titanesses — he pursued them all and usually caught them. However, exceptions were the fiercely virginal Pleiades, daughters of Atlas. They fled from him across hill and valley, through field and copse, until Zeus snatched them up and placed them among the stars where they became the constellation Pleiades. Next, Orion wooed the lovely Merope, daughter of Oenopion, who treacherously blinded the giant. But Orion regained his sight and forced the false king into perpetual hiding. See *Oenopion*. Then, Orion consorted with Eos, goddess of dawn, and visited her in her eastern castle, amusing himself at the chase while she was out heralding the day. It is said the dawn shortened during this episode as Eos hastened back to Orion. But Artemis, goddess of the moon, riding in her silver chariot, grew curious as to what was hastening the dawn and went spying about the eastern castle. She saw Orion and fell in love with him. Being goddess of the hunt as well as of the moon, she offered irresistible attractions for the great hunter. He abandoned Eos and went hunting with Artemis and they led each other on an enchanted chase for a year. But Apollo grew jealous of his sister's preoccupation, for she had formerly scorned men and reserved all her love for him. Apollo determined that Orion should die. He went to his grandmother, Gaia, earth goddess, and convinced her that Orion was depopulating her realm of wild animals by his ruthless hunting. Gaia sent a giant scorpion to kill Orion. He fought the scorpion with arrow, torch, spear, and battle-axe, but the insect's huge jointed body was plated with an armor beyond any that mortals wore and Orion's weapons were useless against it. However, Orion fought so well that the scorpion was not able to inflict a mortal wound. Finally, Orion leaped into the sea and swam away, knowing that scorpions hate water. Now began the second step of Apollo's plot. He led Artemis to the shore of the sea and pointed to a head bobbing in the water. It was Orion's, but too far away for Artemis to recognize. Apollo informed her that the swimmer was a brutish brigand who had assaulted one of Artemis' nymphs and had leaped into the sea at Apollo's approach. The chastity of her attendants was very important to Artemis. She strung her silver bow, notched her unerring silver arrow, and sent the shaft winging over the sea through Orion's head. The giant sank beneath the waves. When she learned the truth, Artemis snatched Orion from the depths of the sea and made him immortal. She placed him in the vault of heaven, in a place where he might follow his favorite pursuits among the starry realms. For the constellation, Orion, pursues the Pleiades. The dog, Sirius, hunts with him. And the Scorpion, also a constellation, crawls far behind, nipping vainly at the hunter's heels.

Orpheus (OR foos; OR fee uhs): Greatest poet and musician of his time. He invented the seven-stringed lyre and drew such ravishing melodies from it that trees would pull themselves out of the earth and hobble on their roots to follow him as he played. Wild beasts and gentle beasts came out of the forests to stand in a listening circle at peace with each other. His most famous adventure was his journey into Tartarus to reclaim his wife, Eurydice, from the dead. See *Eurydice*. However, there are other legends equally significant. For Orpheus was a great religious leader and an innovative mystic. It was he who formulated the notion of the soul as a separate entity. He coined the word "soma" for body, and "sema" for tomb, a play on words meaning that the body was the tomb of the soul which, when released from the corruption of earth, would soar to empyrean heights and abide among celestial harmonies. In a brutal age he was prematurely compassionate and paid for it with his life. He preached vehemently against the custom of human sacrifice. He provoked further antagonism among the followers of Dionysus by arising at dawn, climbing a hill, and hymning the sun as it climbed out of the horizon, celebrating it as the source of life. This the Bacchantes took as an affront to Dionysus whose great rival was the sun-god, Apollo. And, according to one legend, the Bacchantes, maddened beyond scruple, pursued Orpheus and tore him to pieces. However, his head was preserved and was placed in a Lemnian cave where it spoke prophecy, such accurate prophecy that Apollo found his own oracles at Delphi cast in the shade, and decided to bury the head. Where the head of Orpheus was buried, trees grew, and the movement of the wind through these trees is more musical than anywhere else. Also, nightingales abide there and sing more sweetly than birds anywhere else. Apollo, however, finally made Orpheus immortal. He set his lyre among the stars. And, it is said, those gods who particularly loved music often tethered their chariots in that part of heaven. Many of those animals too, who used to sit in a silent circle, eyes gleaming, listening to Orpheus, became lesser stars, and still sit in a circle about the Lyre, listening. "Zodiac" in Greek means "circle of animals."

Palamedes (pal uh MEE deez): A prince of Euboea; among the best of the Greek leaders who fought against Troy. He was an extremely able tactician, rivaling Odysseus, and was credited with innovating many military maneuvers, such as the posting of sentries and the instilling of close-order discipline among foot-soldiers, enabling them to act as one unit in close combat. However, Palamedes was unfortunate in having earned the enmity of Odysseus. It was he who thwarted the Ithacan's attempt at draft-dodging. An oracle had warned Odysseus that if he went to Troy, he would not return for twenty years, and would come back then a beggar and outcast. However, when he heard of Helen's abduction, he knew that he would be summoned to fight, especially as he had been the author of the agreement which bound all former suitors of Helen to go to the aid of Menelaus if Helen were taken from him. When Palamedes and Agamemnon came for Odysseus, he feigned madness. Yoking an ox and a donkey to a plough he sowed the furrows with salt, singing foolishly as he ploughed. But Palamedes tested his sanity by placing Odysseus' son, Telemachus, in front of the plough. When Odysseus reined his animals up short and leaped to save the child, Palamedes accused him of seeking to break his pledge and demanded that he come to war. Odysseus did sail to Troy, of course, and played a pivotal role in that conflict. But he never forgave Palamedes. His vengeance took this form: He wrote an anonymous letter to Agamemnon accusing Palamedes of appropriating a huge store of gold intended for the troops' pay. Then he planted bags of gold in Palamedes' tent. When Agamemnon's men came to search, they found the gold and Palamedes was accused of theft. Despite his impeccable reputation and his protests of innocence, Odysseus swung too much weight and Palamedes was stoned to death. This deed has always stained Odysseus' reputation. Homer, who wished to preserve intact his hero's image, makes no mention of this episode. But many other mythographers have related the tale. Palamedes' murder was avenged by his brother, Oeax, and his father, Nauplius. See *Oeax*.

Palladium (puh LAY dih uhm): A statue of Athena, most sacred of her relics. It took its name from her old playmate, Pallas, daughter of Triton. Once, when the young goddesses were engaged in a mock duel, Athena accidentally killed Pallas. She felt so keen a grief that she added her friend's name to her own, and was thereafter called *Pallas Athena*, and her statues were called Palladium. The most famous of these statues stood in the sanctuary at Troy. According to prophecy, Troy could not be taken so long as the Palladium stood there. It was one of the great exploits of Odysseus to disguise himself as a beggar, make his way within the walls, and carry off the Palladium.

Pan (PAN): God of shepherds and goatherds. He resembled a goat himself with his pointed beard, shaggy legs, and cloven feet. He was goatlike in his habits too, pursuing every nymph he saw — diving into the river to swim after naiads, and searching the groves for dryads. His parentage is uncertain although Hermes is often claimed to have been his father. Other stories say he is the eldest god of all, the original nature god, older than Zeus, and he has been named as father of all fauns and satyrs. One legend says that it was he, not Hermes or Apollo, who invented music; that one day he pursued a nymph named Syrinx, who fled from him across the field and down to the river bank and changed herself into a reed. The bank was thick with reeds and Pan did not know which one she was. He picked a bunch of reeds and cut them into the first Panpipe upon which he blew enchanting melodies, inspired by the sound of the wind moving among the river reeds. Later, it is said, Hermes stole this pipe from him and sold it to Apollo. Pan was useful to Zeus and the young gods in their fight against Cronus. For Pan had a war cry which paralyzed whoever heard it. At a critical point in the battle he shouted, freezing the Titans with fear, and tipped the odds in favor of the Olympians. The fear inspired by his cry gives us our word, "panic." For this deed, Zeus forgave Pan much mischief. In Roman mythology, Pan was known as Faunus.

Pandareus (pan DAIR ee uhs): A prince of Miletus rash enough to steal a golden dog from the temple of Zeus in Crete. Now, this dog was dear to Zeus because it had guarded the goat Amalthea, whose milk had nourished the infant Zeus. When the dog grew too old to fight off wolves, Zeus had given it the light task of watchdog for his temple. Zeus punished Pandareus by chaining him to the roots of a mountain but denying him death, so that he rotted underground forever. The daughters of Pandareus became servants of the Harpies.

Pandarus (PAN duh ruhs): A Trojan chieftain who broke the truce which was to prevail while Menelaus and Paris met in single combat to determine victory for one side or the other — thus sparing thousands of lives. But Athena did not wish the war to end so soon; nor did Hera.

Athena appeared to Pandarus, counseling him to launch an arrow toward Menelaus, promising him eternal fame as an archer if he killed the Greek. Pandarus shot his arrow; he wounded Menelaus and broke the truce. The armies attacked each other just as Athena and Hera had planned. Pandarus later figures in another legend. He carried messages between Troilus and Chryseis, abetting their secret love affair. Our word "pander" derives from this.

Pandora (pan DOH ruh): Her name means "all-gifted." She was so named because she was the first mortal woman to whom all the gods gave gifts: Hephaestus molded her of clay and gave her form; Zeus breathed life into her; Athena gave her sagacity and skill at spinning and weaving; Aphrodite gave her radiant physical beauty; Apollo gave her a lovely singing voice and a gift for healing; Demeter instilled her with a passion for gardening; Artemis taught her certain important secrets concerning the moon; Poseidon gave her the power of sea-change. Hermes saved his offerings for last; he gave her a curiously carved golden box, telling her never to open it because it contained a forbidden mystery. Then Hermes gave her . . . curiosity! Actually, all this was part of a terrible plot. Zeus, still smouldering with rage because Prometheus had succeeded in teaching mankind the use of fire, had evolved a long-range plan to subdue man's pride. The creation of Pandora was the first step in this plan. The second step was to marry the beautiful gifted girl to the Titan, Epimetheus, ostensibly to compensate him for the loss of his brother, Prometheus, who had been condemned to eternal punishment. They were married and lived happily for some weeks. But Pandora could not forget the golden box. She kept gazing at it by day and dreamed of it at night. Finally her curiosity, spiced by taboo, proved irresistible. She opened the box. Out rushed a throng of hairy, fanged creatures, all the troubles that have plagued mankind since — disease, poverty, crime, and so on. But the cruel plan of Zeus was not quite fulfilled. For Pandora slammed shut the lid of the box, trapping one creature inside, *foreboding*, the final spite. If it had flown free, everyone in the world would have known exactly what misfortunes were to happen to him throughout his life. No hope would have been possible and the race of man would have perished off the earth. For while it is possible to survive disaster, it is impossible to live without hope. But foreboding was trapped, and man still lives.

Paris (PAIR ihs): Youngest son of Priam and Hecuba; prince of Troy. His abduction of Helen was the prime cause of the Trojan War, although there were others. According to legend, he seems to have been a better lover than warrior. He lost a duel to Menelaus and would have been killed if he had not been rescued by Aphrodite. He was usually to be found in Helen's chamber rather than on the battlefield, much to the displeasure of his warlike brothers, Hector and Deiphobus. However, he was an excellent archer, skilful enough to send an arrow into Achilles' one vulnerable spot, the tendon above his heel, although he was very careful to shoot from ambush. See *Apple of Discord; Helen; Menelaus; Achilles*.

Parnassus (pahr NASS uhs): One of Apollo's two sacred mountains; the other was Helicon. The caves of Parnassus housed Apollo's Delphic Oracles. The Muses danced there when they were not dancing upon Helicon. It was a favorite haunt too of Dionysus, who often led his revelers there when Apollo was elsewhere.

Pasiphae (puh SIHF uh ee): Daughter of Helios; wife of Minos; mother of Ariadne, Phaedra, and of that monstrous offspring, the Minotaur. She offended Aphrodite by comparing her own beauty to that of the goddess. Aphrodite retaliated by instilling her with an inconvenient love for one of her husband's prize bulls. The product of their passion was the Minotaur. See *Daedalus*; *Minos*; *Minotaur*. Minos imprisoned her in the Labyrinth, also constructed by Daedalus, and she died there.

Patroclus (puh TROH kluhs): Achilles' dearest friend and a key figure in the events of the *Iliad*. According to some legends, he was Achilles' elder cousin. In any case they were raised together and tutored together by Cheiron, who taught them hunting, woodcraft, and the arts of healing. When Achilles sailed for Troy, Patroclus sailed with him as second in command of the Myrmidons. Later, when Achilles retired from the fray because of his quarrel with Agamemnon, Patroclus also quit the field. But he was stricken to the heart by the Greek disasters, for after Achilles stopped fighting, the Trojans were everywhere victorious. Thus he was easily persuaded by Odysseus to don Achilles' golden armor and appear on the field in the guise of that invincible hero, so that the Trojans might be discouraged. Although Achilles did not easily accede to this plan because he had a foreboding of disaster, Patroclus finally persuaded him. He put on Achilles' golden armor and entered the battle, fighting exceedingly well and routing the Trojans, until Hector sought him out and killed him. Driven half mad by the death of his beloved friend, Achilles re-entered the battle, killed Hector, and caused the final defeat of the Trojans — all of which had been part of Odysseus' plan. See *Achilles*; *Hector*. Achilles, however, outlived his friend only by a few days. Their funeral pyres were erected side by side and their shades glided off to dwell together through eternity on the White Isle raised for them by Achilles' sea-goddess mother, Thetis.

Peirene (py REE nee): A spring sacred to the Muses.

It was formed when their flying horse, Pegasus, struck the ground with his hoof. The spring that gushed forth from that deep hoof-mark was of crystal clear musical waters, said to inspire anyone who drank from them. Poets came there to drink and all claimed inspiration.

Peirithous (py RITH oh uhs): King of the Lapiths; son of Ixion; and life-long friend of Theseus. His nature was as daring as that of his father, who had attempted to abduct Hera, and had been condemned to eternal punishment. See *Ixion*. Peirithous went campaigning with Theseus and they had many amazing adventures together. They raided the Amazons; they fought the Centaurs, and defeated them. Most amazing of all, however, they made a pact each to marry a daughter of Zeus. First they abducted the fifteen-year-old Helen, Zeus' daughter by Leda. They cast lots for her and Theseus won. But Helen was soon reclaimed by her formidable twin brothers, Castor and Polydeuces. Then, it is said, they decided to raid Tartarus and abduct Persephone, wife of Hades and Zeus' daughter by Demeter. However, the three-headed dog, Cerberus, was vigilant. He raised the alarm, barking furiously. Hades mustered his demonish hosts, the Harpies, as well as the Empusae and various other bestial troops, who captured the two heroes. Hades had them chained to two rocks where they were tormented by relays of demons. There they remained until Heracles came to raid Tartarus. This mighty hero put the forces of Hades to flight and struck the shackles from Theseus. But it is said that when he attempted to bear off Peirithous, the man's feet had grown into the ground and the earth shook when he was lifted. Heracles had to abandon him and bear Theseus to the land of the living unaccompanied by his old friend. But Theseus never forgot Peirithous. He commanded the Athenians to grant him semi-divine honors and mourned him to the day of his own death.

Pelasgus (peh LAZ guhs): The first man created by the gods, according to the most ancient myths. He was entirely mortal and ruled the land later to be known as Arcadia. The gods instilled him with enough rudimentary wisdom to raise his people out of barbarism. He taught them to erect wooden shelters and sew the skins of animals into garments. He is the ancestor of those people later called the Pelasgians, who made up the pre-Hellenic tribes inhabiting the Peloponnese and the islands of the Inner Sea, and who worshipped the great mother-goddess. In Crete they became a sea-faring nation and sent raiding parties to the eastern shore of the Inner Sea, to Phoenicia, and to the arc of land to the south of Phoenicia. It is thought that the names *Philistine* and *Palestine* derive from "Pelasgian."

Peleus (PEE loos; PEE lee-uhs); King of Phthia; great warrior; and an Argonaut. But his greatest claim to fame was as the father of Achilles. Peleus was an extraordinarily handsome man and extraordinarily brave. Thetis, the sea-goddess, loved him, and amazed the other gods by declaring that she meant to marry him, although he was mortal and she was bound to outlive him by centuries. The wedding of Peleus and Thetis was the most glittering fête ever to be held on Olympus. The groom received splendid gifts. Hephaestus gave him a suit of golden armor and Poseidon gave him those immortal stallions, Xanthus and Balius, whom Achilles later inherited. It was at this wedding that the seeds of the Trojan War were planted when Eris, rankling because she had not been invited, tossed her Apple of Discord onto the banquet table. See *Apple of Discord*. Peleus outlived both his son, Achilles, and his grandson, Neoptolemus. It is said that when he finally died, Thetis, unreconciled to losing her husband, prevailed upon Zeus to make him immortal and allow him to join the shades of Achilles and Patroclus on her White Isle.

Pelias (PEE lih uhs): Jason's uncle, who usurped the throne of Iolchis and dispatched Jason on a quest for the Golden Fleece — an expedition which he hoped would be fatal. Pelias was later killed by his own daughters whom Medea had befuddled by certain magical spells.

Pelops (PEE lah'ps): Son of Tantalus; king of Phrygia. In his infancy he unwittingly became the instrument of his father's eternal punishment. For Tantalus, a son of Zeus, also had an incorrigible yen to offend the gods. When Zeus visited him, he killed his infant son, Pelops, had him roasted, and served him to Zeus. Zeus recognized the flesh as human, and condemned Tantalus to unique torments. See *Tantalus*. Zeus then resurrected his grandson; and since the child's shoulder had been consumed by the cooking fire, he fashioned him an ivory shoulder. Pelops grew to be an extremely beautiful youth. Later, he courted Hippodemia and became the father of those ill-fated twins, Thyestes and Atreus. See *Oenomeus*; *Atreus*. Pelops was a king out of very early times. The southern peninsula of Greece, the Peloponnese, was named for him.

Penelope (pee NEHL oh pee): Queen of Ithaca; model wife of mythology. She waited patiently for her husband, Odysseus, who was away for twenty years — ten years fighting at Troy, ten years trying to sail home in the teeth of Poseidon's hostility. During that time, Penelope was beseiged by suitors, one hundred and eight of them, the most powerful of those chieftains who had not gone to Troy or who had returned earlier. They believed Odysseus to be dead. Each of them wished to become king of Ithaca and they were also drawn by Penelope's great beauty. They were a brawling rambunctious lot, these suitors; many of them became very obstreperous, threatening to abduct her and take Ithaca by force of arms. However, she followed the advice of her wise old counselor, Mentor, and adopted her famous weaving ruse. She claimed that she had vowed an altar cloth to Artemis and that she could not choose a suitor until she had finished that gift for the chaste goddess. Each night, however, she unraveled what she had woven that day. The altar cloth was never finished and the suitors were forced to wait. See *Mentor*. In one legend, it is told that Oeax, brother of Palamedes, seeking to avenge his brother's death at the hands of Odysseus, came to Ithaca and told Penelope that Odysseus had been killed. Penelope flung herself off a cliff into the sea. But Thetis, the sea-goddess and mother of Achilles, sent a flock of ducks to swim alongside Penelope and support her so that she could not drown. Then Thetis herself appeared and told her that Odysseus was still alive. In another touching incident, Odysseus summons her from her chamber after he has slain all the suitors. But she had not seen him for twenty years, and was not sure that she recognized her husband in this blood-stained voyager. However, he recalled to her the construction of their marriage-bed — how, conforming to her wish that they use a bed never before used, he had gone into the forest and cut down a pine tree and fashioned headboard and footboard. Upon hearing this she flung herself into his arms, weeping tears of joy. All in all, Penelope emerges as one of the most attractive personalities in Greek myth, man or woman, god or goddess, a unique wife for a unique hero.

Penthesilea (pehn thuh sih LEE uh): Daughter of Ares; queen of the Amazons. She led a detachment of her sisters-in-arms to Troy after Hector had been killed by Achilles, and attacked the Greeks so fiercely that she almost brought victory again to the Trojans. But Achilles finally sought her out. They fought a savage hand-to-hand combat. It is said, however, that Achilles was so much struck with the beauty of this warrior-girl that he fought less effectively than usual. Penthesilea was more single-minded; she remained undistracted by Achilles' beauty and took advantage of his lapses in concentration to strike some blows he was barely able to parry. Finally, his reflexes took over, and he killed her. However, when he saw her lying there on the battleground he was struck again by her superb beauty and he wept for what might have been had they met at another time, in another place. He was observed in his grief by Thersites, a great scoffer among the Greeks, a mishapen, foul-mouthed man. Thersites jeered at Achilles, who turned, and killed the scoffer with one blow of his fist. It is said that Zeus, who had been watching the battle from Mt. Ida, was so moved by this episode that he had Hephaestus carve upon his Olympian throne a bas-relief of the dying Amazon in Achilles' arms.

Pentheus (PEHN thoos): A king of Thebes who refused to acknowledge Dionysus as a god and sought to expel him and his followers from the kingdom. Dionysus took a terrible vengeance. He provoked curiosity in Pentheus, making him wish to spy upon the secret revels of the Bacchantes. The king put on women's clothes and joined the throng of moon-intoxicated revelers who rushed up the hill. Then he hid behind a tree to watch the secret rites. He saw with dismay that his own mother, Agave, was among the revelers, as well as his two sisters. Then, Dionysus raveled skeins of moonlight, deranging the vision of Agave, who screamed that she saw a lion in the underbrush. In her ecstatic fury she rushed upon her son — whom she took to be the lion — followed by her daughters, and tore him to pieces. It is said that Agave's madness persisted throughout the night and that she carried Pentheus' head home on a pole, thinking it a lion's head and wishing to show the trophy to her son. Never again was Dionysus' divinity denied in Thebes.

Periclymenus (pehr ih KLY mee nuhs): King of Elis; and an Argonaut. His grandfather, Poseidon, had bestowed upon him the power of transformation, enabling him to turn himself into any animal or tree he wished. He captained the forces of his father, Neleus, in a campaign against Heracles. He engaged the hero in single combat, changing himself into a bull; Heracles broke off his horns. He changed himself into a lion and Heracles broke his teeth. He changed himself into a huge serpent and attempted to enwrap Heracles, who knotted him around a tree trunk. Finally, Periclymenus turned himself into a bee, not an ordinary bee, but one as large as an eagle with a barbed stinger longer than a spear. Heracles dived into the river, pursued by this fearsome creature. When the bee swooped too close, Heracles reached out of the water and pulled the bee in, drowning him. Death was Periclymenus' final transformation.

Persephone (pur SEHF oh ne): Daughter of Zeus and Demeter; wife of Hades. Beloved daughter of the harvest-goddess, she led an enchanted life among the growing fields. Her mother gave her a magic paint-box, which she took among the spring flowers, coloring them according to her fancy and drawing them faces that they have worn forever. One morning in April as she was dipping her brush into a shadow of special blueness that she needed for a gentian, she heard a strange rumbling sound that seemed to be coming from beneath the field. The field opened. Out of the pit surged six black horses drawing a black chariot, driven by a tall, black-bearded, black-robed figure. Before she could call for help, she was snatched into the chariot, which plunged again into the pit. Then she saw that her abductor was her uncle, Hades. She did not know what he wanted of her. Then he showed her. His dark lips drank her tears, as the stallions thundered down the passage to Tartarus. But she was stubborn, this young goddess. She refused to accept her captivity. She refused to eat, refused to speak to her captor. In Hades' kingdom lay the world's troves of gold and silver, of diamonds and rubies and sapphires. He heaped her with jewels and had his slaves spin her gowns of silver and gold thread. He called out the nimblest acrobats, the most graceful dancers, the most eloquent actors, and the sweetest singers from among his shades to provide her with entertainment. Still she would not speak to him; still she would not eat. During this time, her mother, Demeter, was coursing the earth like wildfire, searching for her abducted daughter. At first she could not discover what had happened to the girl. Then, in Eleusis, she heard birds gossiping. Piecing together their chirps, she realized that it was her brother, Hades, who had taken her daughter. She rushed to Zeus for justice. But Hades had bribed Zeus with a wonderful volt-blue, zig-zag lightning shaft, more beautiful than any thunderbolt he had ever owned. And Zeus informed Demeter that Hades wished to marry Persephone and that she, being a goddess, would have to marry within the family if she were not to lower herself. Demeter refused to accept the judgment of Zeus, and raged. Her rage was famine. Crops failed, the earth parched, cattle died, people died. Hunger stalked the land; death stalked behind. Finally, Zeus had to yield. He informed Demeter that she could reclaim her daughter so long as Persephone had eaten nothing during her sojourn underground. But if she had accepted food, then, under the ancient Law of Abode, she would have to be considered a guest, not a captive, and must remain as Hades' bride. As Demeter rejoiced, Hermes flew off on his winged sandals to fetch Persephone. But just before Hermes arrived in Tartarus, a treacherous gardener, who hated Demeter because the goddess had once changed him into a lizard for laughing at her, tore a succulent pomegranate in half, and offered it to Persephone who was suffering from hunger and thirst. Before she could stop herself she had plucked six of the juicy red seeds and eaten them. Just then she heard Hermes' bright herald cry and saw his lithe form swooping toward her, and knew that she was saved. But not quite. Hades had already sped to Olympus and claimed Persephone as his bride under the Law of Abode, because she had eaten the seeds. Whereupon Demeter decreed that no crops would grow if her flower-princess had to become the bride of Death. Zeus compromised, and his judgment was final. Persephone would have to spend six months with Hades, a month for each seed. The other half of the year she could spend with her mother. But Demeter kept her word too. For those six months that her beloved daughter spent underground, no crops grew. In the spring, when Persephone returned, the fields could flower again, and the trees bear fruit. In Roman mythology Persephone was known as Proserpina.

Perseus (PUR soos; PUR see uhs): Son of Zeus and Danae; first king of Mycenae. He was the earliest of the seven great Greek heroes and there is a unique dawn freshness to his legend. Quite literally, he was the golden boy of mythology. He was engendered by a golden shaft of sunlight, which was the guise adopted by Zeus for visiting Danae in her prison cell. He and his mother were penned in a wooden box and cast out to sea by his grandfather, Acrisius, but the box floated ashore on Sephiros. When the lid was lifted, golden sunlight poured in and Danae rose from the box in such radiance, holding her infant son, that the king of that place fell madly in love with her. Later, the king, Polydectes, tried to get rid of Perseus, now grown into a youth, by sending him to fetch Medusa's head, believing he must perish on the mission. But Perseus, not at all afraid, though Medusa was a dreadful monster, climbed a hill at dawn to hymn the rising sun, feeling himself fill with its golden power. Hermes appeared then, and Athena; they gave him golden gifts. Athena's was a shield of gold, polished to such a high gloss that it could be used as a mirror. She warned him that he must look upon Medusa only mirrored in this shield, for the direct sight of her would turn him to stone. Hermes' gift was a new-moon sword of pale gold, the only blade sharp enough to cut off Medusa's head. Hermes also gave him a pair of gold-winged sandals, called *tallaria*, which would allow him to fly faster than an eagle. But there were two other pieces of equipment he would need to complete his mission, Hermes told him. And they were lodged with the Nymphs of the West, whom Hermes had visited once, and whose hospitality had so pleased him that he had left them magical gifts. However, these nymphs dwelt in a secret place, and only the three gray sisters, called the *Graeae,* knew the secret which Perseus would have to extract from them. Perseus shouted with joy, thanked the gods, seized the golden shield and the golden sword, and flew away upon his gold-winged sandals. Glittering, he flew into the mist . . . down, down into mist-shrouded regions to the ice-floe upon which the three gray hags dwelt. They owned but one tooth and one eye among them, and passed them from one to the other so that they could see and bite. Perseus asked them where he could find the Nymphs of the West but they refused to tell. Whereupon he seized their eye and their tooth and refused to return them until the secret was revealed. Pleading for their return, the hags told him that the nymphs lived in the Garden of the Hesperides, where Hera's tree of golden apples grew and where Atlas held the western rim of the sky on his shoulders. Perseus leaped into the air and flew to the golden orchard where the nymphs, who did not see a stranger from one century to the next, greeted him with great joy. When he departed they gave him the gifts Hermes had left with them: a helmet which cast darkness about its wearer, making him invisible, and a wallet woven of golden thread called a *kibesis*; only this magic wallet could contain the strong poison of Medusa's snake-haired head. Perseus climbed into the golden air again and sped over sea and land to a place of dreadful gloom. He descended into a giant swamp full of the stench of rotting things, a place where no light penetrated except the weird green fires that flickered off the putrescent marshes. He followed a stinking stream until he came to three figures lying asleep. They were huge, with brass scales and brass wings, and he knew he had come to the place of the Gorgons. Looking into the mirror of his shield he examined the image of each head in turn. The last one was horrid; each hair was a hissing snake. Stepping carefully, keeping the reflection of the head centered in his mirroring shield, he raised his new-moon sword and slashed downward. The head rolled. A fearful shriek rent the air as the Gorgons awoke. He scooped up the head, stuffed it into his golden wallet, and flew away. The Gorgons gave chase, but he outdistanced them. On his way home, he used Medusa's head to turn a sea-monster to stone and rescue Andromeda, who became his wife. See *Andromeda*. Then he returned to Sephiros just in time to interrupt his mother's forced marriage to Polydectes. Again he drew the snake-haired head from his golden kibesis, and turned the groom and all the wedding guests to stone. See *Danae*. Perseus lived to a great old age, founded Mycenae, and became its first king. It is said that he gave the Medusa-head to Athena, who attached it to her shield. Others say, however, that he wished to rid the world of so horrid an object and threw it in the sea, where it still moves upon the tides, making coral as it rolls.

Phaea (FEE uh): A robber-woman; one of those bloodthirsty bandits who infested the mountain road from Troezen to Athens, which the young Theseus had to travel. She was exceedingly savage with her victims. After depriving them of their wallets, she would take their lives. In addition to her other charms, she had the habit of turning herself into a wild white sow when too closely pressed. Theseus encountered Phaea on the mountain road and battered her so with the brass club he had taken from Corunetes that she took refuge in transformation. She became a white sow and attacked him with her murderous tusks. But he was ready with his club and battered the sow to death.

Phaedra (FEE druh): Daughter of Minos and Pasiphae; third wife of Theseus. Her thwarted love for her husband's son, Hippolytus, caused the death of the young man and herself. See *Hippolytus*. In general, any relationship with Theseus was apt to be fatal for any member of the royal house of Crete. Theseus broke the power of Minos, killed the Minotaur, abandoned Ariadne, and became Phaedra's widower.

Phaeton (FAY uh thuhn): A son of Apollo, who persuaded his father to let him drive the sun-chariot. Apollo demurred; the sun-stallions were of titanic strength and needed a god at the reins. But he had promised the boy and could not refuse. However, he made Phaeton agree to drive the chariot at moderate speed across the blue meadow of the sky, not too high, and not too low, but keeping always to the middle of the way. The lad promised and sped off in the sun-chariot. At first, he kept the middle way and the fire-breathing stallions trotted easily, the whirling golden spokes of the chariot wheels casting daylight upon the earth below. But when Phaeton reached his own village he felt an overwhelming desire to impress his playmates, who had never believed he was Apollo's son. He urged the stallions downward till they hovered over the roofs of the village, which immediately burst into flame. The fields caught fire, the forests broke into flames, rivers and lakes turned to steam. The sun-stallions, frenzied by the commotion, rushed up, up, up, until the earth was gripped in a paralyzing frost. The salt sea itself froze, and ships were stuck in the ice, motionless. People and cattle froze to death. Phaeton pulled on the reins desperately, trying to swerve the stallions downward. They rushed toward earth again. The icy waters melted making great floods, threatening to drown the earth completely. Zeus, on Olympus, heard the cries of grief arise from earth. He looked down and saw the runaway chariot of the sun, with a strange youth in the driver's seat. He hurled his thunderbolt, killing Phaeton instantly, and Apollo flew down to take the reins. The earth still bears marks of Phaeton's wild ride. He left great scorched places when the chariot dipped too close. The Sahara Desert is one and there are smaller deserts too. Our word "phaeton," meaning "light swift carriage," is derived from the name of Apollo's reckless son. See *Heliades*.

Philammon (fih LAY muhn): Son of Apollo and Chione; noted musician and sweet singer. See *Chione*.

Philoctetes (fihl uhk TEE teez): A remarkable archer whose career spanned two generations. In his youth he was a companion of Heracles and was entrusted by him to erect his funeral pyre and to set the torch to it with his own hands. Heracles considered his manner of death — poisoned by the shirt of Nessus — to be a disgrace, and he wished no one to attend his last rites. Philoctetes did everything Heracles asked. In return, Heracles gave him his own wonderful bow and those arrows which had been dipped in the Hydra's blood and meant instant death to anyone they pierced. Philoctetes kept that bow and used it in many battles. Only Apollo, it was said, was a better archer; but no mortal could rival Philoctetes. Later, he sailed for Troy but, while on the island of Lemnos, accidentally scratched himself with one of the envenomed arrows. His wound festered and would not heal. The stench that arose from it was unbearable to his comrades. Nor did they wish to listen to his moans of pain. They were not in a compassionate mood, these Greek chieftains; they were afire with battle-lust and wild to reach Troy. And so they abandoned Philoctetes on the island of Lemnos, where he lived, in pain, for ten years. However, in the tenth year of the war, it was foretold by an oracle that Troy could not fall until the bow of Heracles appeared on the field. Odysseus and Diomedes went to Lemnos to ask the aid of the man they had treated so vilely. But the ordeal had refined rather than coarsened him; he did not indulge his grudge, but went to Troy. There, it is said, his wound was healed by the great Machaon, son of Asclepius. The next day, Philoctetes strung the bow of Heracles and killed Paris. A few days later, Troy fell.

Philyra (FIHL uh ruh): A lesser sea-deity who attracted the notice of Cronus. But his attentions were unwelcome. She turned herself into a mare and galloped away. He turned into a stallion and galloped after. She bore him Chiron, half man and half horse, wisest of the centaurs and the only one not sired by Ixion. She grew weary of being a mare and was not particularly fond of Chiron. She petitioned Cronus to change her shape, telling him she wished to dwell modestly in solitude, and without irksome care. He changed her into a linden tree.

Phlegethon (FLEHG eh thuhn): One of the rivers that flowed through Tartarus. But it ran with fire, not with water. It was of special dread to sinners for they were often thrown into it.

Phlegyas (FLEHJ joos): A king of the Lapiths; father of Ixion and Coronis. Now, Coronis was the abducted

184

maiden who became the mother of Asclepius, and was later killed by Apollo in a jealous rage. Her father attacked Apollo's temple at Delphi and destroyed it. He was killed by Apollo and condemned to eternal torment, which took this form: He was shackled hand and foot under a rock suspended by an invisible thread in mid-air; it perpetually threatened to fall and crush him. Thus, three generations of the Lapith royal house defied the gods and incurred unique penalties after death. Phlegyas himself; his son, Ixion, who attempted to abduct Hera and was chained to a flaming wheel for eternity; and his grandson, Peirithous, companion of Theseus, who tried to abduct Persephone, and was shackled forever to the roots of a mountain in Tartarus. See *Ixion; Peirithous.*

Phoebe (FEE bee): The word means "bright," and is sometimes applied to Artemis as goddess of the moon.

Phoebus (FY buhs; FEE buhs): Masculine form of "Phoebe." It is often attached to the name of Apollo, the sun-god.

Phoenix (FEE nihx): A legendary bird without parent and without offspring, it nurtured itself on sunlight and sea spray. When about to die, it drew new life from those primal elements of fire and water and was born again. Its feathers were gold and red and blinding white as the sun; its eyes were green as the sea. It is sometimes described as building its nest in the form of a funeral pyre, setting the nest afire, and then, when consumed, rising from its own ashes.

Phorcys (FOR sihs): Brother and husband of Ceto; and father of monsters. See *Ceto.*

Pittheus (PIHT thoos): King of Troezen; son of Pelops

and Hippodamia. He was the only virtuous one of the criminal brood sired by Pelops. When an oracle told him he was destined to become the grandfather of a great hero, he gave his daughter, Aethra, in marriage to Aegeus, king of Athens. Aethra became the mother of Theseus. Some legends claim, however, that Poseidon was his father, not Aegeus. But Aethra was indisputably the hero's mother and Pittheus his grandfather.

Pleiades (PLEE uh deez): Seven daughters of Atlas who became a constellation after their death. Pursued in life by the hunter Orion, they are still pursued by him across the arch of heaven — for he too is a constellation. See *Orion; Merope*.

Pleisthenes (PLIHS thuh neez): A son of Atreus whom his father killed in error, one of the few inadvertent homicides by this bloodthirsty king of Mycenae whose killing was usually intentional.

Pluto (PLOO toh): Variant name for Hades, king of the dead. It is a form of the Greek word "Plouton," meaning "rich," and was used as a term of flattery for Hades by those who wished to placate the stern god. There is no evidence, however, that Hades was ever flattered out of his somber intentions. See *Hades*.

Podilarius (poh duh LY rih uhs): Son of Asclepius; and master diagnostician. He and his brother, Machaon, the great surgeon, went to Troy, where their skill allowed thousands of the wounded to survive. See *Machaon*.

Polites (poh LY teez): Last of Priam's fifty sons to be killed during the sack of Troy. He was cut down by Neoptolemus. Only one of Priam's sons survived: Helenus, who had aided the Greeks.

Polycaste (pahl uh KAS tee): A sister of Daedalus; mother of Talos whom Daedalus killed in a jealous rage because he was displaying an inventive talent to rival his own. When her son was killed, Polycaste was transformed by a compassionate god into a bird — some say a gull. And this gull shrieked with joy when Daedalus' son, Icarus, fell to his death because the sun had melted the wax from his wings. See *Icarus.*

Polydectes (pahl ih DEHK teez): King of Sephiros. His attempt to force Danae into marriage caused him to be ossified by her son, Perseus, who had brought him Medusa's head as a wedding present. See *Perseus; Danae.*

Polydeuces (pahl ih DOO seez): Son of Zeus and Leda. Brother of Castor and Helen. See *Castor and Polydeuces.*

Polyhymnia (pahl ih HIHM nih uh): Muse of song; and of geometry. This may seem an unlikely combination, but the goddess of the lovely voice taught those who make song that the most exquisite contrivances require an inner order for their structure. There has always been an affinity between mathematics and music.

Polyneices (pahl ih NY SEEZ): Son of Oedipus and Jocasta; brother of Eteocles and Antigone. His perpetual rivalry with his twin brother as to who should rule Thebes led to plot, counterplot, war, and murder. See *Antigone; Eteocles.*

Polyphemus (pahl ih FEE muhs): A Cyclops; outwitted and blinded by Odysseus after he had devoured many of the voyager's crew. See *Cyclopes.*

Polyxena (poh LIHK see nuh): Lovely daughter of Priam and heroine of a non-Homeric legend about the Trojan War. Achilles, it is said, while battling the Trojans, allowed his attention to be distracted by the sight of a beautiful maiden watching from the wall. He immediately decided that the maiden must be his and killed the man he was fighting, so that he could open negotiations without delay. Discovering that the girl was Priam's daughter, he sent envoys to the king. Priam tended to approve this match for, if Achilles were neutralized by becoming his son-in-law, then the Greeks would have to retreat; without Achilles, they could not win. However, Hector opposed the match. After several years of fighting, he now hated the Greeks — particularly Achilles. Paris supported Hector. He was afraid that any truce would mean that he would be forced to yield up Helen to her husband. A courteous refusal was sent to Achilles who, soon afterward, quit the fighting because of his quarrel with Agamemnon. But he kept prowling near the walls trying to glimpse the beautiful maiden. And Polyxena formed the habit of walking the walls at night so that she might be glimpsed. Then occurred the combination of bloody events which ended the war. Patroclus was killed by Hector and Hector was slain by Achilles, who bound his body to the axle of his chariot and dragged it seven times around the walls of Troy. Priam went to Achilles to plead for the return of his son's body. According to ancient belief, unless a body was burned decently on a funeral pyre, or buried with proper ceremonies, its unquiet ghost would roam forever. Achilles at first refused to listen to Priam's pleading, until a cloaked figure that had accompanied the king drew the cloak from its face and Achilles saw that it was Polyxena. The sight of this lovely tear-stained face melted Achilles' cruel resolve and he allowed Priam to take his son's body back to Troy. But he told the king he now intended to press his suit for the girl's hand and that this time he expected a favorable reply. When king and princess returned to their castle, Paris craftily pretended to change his mind. He suggested to Polyxena that she arrange a tryst with Achilles at a certain grove sacred to Apollo, just outside the Trojan walls. Polyxena joyfully sent a message to Achilles, who came to the grove the next day. Paris, hiding in ambush behind a statue of Apollo, launched the arrow that severed the tendon above Achilles' heel — his one vulnerable spot — thus killing the hero. Polyxena, maddened with grief by the death of the only man she had ever loved, took up the arrow and stabbed herself in the heart. According to some legends, when Thetis transported the shade of Achilles to the White Isle she had raised in the sea as his eternal home, he refused to dwell on that isle unless his mother would bring the shade of Polyxena there. Thetis demurred, but the shade of her son threatened to leave the isle and take his chances in Tartarus. So Thetis brought Polyxena to the White Isle where the two shades embraced and dwelt together through eternity.

Porphyrion (por FIHR ih uhn; por FY rih uhn): Leader of the race of Giants who were the offspring of Gaia and Uranus, and younger brothers of the Titans. Embittered because Zeus had defeated and imprisoned their elder brothers, the Giants launched a sudden attack. Now, these Giants were fearsome creatures, huge as Titans, possessed of volcanic strength and incredibly savage dispositions. According to some legends, their legs were serpents. The Giants uprooted two mountains, piled Pelion on Ossa, and scaled Olympus. It had been foretold that the gods could defeat the Giants only with the help of a lion-skinned mortal. Zeus decided that this must be his son, Heracles, and sent Hermes speeding through the twilight to find him. While the Giants were scaling Olympus, their mother, Gaia, who favored their cause, was searching for a certain herb she knew would confer invulnerability upon her sons and make their victory certain. Zeus, however, realized what his grandmother was planning, and commanded Helios to keep his sun-chariots stabled and the dawn-goddess, Eos, to keep out of the sky. Darkness held upon the earth and Gaia groped about without finding the magic herb. Now, the battle was joined. Porphyrion led his Giants in a wild charge. Many of the gods were injured. They retreated. Just then, Hermes returned with Heracles, who beat back the first wave of Giants with his brass club, then fell to one knee and launched arrow after arrow. Each one found its mark, killing a Giant. The gods rallied. Hecate wielded her scorpion whip. Hephaestus hurled ladles of hot lead. Athena thrust valiantly with her spear. Apollo shot arrows of golden fire; Artemis shot arrows of silver fire. But the gods could only wound the Giants; in each case Heracles, conforming to prophecy, had to deal the death-blow. But Porphyrion could not be killed. Wounded, battered, but still ablaze with ferocity, he led the remnants of his Giants down off Olympus, vowing that he would return one day after Heracles had died, and seek vengeance. And, it is said, that is why the gods did not accept Heracles' death, but resurrected him as a god, and took him among the company of the Immortals. As for Porphyrion, no one knows exactly what happened to him but there are those who say that it is his festering grudge that is behind all the secret malice of nature, which occasionally erupts, causing slaughter and destruction, and shaking mankind's faith in itself and in its gods.

Poseidon (poh SY duhn): Son of Cronus and Rhea; god of the sea. Green-robed, wearing a crown of pearl, he whirled over the sea in a dolphin chariot, shaking storms out of his beard, raiding the shoreline with his legions of white-maned combers, sending waterspouts high, feuding with his brothers and sisters, making claim on land and air. This was Poseidon, gigantic brother of Zeus, most fearsome of the Olympians, whom men spoke of in hushed voices as the "earth-shaker." He was a very changeable god, hot-tempered and loving, cruel and kind. His bounty supported generations of sailors and fishermen; then, all of a sudden, his mood would change — his smiles would turn to rage, a storm would boil out of the blue sky, wrecking fleets, drowning those who had dared the sea on ships. He was generous. His underwater domain held riches beyond calculation. And he was inventive with forms of life. He liked to surprise nymphs with monsters, and concocted the octopus, the blowfish, and the seapolyp for their entertainment. Once, to appease the jealous wrath of his wife, Amphitrite, he thought up the dolphin and gave it to her as a gift. But his handsomest creation was the love-token he contrived for Demeter. The harvest queen had always repulsed his rude wooing, and fled him down inland ways, until one day he presented her with the most beautiful creature ever seen on earth. It was the horse, which delighted the goddess and made her change her opinion of Poseidon. It had taken him many trials to make the horse and he cast aside his unsuccessful attempts: camel, hippopotamus, giraffe, donkey, zebra. Poseidon was revered by those who lived near the sea and feared by inland folk as well — for his floods reached far. Travelers sacrificed to him before each voyage, petitioning him as "Grantor of Safe Passage." The horse was sacred to him; also the pine tree — father of ships. In Roman mythology, Poseidon was known as Neptune.

Priam (PRY uhm): Father of the fifty princes who fought the Greeks at Troy; the son of Laomedon; husband of Hecuba; and last king of that fabled city — Troy. He had ruled for many years before the war struck and had rebuilt the city and the treasury ruined by his father, Laomedon. He was finally killed by Neoptolemus, son of Achilles, during the sack of Troy.

Procne (PRAHK nee): Wife of Tereus, king of

Thrace, and sister of Philomela. See *Philomela*.

Procrustes (proh KRUHS teez): Most infamous of those monstrous brigands who made life miserable for travelers along the mountain road from Troezen to Athens. He kept an inn in which there was a special bed-chamber with a very special bed. Guests who sought repose there found themselves shackled to the bed frame. If they were too short for the bed, he attached ropes to their ankles and stretched them until their bones cracked. If they were too long for the bed, Procrustes lopped off their feet or their head. In any case, he always ended by killing his guests and appropriating the contents of their wallets. His final guest was Theseus who, dismayed by the pile of bones that lay about the inn yard and further dismayed by the bloodstained bed frame, decided not to lie upon the bed — but suddenly pushed Procrustes upon it. Thereupon he treated his host as his host had treated guests. Procrustes was too long for the bed, so Theseus cut off his head. And that short stretch of the road became safer for travelers.

Proetus (proh EE tuhs; PREE tuhs): Twin brother of Acrisius, thus great-uncle to Perseus. He and his twin began fighting while still in their mother's womb and this dissension continued throughout their lives. Acrisius shared the kingdom of Argos with Proetus, but then suspected him of designs upon his daughter, Danae, and succeeded in expelling him. Proetus then became king of Tiryns, where he entertained the hero Bellerephon, and plotted his death. He had three daughters who were sent mad by Hera for mocking her image but were cured later by the wise Melampus. All in all, he emerges as a vile petty-minded character and was much loathed by his subjects.

Prometheus (proh MEE thee uhs; proh MEE thus): Noblest of the sons of Uranus and Gaia; arch-rebel; and friend to man. Prometheus belonged to the race of Titans who were cousins to the gods. One day he looked down upon the earth and did not like what he saw. Men and women crouched in dark caves, cold, almost naked. They used tools chipped out of stone and ate their meat raw. They were dulled, brutish, speaking to each other in grunts. Prometheus went to Zeus and said:

"Why, oh Thunderer, do you keep the race of man in ignorance and darkness?"

"What you call ignorance is innocence," said Zeus. "What you call darkness is the shadow of my decree. Man is happy now, and will remain happy until someone persuades him he is unhappy. Do not meddle further with my designs."

"I know that everything you do is wise," said Prometheus. "Enlighten me with your wisdom. Tell me why you refuse man the gift of fire?"

"Because hidden in man is a pride that can destroy us. Give him the great servant called fire, and he will try to make himself as powerful as the gods. Why, he would storm Olympus. Go now and trouble me no further."

But Prometheus was still not satisfied. The next morning he stood tiptoe on the mountaintop and stole some fire from the sunrise. He hid the spark in a hollow reed, then went down to earth. Zeus looking down later could not believe what he saw. Everything was changed. Man had come out of his cave. Zeus saw huts, farmhouses, walled towns, a castle. He saw men cooking their food, carrying torches to light their way at night. Forges blazed; men were beating out ploughs, keels, swords, spears. They were raising white wings of sails and daring to use the fury of the winds for their voyages. They were wearing helmets, riding out in chariots to do battle like the gods themselves. Zeus was infuriated. He knew whom to blame. He ordered Prometheus to be seized and bound to a mountaintop in a place where it always snows and the wind howls ceaselessly. There the friend of man was sentenced to spend eternity, chained to a crag, two vultures hovering about him, tearing at his belly and eating his liver. He could not die because he was immortal, but he could suffer. And suffer he did through long centuries for giving man the gift of fire. Finally, another hero was born brave enough to defy the gods. He struck the chains from Prometheus and killed the vultures. But that deed belongs to the story of Heracles.

Prosperina (proh SUR pih nuh): Roman name for Persephone, daughter of Demeter, and Hades' queen. See *Persephone*.

Protesilaus (proh tehs ih LAY uhs): A king of Thessaly who sailed with forty ships against Troy. When the Greek ships were drawn up at their moorings and the Trojan army was ranked on the beach ready to meet the invaders, the Greeks, it is said, hesitated. No one wished to be the first to charge that hedge of spears. Protesilaus leaped from the deck of his ship, shouting to his men to follow, and was the first Greek to set foot on the Trojan shore. His war was a brief one. He had not advanced ten paces before Hector came charging out of the ranks and transfixed him with his spear. Now, the wife of Protesilaus, who was named Laodamia, was inconsolable when she heard of her husband's death. She prayed to Hermes, who conducted the dead to Hades, to come and fetch her so that she might join her husband. Hermes came, was struck with compassion, and made her an unprecedented offer: He would bring her husband home from the Land of the Shades for three hours each day so that she might converse with him! She accepted this offer. Each day, Hermes made the journey to Tartarus and conducted Protesilaus to Thessaly, withdrawing while the dead king conversed with his wife, and then conveying him back to Hades. Finally, however, Laodamia, could not bear these daily farewells. She pleaded with Hermes to allow her to accompany her husband to the Land of the Dead and abide there with him forever. Hermes agreed to do so.

Psyche (SY kee): Youngest daughter of a king who had three daughters; she was so beautiful that Aphrodite grew envious. The goddess of love dispatched her son, Eros, to pierce Psyche with one of his arrows and instill her with a passion for her father's swineherd, or perhaps for one of the swine, this being Aphrodite's notion of what a girl deserved who dared be as beautiful as herself. However, when Eros approached the sleeping girl with his arrow notched, he accidentally scratched himself, fell in love with Psyche, and bore her away to be his bride. Now, god may marry mortal only on condition that the god remain invisible — for the sight of the naked god can consume a mortal with the divine fire, as happened to Semele when Zeus appeared before her in his own form. Therefore, Psyche never saw her husband, nor any of his servants. Her way was lighted by torches carried by invisible hands. Invisible servants brought her food and drink. Trees were pruned by invisible gardeners. At night, all torches were extinguished; her husband visited her in total darkness. She received him joyfully, but never saw him. When morning came, he was gone. She was very happy for a while, but then decided to invite her sisters to the castle so that they might see her in her happiness. The sisters came and immediately began to instill the poison of suspicion in her mind, drop by drop: one suggesting that her husband must be a monster too ugly to allow himself to be seen; the other suggesting he might be a dissolute prince with a different castle every ten miles, and and a different bride in each. The sisters departed but the evil doubts they had brewed did not. They remained lodged in her thoughts and festered there. Finally she could stand it no longer. One night when her husband was asleep she arose, lighted a wax taper, and bent to look at him. There, lying on the bed, was a youth more beautiful than any she had ever imagined ... marble-skinned, with hair the color of pale flame, and a pair of large, white, smoothly feathered wings. A drop of hot wax fell from the taper onto his shoulder. He awoke. He looked at Psyche, but not with anger, his eyes were filled with such grief and pity that she fell into a swoon. When she awoke the castle was gone. The courtyard was gone. She stood among weeds and brambles. All the good things that had belonged to her had vanished with her love. From that night on she roamed the woods, searching. And some say she still searches the woods and dark places. Some say that Aphrodite turned her into an owl that sees best in the dark and cries, "Who ... who ...?" Others say her husband forgave her, finally, and took her up to Olympus. It is her special task to undo the talk of the bride's family, and the groom's. When mother or sister visit bride or groom and say, "This, this, this ... that, that ... Better look for yourself, seeing's believing" — then she whips them away and she herself, invisible, whispers that none but love knows the secret of love, that believing is seeing.

Pygmalion (pihg MAY lee uhn): A young sculptor of Cyprus so talented that his fame reached Olympus and Aphrodite herself came to pose for him. He was inspired by the beautiful goddess and carved a masterpiece, a statue so beautiful he fell in love with it as though it were living. He could not work or eat or sleep — he just sat in his studio looking at the marble girl. "If I can't have her," he said, finally, to himself, "I don't want anything. I shall jump off the cliff into the ocean, and die before nightfall." Aphrodite heard him. She appeared and said: "I have come to help you. What do you want?"

"Her," said Pygmalion, pointing to the statue. "Nothing else, only her."

"Highly irregular," said the goddess. "But I admire your

196

taste; she looks like me. Put your hand in hers..."

Pygmalion took the statue's hand and kissed its lips. Immediately the cold marble flushed into life. A rosy girl stood there on the pediment; her hair, yellow as daffodils, hung to mid-thigh. "Her name is Galatea," said Aphrodite. "Be happy..." In gratitude, the sculptor spent the rest of his life making images of Aphrodite for her temples all over the world. See *Galatea*.

Pygmies (PIHG meez): A race of Egyptian dwarfs, one cubit high — a cubit being twenty-two inches, or the length of a man's forearm between fist and elbow. The word "pygme" in Greek means "first." Once a mortal girl of normal size came to live among them; they were so impressed by her stature that they worshipped her as a goddess. When Hera learned of this she became incensed, as was the habit of gods when they heard of mortals worshipping each other. Hera changed herself into a crane. This long-legged, long-beaked bird stalked over the marshes into the Pygmy village and began to peck the little creatures to death. When she had killed a sufficient number to sate her rage, Hera departed — but thus began an annual war between cranes and pygmies. Each spring when the Nile floods, the cranes come and attack the pygmies, who do their best to fight them off. Once, Heracles came to Egypt. Weary after his bout with Antaeus, he fell asleep on the banks of the Nile. The pygmies, confused by his name, and identifying him with their enemy Hera, besieged the recumbent hero as if he were a city — placing ladders against him, scaling them, and swarming over him with their needlelike swords. Heracles awoke, gathered them up in his lion-skin, and carried them home in a bundle to Eurystheus. They were the only creatures on earth, it was said, that the king did not fear. They were too small.

Pylades (PIHL uh deez): Beloved companion of Orestes; and husband of Electra. See *Orestes.*

Pyramus and Thisbe (PIHR uh muhs) (THIHZ bee):
A young couple whose parents disapproved of their love.
They could speak to each other only through a crack in
the wall that divided their gardens. Finally, however,
they decided they must see more of each other and arranged a tryst outside the city under a certain mulberry
tree. Thisbe arrived first but was frightened by a lioness
prowling out of the shadows. She fled, dropping her veil.
The lioness tore the veil and stalked away. Pyramus arrived, saw the torn veil, and thought Thisbe had been
devoured by a wild beast. He drew his sword and killed
himself. Thisbe returned and saw Pyramus lying there,
dead. She picked up his sword, stabbed herself and fell
across his body. From that time on, mulberries — which
had been white — have been red as blood.

Pyrrha (PIHR uh): Daughter of Pandora and Epimetheus; and wife of Deucalion. She survived the great
flood with her husband and became the mother of a
new race of man. See *Deucalion.*

Pyrrhus (PIHR uhs): Variant name for Neoptolemus,
son of Achilles. See *Neoptolemus.*

Python (PY thuhn): The enormous serpent sent by
Hera to harry Leto from one end of the earth to the
other. For Hera knew that Leto had been loved by Zeus
and that the children she would bear were destined to
outshine any of Hera's own. The serpent hunted Leto
ruthlessly. Night and day it glided after her displaying
its great fangs. Night and day she saw its scaly coils
writhing after her, the glare of its poisonous red eyes.
She could find no safe place to lie down and bear her
children. Finally, Zeus raised an island from the depths

of the sea, chaining it to the bottom, and placed Leto upon it. Then he flung reefs and rocks about the island and giant sharks among the reefs so that the python might not approach. There, upon this island called Delos, Leto bore the divine twins, Apollo and Artemis, who, indeed, did outshine Hera's children; they became sun-god and moon-goddess. When Apollo had grown, his first act was to hunt the Python. He pursued the monster across the Peloponnese, until it took refuge in the deep caves of Delphi. Apollo followed it into the cave, stringing his golden bow. The blackness of the cave was brightened by the flight of his golden arrows — until the Python was pierced in a hundred places and lay dead. This place, Delphi, became sacred to Apollo. There he built his temple where his oracles dwelt. This story is significant because it illustrates the elegant mechanism of Greek metaphor, which never moralizes and is never coarsely sententious, but in which ideas become action. In the tale of Apollo and the Python the exquisite process reveals itself in the nomenclature. *Python* in Greek means "rot." Apollo was the sun-god; his arrows were shafts of sunlight. Now it is an axiom of medical science that rot breeds in the dark — that sunlight and ventilation arrest the festering process and heal the organism. Thus, when Apollo followed the Python into the darkness and slew the very body of putrescence with his golden bolts of sunlight, he was not only avenging his mother and establishing his godhead, but also setting into motion those remedies which became sovereign to him as god of medicine. The temples of Apollo, incidentally, were the first hospitals. The treatment followed in these sanctuaries is interesting in the light of contemporary notions. The patients underwent a regime of hydrotherapy — that is, they bathed daily in running water. They did light work each day in the sun, subsisted on a diet of herbs, and spent hours in contemplation of the divine mysteries.

Rhadamanthys (rad uh MAN thuhs): Eldest son of Zeus and Europa. His legend is confused. Some say he shared the kingship of Crete with his brother, Minos, and was finally expelled by Minos, taking refuge in various Aegean islands. Others say he lived at peace with Minos, acting as counselor to the king and conducting himself with such wisdom and discretion that Minos, following his advice, was able to give Crete a model set of laws. At any rate, in his later years, Rhadamanthys did leave Crete and go to Boetia, where he fell in love with Heracles' mother, Alcmene. When she became a widow, he married her. After his death, Hades, who had been very much impressed by the help Rhadamanthys had given to Minos, made him one of the three great judges of the dead.

Rhea (REE uh): Daughter of Uranus and Gaia; sister and wife of Cronus; mother of Demeter, Hera, Hestia, Poseidon, Hades, and Zeus. She outwitted her child-devouring husband, Cronus, and was able to save Zeus from his father's monstrous appetite (teaching him also how to rescue his brothers and sisters); finally, he deposed his father as king of the gods. See *Cronus*. Rhea reigned as earth-goddess during the sovereignty of the Olympians and, while seldom meddling in their affairs, was always ready with help or advice.

Rhesus (REE suhs): A king of Thrace who owned the swiftest stallions in the world, except for the magical steeds of Achilles. It had been foretold by an oracle that if these stallions of Rhesus were ever to drink from the river Scamander, which cuts across the Trojan plain, then the city of Troy would never fall. Priam sent for Rhesus, who came with forty ships and his marvelous white stallions. However, the Greeks were aware of this prophecy. The night that Rhesus debarked, Odysseus and Diomedes put on dark clothing, blackened their hands and faces, and made a daring night raid through the Trojan lines to the king of Thrace's encampment. They killed Rhesus and made off with his stallions, which they never allowed to drink from the Scamander. This was in the tenth year of the war. Shortly after, Troy fell.

Rhoecus (REE kuhs): A young woodsman who spent much time searching hollow trees for beehives because his old mother was toothless and ate nothing but honeycombs. Thus, he incurred the enmity of bees who swarmed angrily about him. But like all the best searchers for honey he had trained himself to ignore bee stings. One day he came upon another woodsman, a huge burly fellow who was preparing to cut down a beautiful old oak. Rhoecus, who was very fond of that oak, forbade the stranger to put his axe to it. Wordlessly, the stranger attacked him. They fought with axes and Rhoecus drove the intruder away. Out of the tree came a lovely dryad who embraced the young man and thanked him for saving her home and her life. For a dryad dies when her tree dies. The dryad told him that she loved him, but had to hurry off to go hunting with Artemis, an engagement she dared not break. However, she said, she would meet him the next day, sending him a messenger to tell him when and where. She glided away among the trees. Everything that had happened to

201

Rhoecus that afternoon seemed so beautiful that he thought he was dreaming. He returned to his mother laden with honeycombs. Now, the messenger the dryad had chosen to send to Rhoecus was a bee. Dryads often sent bees on errands. This bee, like all bees, hated Rhoecus, and therefore took him no message. Later, the bee returned to the dryad and informed her that he had, indeed, borne her message to Rhoecus — but that the man had laughed scornfully and brushed the bee away. The dryad could not believe this to be true. She hurried to the trysting place; she waited and waited but Rhoecus did not appear. In a fury of thwarted love she turned herself into a wasp whose sting is more envenomed than that of a bee. She sought out Rhoecus and stung him to death. Then she stung herself to death. But Artemis, Lady of Wild Things, took pity on the pair of misguided lovers and changed them into bears so that they might go about the forest together searching hollow trees for honey.

Ripheus (RIHF oos): A Centaur of enormous size and extremely vicious temperament. He appeared, uninvited, at the wedding of Peirithous, the dear comrade of Theseus. Ignoring the ceremony taking place, he seized the bride and galloped off with her. But Theseus raced after him and caught and killed him. The bride was returned and the nuptials were resumed.

Rumor (ROO mur): She is not widely recognized but, according to some legends, was the youngest daughter of Gaia and Uranus, a swift-footed, barb-tongued demon, full of malice. Her greatest pleasure was to dart about whispering tales to all who would listen and almost everyone would. She did not care whether the tales were true or false as long as they could harm someone.

Salmacis (SAL muh sihs): A fountain of dubious waters. Whoever drank of this fountain — men or women — found themselves seized with a sudden preference for their own sex. According to legend, the fountain acquired its properties when its titular deity, the nymph Salmacis, found herself attracted to the beautiful youth Hermaphroditus, son of Hermes and Aphrodite. She prevailed upon a powerful god — whose identity varies from myth to myth — to unite her body forever with that of her beloved. The god assented and their bodies were joined as a single organism, sharing the attributes of male and female. See *Hermaphroditus*.

Salmoneus (sal MOH nee uhs; sal MOH nuhs): King of Elis. He was a brother of Sisyphus and shared his elder brother's contempt for the gods. Salmoneus grew so arrogant that he commanded his subjects to address him as "Zeus." To validate his claim to divine honors he clanged iron pots together, calling it thunder, and hurled torches into the night sky to mimic lightning. Zeus, of course, viewed such pretensions with enormous displeasure, which he expressed by hurling a thunderbolt at Salmoneus, killing him instantly. After his death, Salmoneus was consigned to a part of Hades near where his brother, Sisyphus, was undergoing his own special torment. As Salmoneus observed his brother's ordeal, turnspit demons were basting him over a flame, so that he sizzled through eternity as his brother eternally rolled his rock.

Sangarius (sang GAHR ih uhs): A river-god whose daughter told him one day that he was soon to become a grandfather. When Sangarius demanded to know the name of her lover, she declared that she had never had one, but had become pregnant by eating an almond. Her father found this hard to believe and was about to fall into a murderous rage when his daughter also told him she had been visited in a dream by Aphrodite and was told that her grandson would be an immortal hero, shedding luster upon all his ancestors. Such dreams were taken seriously in those days and Sangarius found himself quite willing to become the ancestor of an illustrious hero. And so it came to pass. The child born to the river-god's daughter was Hecuba, who became Priam's wife, and the mother of Hector. The almond part of the story has never been properly explained; but then, no one pressed for an explanation.

Sarpedon (sahr PEE duhn): Third son of Zeus and Europa. He was a bellicose youth. His brother, Minos, recognizing in him a potential rival for the throne and a fomentor of civil war, exiled him from Crete. Sarpedon then sailed for Troy with many ships and fought valiantly against the Greeks. He was finally killed by Patroclus, dearest friend of Achilles. Of the three sons of Zeus and Europa, he was the only one whom Hades did not think wise enough to appoint as one of the three great judges of the dead. Minos and Rhadamanthys were two of the judges; Aecus, father of Pelops and grandfather of Achilles, was the third.

Saturn (SAT urn): Roman name for Cronus, father of Zeus. See *Cronus*.

Satyrs (SAT urz): Goat-footed, goat-horned woodland deities, descendants of Pan and followers of Dionysus.

Scamander (skuh MAN dur): A river-god, titular deity of the river that flowed over the Dardanian plain. This river was fed by two springs, one warm, one cold — imparting variety to its waters. They were luxuriantly warm in winter and refreshingly cold in summer. Also, it was said, they conferred a marvelous luster to the skin and hair of all who bathed therein. Hera, Athena, and Aphrodite made sure to swim in the river before appealing to the judgement of Paris in their competition for the golden apple. Scamander, the river-god, intervened in the Trojan War on behalf of Hector. Andromache had bathed in the river the night before Hector was to meet Achilles. She pleaded with Scamander — who was very partial to beautiful women — to help her husband by drowning Achilles. She promised that she would persuade Hector to lead Achilles to a bend in the river so that Scamander might hurl his fathoms upon the Greek hero. The battle between Scamander and Achilles is one of the epic struggles of the war. Scamander was unable to drown Achilles, the son of a sea-goddess and undrownable. Achilles emerged from the flood waters to pursue Hector and slay him. See *Hector*.

Sciron (SY ruhn): One of the bandits whom Theseus encountered on his journey to Athens. It was Sciron's habit to force travelers to wash his feet. He extorted such attentions while seated on a natural throne of rock at the edge of a cliff. When his victim finished the foot-washing, Sciron kicked him off the cliff into the jaws of a giant turtle, who waited beneath and whose patience was always rewarded. Sciron accosted Theseus in the same manner. Theseus knelt before him, took his foot, and then, using the brigand's leg as a lever, threw Sciron over his shoulder into the jaws of the turtle — who was without prejudice in such matters and ate his master with impartial gusto.

Scylla (SIHL uh): A sea-monster who devoured six of Odysseus' crew. She had not always been a monster. Once she had been a beautiful sea-nymph, but had been loved by a sea-deity named Glaucus who, in turn, was much admired by the island sorceress Circe. Now Circe, mistress of transformations, was a very dangerous rival. She brewed a broth of poison herbs and poured it into the tidal pool where Scylla bathed. The water boiled and bubbled and Scylla was hideously transformed. From the waist up she remained a beautiful nymph, but the lower part of her body became six ravening dogs. Whenever a ship passed too close these dog-heads would dart out, seize sailors, and devour them. Scylla dwelt on one side of a narrow strait off the coast of Sicily. Right across from her, on the other side of the strait, was the monster, Charybdis, once a greedy woman whom Zeus had changed into a gross bladderlike creature who drank the tides and everything that floated upon them. Between them, Scylla and Charybdis became classic navigational hazards. Odysseus had to sail between them. His only chance was to sail exactly in the middle of the strait. If the ship swerved inches to one side or the other it would either be swallowed by the whirlpool or its crew devoured by Scylla. The ship was too wide, so he had to make a choice. He steered closer to Scylla, choosing to sacrifice some of his crew rather than lose the whole ship. The dog-heads reached out and devoured six sailors — but Odysseus was able to shear off two of the heads. See *Charybdis*.

Selene (suh LEE nuh): Variant name for Artemis, moon-goddess. See *Artemis*.

Semele (SEHM uh lee): Lovely daughter of Cadmus and Harmonia who was visited by Zeus and became the mother of Dionysus, god of the vine. She was consumed by divine fire when Zeus appeared to her in his own guise. See *Dionysus*.

Seven Against Thebes (THEE'BZ): Classic name for the campaign led by Polyneices against his twin brother, Eteocles, who had usurped the throne of Oedipus. The war led to the death of Eteocles, Polyneices, and their sister, Antigone. See *Eteocles; Antigone*.

Sibyls (SIHB uhlz): Mortal women, endowed with unearthly powers of prophecy, in whom the gods confided secrets of the future. Under certain circumstances they shared these secrets with mankind, but were not always believed. According to legend, there were ten of these prophetic women in ancient times. Cassandra was possibly the most famous of them. Others deny that she was a Sibyl at all. Sibyls were sometimes believed, but Cassandra never. Sibyls enter Roman as well as Greek legends.

Silenus (sy LEE nuhs): Bald, pot-bellied, merry-hearted son of Pan, who became tutor to the young Dionysus. He is usually depicted as vine-clad, riding on a donkey, attended by nymphs and satyrs. His own descendants, the Sileni, were very much like satyrs themselves, except that they were hornless, and their nethers were like horses instead of goats. But their antics were similar.

Sinis (SY nihs; SIHN uhs) : A giant who dwelt in the forest; and first brigand encountered by Theseus on his journey to Athens. He would seize travelers and, after divesting them of their moneybags, tie their feet to a pine tree he had bent to the ground, and their arms to another pine tree similarly bent. Then he would release both trees, which would fly up, tearing the victim in half. Theseus grew suspicious as he followed a path through that forest, because the trees bore dreadful fruit; bloody bones hung from their branches. Thus, when Sinis approached, Theseus was prepared. He allowed his arms to be tied to one bent pine, but then, as Sinis was bending the other pine, Theseus kicked free suddenly. The pine whipped up and he kicked Sinis under the jaw with all the enormous elasticity of the springing tree adding force to his kick. The brigand's neck was broken. Theseus was about to go on his way when he saw a beautiful girl vanishing into a copse. It was the daughter of Sinis, Perigune, who concealed herself in an asparagus bed. She whispered to the tall stalks, promising that if they would protect her from the man who had killed her father, she would never pick asparagus or burn its thorns. However, when she took a closer look at Theseus, she freely came out of hiding. Theseus stayed with her in the pine forest a few days and she later bore him a son, Melanippus, who became a runner of legendary speed. The inhabitants of that place, forever afterward, viewed the asparagus as a sacred plant.

Sinon (SY nuhn): Son of Sisyphus; half-brother to Odysseus. He owned his share of the family craftiness and proved a great help to Odysseus in carrying out the ruse of the Wooden Horse. After the Greeks had built the Wooden Horse and hidden their warriors inside, they boarded their ships and sailed around the headland, pretending to depart for Greece. Sinon remained on the shore as if abandoned by his comrades. The Trojans took him prisoner and he told them that the Wooden Horse was sacred to Athena, and that if the Trojans brought it within their gates, the goddess — who had opposed them throughout the war — would forevermore protect them from the Greeks. The Trojans followed his advice. Later that night he slipped his bonds, opened a door in the horse's belly, and allowed the armed men inside to emerge and begin the sack of Troy.

Sirens (SY rehnz): Three sisters; half women, half birds, who enter the story of Odysseus. They were beautiful girls, but with birds' wings, and voices that combined all that was loveliest in the voices of singing birds. It was their custom to perch upon rocks along a coast and, when a ship passed, sing seductively to the sailors. The men, forgetting everything as the enchanting melody poured over them, would allow their vessel to drift closer and closer until it was wrecked on the rocks. Odysseus had to pass that way, but he had been fore-warned by Circe of the Sirens' powers. He ordered his men to stuff wax into their ears so they could not hear, and he had himself bound to the mast. When he heard the beautiful voices, however, and saw the lovely crea-tures beckoning, he was filled with such desire that he tore the mast out of the deck and tried to jump over-board. Fortunately, however, his comrades were able to subdue him until the ship was safely past. It is said that the thwarted Sirens threw themselves off their rocks and drowned themselves. According to other legends, how-ever, their voices did not die with them, but still abide upon certain land winds in certain seasons and still call sailors to death by drowning.

Sisyphus (SIHS ih fuhs): King of Corinth. He earned the enmity of Zeus by informing an angry father that the king of the gods had carried off his daughter, Aegina, who was to become great-grandmother to Achilles. Zeus decided that Sisyphus must die, but did not wish to honor him by sending Hermes to conduct him to Tar-tarus. He sent a lesser messenger, Thanatos, whose name means "death." However, Sisyphus, a man of infinite re-source and courage, succeeded in binding Thanatos in chains, and returned calmly to take his place among the living. After some time Thanatos was released and sent again to Sisyphus. This time, however, Sisyphus made another plan. He instructed his wife to omit any funeral rites and to offer none of the special gifts to Persephone which were supposed to placate that goddess of the underworld and ease the passage of the one who had died. Persephone, thus, had no knowledge of Sisyphus' death and, when confronted by him, was persuaded that he had been conducted to Tartarus by mistake. She ordered him to be freed. So Sisyphus again escaped Tartarus and resumed his life. Now, Zeus was determined that there should be no third escape. Sisyphus was taken again to Tartarus under strong guard and his impiety was blazoned forth for all to know. Once in Tartarus he was condemned to a unique punishment: to roll a huge rock up a hill; just as the summit is reached, the rock rolls back, and he must resume his task at the bottom of the hill. He was sentenced to roll this stone up the hill through eternity. In another legend, Sisyphus appears as the father of Odysseus. Indeed, the great voyager displayed the same kind of cunning and resourcefulness but never bent them to impious deed.

Smyrna (SMUR nuh): Also called Myrrh; princess of Phoenicia, who conceived a passion for her father, Cinyaras, and made him drunk enough to forget that she was his daughter. When she became pregnant he, maddened by the horror of incest, pursued her into the forest, where he killed her with his axe. She was changed into a myrrh tree and Adonis was born from the tree in the odor of myrrh. See *Adonis*.

Somnus (SAHM nuhs): Roman name for Hypnos, god of sleep. See *Hypnos*.

Sphinx (SFIHING'Kx): A monster who resembled a winged lion with a maiden's face and a serpent's tail. She entered the legend of Oedipus, having been sent by Hera to ravage Thebes. She crouched upon the roadway and devoured every traveler who could not answer her riddle. Oedipus did answer the riddle, then killed her. An admiring populace made him king of Thebes — an honor he would have done well to decline. See *Oedipus*.

Stentor (STEHN tor): A brass-voiced warrior whose war cry was louder than the shout of sixty men, and struck terror into his foes. However, he was rash enough to challenge Hermes, the herald-god, to a shouting match. Hermes borrowed noises from his brother gods: wind-screech from Aeolus; breaker-crash from Poseidon; weapon-clash from Ares; volcanic rumbling from Hephaestus; they all entered his voice and he easily outshouted Stentor who, in humiliation, fell on his own sword and entered silence. We derive our word "stentorian," meaning "loud, reverberating," from the name *Stentor*.

Sthenelos (STHEHN uh luhs): Son of a hero and father of a coward. His father was Perseus, first king of Mycenae; his son was Eurystheus, third king of Mycenae, and Heracles' taskmaster. Eurytheus was frightened out of his wits by his formidable servant, hiding in a brass jar buried in a pit whenever Heracles approached. Sthenelos, however, was a brave man, a good warrior, and a wise king.

Stymphalian Birds (stihm FAY lih uhn bur'dz) : Except for a possible dragon or two, these were the most terrible winged creatures in the world. They were like giant cranes in appearance, with long, lancing, iron beaks that could pierce armor, shield, or helmet. They ate everything in sight — other birds, cattle, goats — but their favorite food was man. To rid the earth of these birds was Heracles' sixth labor. The task was made more difficult by the fact that the birds inhabited a marshland hill of mud that sucked like quicksand. In preparation for his labor, Heracles borrowed a huge rattle from Hephaestus, a rattle with a terrible brassy sound. (It was used by the smith-god to wake the Cyclopes from their slumbers so they could resume work at the forge; thus, it had to be loud enough to be heard over the crash of sledge on anvil and the rumbling of avalanche and volcano.) Heracles stood on the edge of the marsh shaking the rattle. The Stymphalian Birds were startled by this shattering clangor and rose in a great flock. There was no way for Heracles to pursue them in the air; he had to tempt them down. He stood there on the marsh bank and bared his chest. One by one these enormous birds swooped at him and tried to drive their armor-piercing beaks through his chest. Their beaks bent on that massive breastbone. One by one, as they swooped down and stabbed at his chest, he seized and strangled them, until there were none of them left alive. The nature of this task wearied even Heracles. His chest was so bruised he had to rest several days before embarking on his seventh labor, which was to capture the Cretan Bull.

Styx (STIK'X): Known chiefly as the great river that bordered Tartarus and across which Charon ferried the dead. Styx was originally the name of the Titaness who became the presiding deity of the river. Zeus had a special fondness for this daughter of Uranus and Gaia. When the Titans attacked him, she deserted her brothers and came to his aid. When asked what favor she wished, she claimed the greatest river of Tartarus as her own, asking that the most sacred oaths be solemnized by the waters of her river. And so, when any god made an exceptionally important vow, the messenger-goddess, Iris, flew down to Tartarus and returned with a vial of water from the Styx. Whoever made the oath drank of this water and the oath became inviolate. If the oath was broken, he who had sworn falsely was thrust into a deep swoon for nine years. If, after recovering from that swoon, he still failed to abide by the oath, he was expelled from the company of the Olympians forever.

Syrinx (SIHR ingkx): Nymph pursued by Pan. Changed into a river-reed, she inspired him to make the first Panpipes. See *Pan*.

a deep and terrible wail. If, after reaching the bottom
if he swore, he still relied in audes by the oath, he was
expelled from the company of the Olympians forever.

See POLLUX; IXION. [Nicola Djumenco]

Talaria (tuh LAY rih uh): Literally "ankle-wings," the
word came to mean the winged sandals worn by the
messenger-gods, Hermes and Iris. Perseus borrowed them
from Hermes so that he might fly about the world on
his hero-tasks.

Talos (TAY luhs): A nephew of Daedalus who invented the compass and the saw before be was twelve
years old. But his precocity cost him his life. Daedalus,
who was indisputably the master artificer of ancient
times, grew so envious of the inventive genius displayed
by the lad that he decided to curtail that career. He led
the boy to the edge of a cliff and pushed him off. Some
say he pushed him off the roof of Athena's temple. In
any case, Daedalus earned the displeasure of the goddess and had to flee Athens. See *Daedalus; Polycaste*.

Talus (TAY luhs): A living statue cast in bronze by
Hephaestus at the request of Zeus, who wished an in-
destructible sentry for the island of Crete, where he had
left Europa and her three sons. Although Talus was
made of bronze, he had to be endowed with life so he
might pursue his duties with some intelligence. Hephaestus ran a single vein down his body from throat to
ankle where flowed the single stream of blood that gave
him the life he needed. The vein was stoppered with a

single bronze pin at the ankle. There was never a sentinel like Talus. Tall as a tree, tireless, invulnerable to weapons, and completely obedient to the orders given by Zeus, he circled the island three times a day. Whenever a ship approached he would hurl huge boulders at it, driving it off. Then the Argonauts came; they wished to land upon Crete to take on food and water. But Talus pelted them with boulders and they could not approach. Then Medea came onto the deck, playing her lyre and singing sweet sorcerous songs. She cast so strong a drowse upon the summer air that even the man of bronze fell under its influence. He went fast asleep, the first time he had ever slept. Thereupon, the Argonauts landed. Medea drew out the bronze pin that stopped Talus' single vein. His blood ran out at the ankle and the bronze sentinel became a heap of scrap metal. The Argonauts took on supplies and departed. Medea, it is said, kept the bronze pin for her hair.

Talthybios (tuhl THY bih uhs): A Mycenaen noble; confidential agent of Agamemnon and thus entrusted with some of the most unsavory errands in mythology. He brought Iphigenia to Aulis to be sacrificed. He was sent by his king to fetch the beautiful slave-girl Briseis, from the tent of Achilles, thus sparking the feud that almost cost the Greeks their victory. After the sack of Troy he was given the task of telling various Trojan widows which Greeks they would have to serve as slaves. It was he who told Andromache that she would become the concubine of Neoptolemus. His most burdensome assignment was to try to persuade Cassandra to stop her wild ravings and go off peaceably with Agamemnon, who had claimed her. Apparently, however, years of this kind of work did not completely corrupt him — he was still capable of one kindly and courageous deed. On that night of blood in the royal castle of Mycenae when he saw Agamemnon cut down before his eyes, he risked his life to help Electra spirit the young Orestes out of the country before the child could be hunted down and murdered by Aegisthus.

Tantalus (TAN tuh luhs): Disobedient son of Zeus; and founder of the most doom-ridden family in mythology. He made it his business to offend his father in every way he could. Although a mortal, he was admitted to the company of the gods by virtue of being the son of Zeus. He repaid their hospitality by stealing nectar and ambrosia — specifically reserved for divine consumption — and selling it to mortals. Also, it was said, he told secrets he had heard at the banquet table on Olympus, and what he had not heard he made up. Zeus was puzzled and incensed by this behavior but kept his patience until Tantalus displayed the stupendous depths of his wickedness: He invited Zeus for dinner, killed his son, Pelops, roasted him, and served him up to Zeus as a saddle of mutton. Zeus recognized the flesh as human. He resurrected his grandchild and killed Tantalus. But he was not satisfied with just killing so dreadful a criminal — he wished him to suffer throughout eternity. This was the punishment: Tantalus was denied food and drink until he was wild with hunger and parched with thirst. Then he was made to stand in a stream of crystal water under apple trees whose boughs, laden with delicious fruit, bent invitingly toward him. But when he tried to reach for an apple, the boughs swayed gently away, keeping their fruit just out of reach, and he could never eat. But worst of all was thirst: When he bent to drink from the crystal pool, the waters shrank away from his lips and he could not drink a drop. There he stood, waist-deep, in his crystal pool under the apple trees, eternally reaching for the fruit, eternally stooping to drink, and eternally denied. We derive our word "tantalize" from his name.

Tartarus (TAHR tuh ruhs): Hades' kingdom; the land of the dead. See *Hades*.

Teiresias (tih REE sih uhs): A Theban prophet whose oracular aptitudes were unequaled and whose counsels were heeded and ignored by several generations of kings, adventurers, and heroes — among them, Heracles, Oedipus, and Odysseus. He was a man of many afflictions. He went blind, or was blinded by an angry god — the legends differ. And, for most of his adult life, he alternated between being a man and a woman — never hermaphroditic, but a complete man at one time, a complete woman at another. These afflictions, however, seemed to sharpen his perceptions. Denied the use of his eyes, he learned the language of birds, who are great gossips and told him many things he would not have learned otherwise. Also, having lived as both wife and husband, he had dimensions of experience that no one else could rival. In one legend, he was the scapegoat of a quarrel between Zeus and Hera as to who derives the most pleasure from love — male or female. They appealed to Teiresias, who had been both. He asserted without hesitation that the female derived ten times as much pleasure as the male. Hera flew into a rage and blinded him. However, this is only one of the legends that surround this remarkable soothsayer. His powers of foretelling the future and, more significantly perhaps, of divining the complexities of human nature were rivaled only by Cassandra, who also was punished for her gifts.

Telamon (TEHL uh muhn): Brother of Peleus; uncle of Achilles; and father of Ajax, who, next to Achilles, was the most formidable warrior in the Greek forces. In his younger days, Telamon had accompanied his hero-brother, Peleus, on most of his adventures and was accounted a hero himself. He hunted the Calydonian Boar; he journeyed with Jason on the Argos; he helped Heracles defeat Laomedon, false king of Troy. For this last he received Priam's sister, Hesione, as part of the booty. He took her back to Salamis and made her his second wife. She bore him another son, Teucer, half-brother to Ajax, who also fought very bravely at Troy.

Telegonus (tee LEHG oh nuhs): Son of Odysseus and Circe who became the living fulfillment of one of the prophecies of Teiresias. The blind oracle had predicted that Odysseus would be killed by his own son and that death would come to him from the sea. Now, Telegonus, voyaging on the Inner Sea, was driven off course by a storm and landed on the coast of Ithaca without knowing where he was. His crew was hungry and began to drive off some cattle. Odysseus saw strangers taking his cattle and rode out to stop them. There was a skirmish. Telegonus killed the old hero with a spear whose head was the spine of a sting-ray. Thus, the prophecy of Teiresias came true. Later legends say that Telegonus married his father's widow, Penelope, and that their son was Italus — from whom Italy takes its name.

Telemachus (tee LEHM uh kuhs): Loving and loyal son of Odysseus by Penelope. His search for his lost father is one of the most touching episodes in the legend of Odysseus. And when his father finally returned to Ithaca, the youth served Odysseus in every way possible, preparing an assault against the suitors, risking his life time after time as he and his father drove off the interlopers. There is an odd symmetry to a later legend: After the death of Odysseus, and after Telegonus, son of Circe, had married Penelope, it is said that Telemachus sailed to Circe's island and married her, thus completing the odd posthumous quadrangle. The son of Circe and Telemachus was named Latinus. With his cousin, Italus, he traveled westward to join Aeneas in creating the Roman nation. According to other legends, Telemachus married Nausicaa, the young princess of Phaeacia, who had also loved Odysseus. In all these tales, however, the sons of Odysseus seem to live in the shadow of the great voyager, able to love and marry only women their father had loved.

Telesphorus (tuh LEHS fuh ruhs): A minor deity appointed to assist Asclepius, the master healer. Telesphorus would drain himself of strength each day and lend his strength to convalescents to carry them through the night, always the most dangerous time for those dangerously ill. Each morning his strength renewed itself and he was ready for that day's task.

Terpsichore (turp SIHK oh ree): Lovely light-footed goddess who is the muse of dancing. She wore a wreath of laurels and carried a lyre. It is said she could run over a meadow without bending a blade of grass and that her sisters had to cry warning before one of her leaps, lest hunters, mistaking her for a bird, launched their arrows at her.

Tethys (TEE thihs): A Titaness; wife of Oceanus; and mother of rivers. She was also the mother of those three thousand lovely sea-nymphs called the Oceanids.

Teucer (TOO sur): Son of Telamon and Hesione; half-brother of Ajax; and an archer of uncanny skill. His father, Telamon, banned him from Salamis for life after Ajax had committed suicide in a rage over being deprived of Achilles' armor. Telamon felt that Teucer could have prevented his brother from taking his own life and he never forgave the young man. See *Telamon*.

Thalia (thuh LY uh) : Lady of Masks; muse of comedy. Her name means "festivity," and wherever she went laughter and joy went with her.

Thamyris (THAM ih rihs): A great musician; only rival of Orpheus. But he grew arrogant and challenged the Muses to a contest. Such was his pride, it is said, that he was unable to bear defeat. When he lost the competition he cried his eyes out and refused to touch his lyre again.

Thea (THEE uh): A deity out of the eldest legends; called the "goddess of light." She married her brother, Hyperion, god of light. Their children were Helios, Selene, and Eos — or the sun, the moon, and the dawn.

Themis (THEE mihs): Daughter of Uranus and Gaia, and most powerful of the Titanesses. A consort of Zeus and much esteemed by him, she was known as the "goddess of necessity." She became the mother of the Fates and the Hours.

Thersander (thur SAN dur): Son of Polyneices; leader of the "Epigoni," those sons of the champions who had fallen in the campaign called the Seven Against Thebes. A generation after his father's death, Thersander led these young men in a second campaign against Thebes. This one was successful. The city fell and Thersander seized the throne that had belonged to his grandfather, Oedipus.

Thersites (thur SY teez): Worst troublemaker among the Greeks who fought at Troy. Bandy-legged, warp-headed, his chief pleasure was to revile his leaders and jeer at heroes. He jeered once too often, however, when he spied Achilles weeping over the corpse of Penthisilea. Achilles smote him so terrible a blow with his fist that he fell lifeless on the spot. See *Penthisilea*.

Theseus (THEE see uhs; THEE soos): Son of Aegeus and Aethra, but some say that Poseidon was his actual father. He was one of the seven great Greek heroes. Moving from peril to peril all his life, he nevertheless lived to a good old age and his career intersected that of Heracles, Oedipus, Jason, Castor, Pollux, Helen, Atalanta, and Peleus. He hunted the Calydonian Boar, was an Argonaut, and reigned as king of Athens for many years, breaking the sea power of Crete, and making his own kingdom great beyond all others. The story of his life is told in three separate myth cycles. The first series of tales, full of youth and charm and simple adventure, relate his journey from Troezen to Athens. This was the worst stretch of road in that part of the world, infested by a lethal band of robbers. These men chopped off travelers' hands and feet, tore them apart on springing trees, and fed them to giant turtles or, when too much in a hurry for such elaborate homicides, simply clubbed them to death. Now, Theseus had been warned of these perils and had been advised to take the sea route to Athens. But he was young and rash. Valuing adventure more than safe arrival, he set off on the mountain road. One by one he encountered and defeated these bandits. His specific encounter with each is described under the names of the brigands involved: Sciron, Sinis, Procrustes, etc. Reaching Athens, he was accepted by his father, king Aegeus, as heir to the throne and began his next series of adventures — the Cretan cycle of the Theseus myth. For Theseus insisted on going to Crete as one of the martyred group of Athenian youths whom Aegeus had to send each year to King Minos. Because Athens had been defeated in a war with Crete the city had to pay an annual tribute of six of their most beautiful youths and six of their most beautiful maidens. These youths were doomed. When they reached Gnossos, they were ushered into the labyrinth where the Minotaur was waiting to devour them. See *Minotaur*. This labyrinth, constructed by Daedalus, was a prison-maze in the castle garden; to escape from it was impossible. Here were penned the Minotaur and his mad mother, Pasiphae. However, Ariadne, daughter of Minos, had fallen in love with Theseus and resolved to help him. She owned a magical ball of thread, also contrived by Daedalus. This thread could unwind itself, turn corners, mark paths, then reel itself up again. With this ball of thread Ariadne was able to guide Theseus to the lair of the Minotaur, where he took the monster by surprise and killed him. Then Ariadne led Theseus out of the maze and fled with him when he rescued his comrades and embarked for Athens. See *Ariadne*. There is a third cycle of Theseus tales, not so sequential as the first two, but relating episodes in his long career. In this cycle he eloped with Antiope, queen of the Amazons, who bore him Hippolytus. He later married Phaedre, younger sister of Ariadne. Incensed by her against his son, Hippolytus, he killed the youth. See *Phaedre*; *Hippolytus*. Then, with his dear friend, Peirithous, Theseus embarked on a series of daring exploits to fulfill a mutual pledge they had made, each to marry a daughter of Zeus. They kidnapped Helen. When she was reclaimed by her brothers, Castor and Polydeuces, they then invaded Tartarus to abduct Persephone. This raid failed. They were imprisoned in Tartarus and lay shackled there, undergoing fiendish torment, until rescued by Heracles. See *Peirithous*. Among the lesser legends of Theseus are the help he gave Oedipus, his assault against Thebes to depose Creon, and his expulsion of Medea from the court of Athens. He found time to be a wise king during all these adventures. After his death, he was accorded semi-divine honors by the Athenians. His personality was so powerful that at one point he emerges from myth into history. It was said that at the battle of Marathon when the outnumbered Greeks were losing, a bronze statue of Theseus led them on a charge that broke the Persian ranks and gained a victory that shifted the balance of power from east to west for the next three thousand years.

Thessalus (THEHS uh luhs): Son of Jason and Medea; he was the first king of a province in northern Greece, which, in his honor, was later called Thessaly.

Thetis (THEE tihs): Loveliest of the daughters of Oceanus and Doris. She was pursued incessantly by Poseidon who offered her marriage. Although she did not fancy Poseidon, she was somewhat tempted by the notion of becoming queen of the sea. However, an oracle told Poseidon that any son born of Thetis would be greater than his father. Poseidon withdrew his offer and married Amphitrite. Thetis, thereupon, fell in love with Peleus, greatest warrior of his day. The wedding of Peleus and Thetis was the most lavish fête ever held on Olympus. It was there that Eris came, uninvited, bringing the most mischievous gift in history — the golden apple which bore the seeds of the Trojan War. See *Apple of Discord*. Thetis had a son and he fulfilled the prophecy. He was Achilles — greater than his father, indeed, the greatest fighting man in all mythology, except for Heracles, who was more than mortal. Thetis was a most tender mother to Achilles throughout his brief and violent career. Failing in her effort to hide him from the war at the court of Sciros, she visited him frequently on the field. She comforted him during his suicidal mood after the death of his friend, Patroclus. She persuaded Hephaestus to make him a new suit of golden armor so that he might venture, gorgeously attired, against the Trojans the next day. And, later that day, she persuaded Hephaestus to hurl red-hot boulders into the river Scamander which was trying to drown her son. After the death of Achilles, she demanded his soul from Hades. Raising an island from the sea, the White Isle, she placed Achilles on it, providing him with Patroclus and Polyxena for company. Later, it is said, when her husband, Peleus, died — as mortals must — she reclaimed his shade and placed it with that of his son on the White Isle, which she visited daily.

Thoas (THOH uhs) : Son of Ariadne and Dionysus. He became king of Lemnos, a very troubled island. During his reign, the women of Lemnos rebelled against their husbands, killed them all — and would have killed the king also had not his daughter, Hypsipyle, spirited him aboard a ship and bade him sail for his life.

Thyestes (THY ehs teez): Brother of Atreus, he involuntarily fed upon his own children whom Atreus had slaughtered, cooked, and served up to him at a banquet. See *Atreus*. Thyestes had earned his brother's displeasure by seducing his wife, Aerope, but the banquet was supposed to have been one of reconciliation. This horrible meal is a key episode in the tale of the house of Atreus, which had been founded by the arch-criminal Tantalus, grandfather of Thyestes. A curse was fastened upon this family. They went from doom to doom. The descendants of Atreus were all to suffer for his foul crime: Agamemnon, Iphigenia, Orestes, Menelaus. Only in the final years of the hard-earned serenity and wisdom of the matricidal Orestes did the curse burn itself out. See *Orestes*.

Thyrsus (THUR suhs) : Vine-twined staff, tipped with pine cone, brandished by the revelers who followed Dionysus. Later it was believed that the staff had become sacred to Dionysus and imbued with some of his potency; when planted it would take root, bear flowers and fruit.

Titans (TY tuhnz): The first brood of divine creatures produced by the marriage of Uranus and Gaia. Cronus and Rhea were the youngest of the Titans, according to some legends. They became the parents of Zeus, Poseidon, Hades, Demeter, Hera, and Hestia. When Zeus deposed Cronus, he was attacked by his uncles, the

Titans, and they engaged in a heaven-shaking, earth-quaking struggle until the young Olympian finally prevailed. Attributes of the various Titans are described under their own names: Atlas, Prometheus, Oceanus, Tethys, etc.

Tithonus (tih THOH nuhs) : Son of Laomedon; elder brother of Priam. This prince of Troy was radiantly handsome. Eos fell in love with him and bore him away to her eastern palace. She begged Zeus to make him immortal so that he might be her consort forever, but she neglected to ask for eternal youth. After fifty years or so he became old and decrepit while the dawn-goddess was as beautiful as ever. He could not bear this contrast and begged Eos to kill him. But she could not, for he was immortal. Therefore, she changed him into a grasshopper whose dry chirping is often heard when dawn begins to ride the sky.

Tityus (TIHT ih uhs): One of the giant sons of Gaia. He was dispatched to help the Python hunt Leto, whom Hera hated with an unassuageable hatred. Later he was killed by Leto's children, Apollo and Artemis, who persuaded their uncle, Hades, to place the giant in a craggy corner of Tartarus where vultures tore at his liver through eternity, the same punishment that Zeus meted out to Prometheus for a much worse reason.

Triptolemus (trihp TAHL uh muhs) : A prince of Eleusis who became a special favorite of Demeter. It is said that he was the first to tell Demeter that it was Hades who had abducted Persephone, thus enabling her to reclaim her daughter with at least partial success. Demeter felt enormously indebted to Triptolemus. She appointed him worldwide envoy of agriculture, equipping him with a chariot drawn by winged dragons upon which he could fly through the air, dropping seed on all the barren places of earth. Where men were too primitive to know the use of the plough, he would descend and teach them. He was also a great protector of animals and warned against needless slaughter. Demeter remembered him after his death. She caused shrines to be erected in his honor and chose his homeland of Eleusis to be the site of her Great Mysteries.

Triton (TRY tuhn): Misshapen prince of the sea; son of Poseidon and Amphitrite. He had a dolphin's tail, green hair, green beard, and scales and gills. He was of kindly disposition and often flew in the wrack of Poseidon's storms, brandishing his smaller trident, and calming the waters.

Troilus (TROH uh luhs): Youngest of Priam's warrior sons. He fought with exceeding gallantry against the Greeks, but fell fatally in love with the beautiful Chryseis, a captive of the Greeks who had been returned to Troy. Chryseis betrayed Troilus in a very heartless way. She extracted military secrets from him and then took them as a love-offering to Diomedes, the Greek chieftain with whom she had fallen in love during her captivity. Troilus became so despondent over her treachery that he lost his zest for fighting and fell easy victim to Achilles. It was even said that he sought Achilles in single combat as an honorable means of suicide.

Trophonius and Agamedes (troh FOH nih uhs) (ag uh MEE deez): Sons of Apollo; said to be the greatest architects and builders of ancient times. They built Apollo's temple at Delphi, a great temple to Poseidon, and many other splendid temples and edifices. After lifetimes of such fruitful labors, they asked their father, Apollo, what reward they might expect. He told them he would give them the greatest gift within his power and bade them enjoy themselves as much as possible for the next six days; on the seventh day they would receive their reward. For six days they devoted themselves to pleasure; on the seventh day Apollo cast a sleep upon them. As they lay asleep, he painlessly took their lives. A peaceful death, in Apollo's opinion, was the greatest gift he had to bestow.

Tros (TROHS): Grandson of Dardanus; and father of Ilus, who founded Troy. King Ilus, who loved and honored his father, named the city in his memory. Tros was also the father of Ganymede, who became the cup-bearer to the gods. See *Ganymede.*

Tyche (TY kee): Sister of Nemesis and capricious assistant to the Fates. See *Nemesis.*

Tydeus (TY doos; THID ee uhs): Father of the great warrior Diomedes, and a fearsome fighting man himself. He campaigned with Polyneices in the war of the Seven Against Thebes. Sent as a herald to demand the surrender of the city, he was ambushed by fifty Thebans and killed forty-nine of them. He finally fell in this campaign, but his son, Diomedes, who, during the Trojan War defeated Ares in single combat, amply upheld his father's reputation. See *Diomedes.*

Tyndareus (tihn DAY ree uhs): King of Sparta; husband of Leda; and foster-father of Helen and Polydeuces, who had been sired by Zeus. Leda presented her husband with two children of his own, Castor and Clytemnestra. It was Tyndareus who, following the advice of Odysseus, persuaded the suitors of Helen to pledge themselves by the most solemn vows to abide by his choice of a husband for her and to go to the aid of that husband if anyone abducted Helen. This pledge, of course, became one of the contributing causes of the Trojan War. See *Helen.*

Typhon (TY fuhn): Youngest and most powerful of the Giants born to Uranus and Gaia. After Zeus had defeated the Titans and sent them into perpetual exile, the Giants, led by Porphyrion, attacked the Olympians. See *Porphyrion*. According to one legend, Typhon almost won the war unaided in its opening skirmish. He had no need to scale the piled up mountains of Pelion and Ossa to reach Olympus; he himself was as tall as a mountain. When he attacked, the gods fled. And, indeed, so terrible a creature as Typhon had never been seen upon earth, under earth, in the skies, or in the yawning gulfs of Chaos. From the great plateau of his shoulders sprouted the scaly stalks of a hundred necks and on each of these necks was a dragon's head each of whose mouths belched flame. When he attacked, the gods fled. Zeus alone held his ground. He seized Zeus and hamstrung him, shackling him hand and foot and penning him in a cave — first, however, cutting off one of his own heads and setting that dragon before the entrance of the cave as a sentinel. There Zeus remained during the opening stages of the battle, until Heracles appeared and routed the Giants. Hermes and Pan raced to the cave where Hermes killed the dragon and Pan unshackled Zeus. Earlier, Typhon had married Echidne, a female monster, and sired a litter of frightful creatures including Cerberus, Ladon, the Chimaera, and the Sphinx. All the whirlpools that swallow ships were also said to have been his children. From his name we derive our word "typhoon."

and how will meet the chorus. That know, nor do you yourself. Go to, go as you have done at mine. The murderer thou murdered and your reign runs true. His own hand. The poet Cronus the throne after of the

Ulysses (u LIHS eez): Roman name for Odysseus. See *Odysseus*.

Urania (u RAY nih uh): Muse of astronomy and astrology, and the mother of two great musicians — Linus, the son of Apollo (and tutor of Heracles, who was killed by his impatient pupil), and Hymnaeus, daughter of Dionysus. As Muse of astrology, she was concerned with the future. Sibyls, oracles, soothsayers, and prophets came to her for inspiration. In one hand she carried a globe, in the other a pair of compasses.

Uranus (U ruh nuhs; u RAY nuhs): Son of Gaia; father of Cronus. His name means king of the mountain and he was the ancestor of the gods. He was born of Mother Earth — whom he later wed, siring the Giants, the Cyclopes, the Titans — and was killed by Cronus, youngest of the Titans and father of the gods. He was slain by a stone sickle sharpened for Cronus by Mother Earth who had quarreled with her high-riding husband and preferred her son. Uranus' body was cut into seven pieces and flung into each of the seven seas. His mighty white-bearded head was flung into that branch of the ocean-stream which can be seen from Olympus. But before it sank the head spoke, calling up to Cronus: "You murder

229

me now and steal my throne. But know this. A son of yours shall do to you as you have done to me." This prophecy of the butchered god was to come true. His grandson, Zeus, deposed Cronus and became king of the gods.

Venus (VEE nuhs): Roman name for Aphrodite, goddess of love. See *Aphrodite.*

Vesta (VEHS tuh): Roman name for Hestia, goddess of the hearth, and patroness of marriage. See *Hestia.*

Vulcan (VUHL kuhn): Roman name for Hephaestus, the smith-god; patron of artisans and inventors. He used a mountain as his smithy; the fires of the mountain tempered his metals. We derive our word "volcano" from the Roman form of his name. See *Hephaestus.*

Xanthus (ZAN thuhs): Twin stallion to Balius, one of the magical steeds owned by Achilles. They spoke Greek and, in the heat of battle, would unyoke themselves from their chariot and fight at Achilles' side. It is said they wept great tears when informed of his assassination by Paris, waived their immortality, and insisted on casting themselves on his funeral pyre, so that they might never serve another master. See *Balius*.

Xuthus (ZOO thus): Brother of Hellen and Dorus, and one of the patriarchs of the Hellenic tribes. His sons were Achaeus and Ion whose descendants formed the two last of those tribal confederations which invaded the Peloponnese and conquered the original inhabitants, colonizing the islands of the Inner Sea and becoming the greatest people of the ancient world. The overall name for these tribes was "Hellenes," but the main branches were the Dorians, the Ionians, and the Achaeans. See *Hellen*.

Zephyrus (ZEHF ur uhs): The West Wind. He was the kindliest of the four brothers. Like all the winds, he was the son of the Dawn and his father was Astreus. The West Wind came in the springtime. He melted snow. He brought warm rain. And the waters of the melting snow and the warm rain waters sank into the earth and brought up flowers and trees and all the crops that fed mankind. According to one legend, he sired Achilles' marvelous stallions, Balius and Xanthus; their mother was the Harpy, Podarge. In another legend, he married Chloris, a beautiful nymph whom the Romans called "Flora," and was a flower deity. As a wedding gift Zephyrus planted a garden for Chloris, and this garden bloomed all the year around, bearing the loveliest of flowers and fruit.

Zetes (ZEE teez): An Argonaut; twin brother of Calais. See *Calais*.

Zethus (ZEE thuhs): Son of Zeus and Antiope who built the walls of Thebes. This is a legend out of very ancient times when Thebes was still called Cadmea. Zethus, a man of enormous strength, and his brother, Amphion, had a blood feud with Lycus, king of Cadmea, because he had mistreated and abandoned their mother.

232

They killed Lycus with their swords and tied his wife, Dirce, to the tail of a bull, then spurred the bull over rough ground, causing Dirce to be dragged to her death. It was a cruel death, but she had tormented their mother in a fiendish way. Zethus and Amphion then shared the kingship of Cadmea. But it was an unprotected city. Zethus dragged huge boulders into place, building a wall around the city. Amphion, a master musician, helped in his own way. When the boulders were too large for Zethus, Amphion played his lyre — making the rocks dance into place. Zethus married the nymph Thebe, and changed the name of the city in her honor.

Zeus (ZOOS): Son of Cronus and Rhea. King of the gods. He was all-powerful. Each of the lesser gods held tenure by his consent. But he chose sky and mountaintop as his special realm. His name meant "bright sky." He married Hera, his elder sister, and honored her beyond all others as queen of the gods. But he had many consorts. He ranged heaven and earth and the depths of the sea for his many women, swiftly changing his shape to escape Hera's vigilance. He appeared to Europa as a bull, Leda as a swan, Leto as a partridge, Danae as a shower of gold, and to Alcmene as her own husband. His wooing was as irresistible as nature itself, his fertility nature's bounty. He bred god, demigod, and hero on those favored with his attentions. King of sky and mountaintop, ruler of god and man, he was father Zeus, omnipotent. He sat on his throne on Olympus under a canopy of clouds, grasping the lightning as his sceptre, and held court among the gods. On certain days of the year he dispensed justice. He heard pleas and mediated quarrels. His opinions were wise and serene, but inflexible; there was no appeal. His will was man's law, his caprice was destiny; the fate of nations hung on his whim. He was sometimes defied — as in the case of Prometheus, who ignored his edict and gave fire to man. He was also sometimes outwitted — by Hera, especially. But his power was great enough to absorb these setbacks and his high dignity was never impaired. In his footfall was thunder. His smile was prosperity, his wrath, catastrophe. Oak and eagle were sacred to him. In Roman mythology, Zeus was known as Jupiter.